The Chamber

By

Connie Stoffel

Cover Design by Connie Stoffel

Copyright © 2017

To Contact the Author
Email: tameionchamber@outlook.com
Website: thetameionchamber.com

*A*cknowledgements

This book is dedicated to my soon coming King, Jesus, and to My Father God who has prepared me to be the Bride of His One and Only Son. I also want to dedicate this book to every seeker of God who is not content staying in the outer courts of prayer and praise, and who desire the fullness of the Holy Spirit's power working in their lives.

I want to say thank you to my husband Greg who is a true son of God, the companion of my heart and the one I love deeply. Thank you for raising me (literally) up to be the woman of God I am today. You have taught me to live with purpose, to love unconditionally and that I am valued.

I also thank my family and all the precious women of God that I have had the honor to know and love throughout the years. I especially want to mention my precious sisters who are Watchman Warriors and Intercessors. We have spent the last six years praying together weekly seeking God's heart on behalf of our families, homes, churches, city and nation. I particularly want to honor my dear friend Nancy Bowser who is not only my mentor and friend, but a kindred spirit. Thank you for all you have done in helping me to get my book done.

*F*orward
By Nancy Bowser

*I*t **is a privilege** for me to introduce this amazing book that my precious friend is sharing with you.

Connie is a powerful intercessor, a watchman and a warrior in the spiritual and physical realms. We have spent countless hours together interceding for each other, our families, churches and community. Through her love for the Lord, His Word, and her desire to know Him as intimately as possible, the Holy Spirit has gifted her with an invaluable, visual key in preparing herself as Christ's Warrior Bride, enabling her to walk with Him in victory.

The things that Connie shares in this book are truly spiritual artifacts of buried treasure from God's Word that He has revealed to her as she has diligently spent time with the Father in an intimate relationship with Him. This deeper understanding has changed my life as I have learned how to draw closer to my God, the importance of being in His presence daily, the discipline and preparation of being spiritually dressed, and the relevance of applying this truth.

This book is for those who are serious about going deeper in relationship with Yahweh. As Christians, we are the Bride of Christ, and we are warriors. We must prepare for war every day, for there is an enemy whose desire is for our destruction and for the destruction of God's Kingdom. It is probably easier for women to relate to the concept of being a warrior than for a man to relate to being a bride, however, God calls all of His people to be warriors, and Jesus identifies His true Church, men and women both, as His Bride.

In this book, Connie brings these two aspects together in a beautiful way, for no warrior would willingly step out into battle without being properly outfitted and trained in warfare, and no bride would attend her wedding without her dress.

May your life be touched in such a way that you will thrive, being prepared to live victoriously, dressed as His Warrior Bride, ready to meet the soon-coming Bridegroom.

Table Of Contents

*I*ntroduction

A **personal story** can be quite powerful. It is a series of experiences, times and places that a person has not only walked, fought and lived through, but have tangibly been touched by. Deeply touched! Your personal story can shape how you see life from that moment on. Simply put, a personal story comes from something you have experienced whether good or bad, which makes it your story, and yours alone. It may be similar to someone else's story, but there are always differences that make it personal just to you.

I have not only been moved and deeply touched by hearing personal stories, but I have one myself that God has used in a powerful way. No matter how wonderful or not so wonderful your personal experience, when God enters the picture of your story, it can become a powerful testimony and He will get all the glory!

Most of the time the process of acquiring a personal testimony is based on the law of the harvest: *"For whatever a man sows, that he will also reap"* (Galatians 6:7). A lot of things we have been through were brought on by ourselves, whether good or bad, but there are also things that we have experienced that were brought upon us by the good or bad actions of others. Either way, it's our story, and it needs to be used for God's glory!

No matter which direction your life has taken, once God gets a hold of your personal story and creates your testimony, it becomes powerful in the hands of a mighty God! It becomes a most precious possession because it is not acquired by logic or reason alone, it cannot be purchased with earthly possessions, and it cannot be given as a present or inherited from your ancestor. It is a gift from God and is to be used to encourage others. No matter what you have experienced, He has a divine appointment for you to keep! Sharing your experience with someone may be exactly what God wants you to do and that person may need to hear exactly what you have to say.

There are many godly character traits that come through in a personal testimony when God is given the glory, such as His wisdom from the lessons learned, encouragement, hope and healing, to just name a few. We could fill pages if we were to list them all. Testimonies can bring people together, uniting us in ways only our God can. This is especially true if you can really identify with the person giving their testimony. Testimonies can create a sense of safety, a place of trust, a knowing that, "If they made it through that, so can I!"

It is often easier to talk about someone else's testimony than to claim one for ourselves. We can tell a person about someone else's testimony, but when we can share our own heart experience, it will deeply affect the hearts and lives of those who are listening. The emotions, feelings, even written words we use in sharing our testimonies can be felt by the listeners as if they had walked right alongside of our experience themselves. My husband, Greg Stoffel, has a wonderful quote that is burned into my spirit and that I will never forget. He says, "Impart something you have only heard or learned about, and people might listen. Impart something you have experienced and lived through, and it will change hearts, lives, cities, nations and the atmosphere around you!" This is so true! Have you ever considered the sheer power in your simple testimony? If not, you need to!

I have met many people who downplay their testimonies calling them "boring or uneventful." I've heard them say, "I don't really have a testimony; I've always just known God!" Or "I don't have a wild past or exceptional conversion story; my testimony is boring." I don't care who you are. As a believer you should never be made to feel that your story with Jesus is somehow useless or immaterial! Just because God has protected you from the pain that many others experienced doesn't mean that your testimony is somehow less powerful or less effective.

You may have grown up in a wonderful Christian home with God-fearing parents; the glory still belongs to God! If you knew Christ at an early age and never really "wandered from the faith" or had a period of doubt, the glory still belongs to God! If you find your testimony boring because you never found yourself sexually abused, drug addicted, having an abortion, homeless or in jail, the glory still belongs to God! If this describes you, know this: your testimony still counts and is very important to God!

My husband Greg and I have two very, very different testimonies. He has always loved the Lord, always walked with God. Me, completely different! Hard hearted for most of my life, no fear of God, life of drugs, etc.! But the truth is that it took just as much grace to keep my husband pure as it did to pull me out of the pit! It's the same grace, it's the same cross of Christ, and it's the same blood! Do you see that? Your testimony is to be shared to the glory of God because it's all about God's amazing grace! Your testimony is to be shouted from the mountaintop! Never let anyone, especially the enemy, make you think that your testimony is not worth sharing. The power of your testimony lies in Gods offering of His faithful arm of protection throughout your precious life!

My testimony is not a pretty picture and sometimes, I am hesitant to share it. Yet I know God can use what is dirty, dark, ugly, blemished and broken to bring about His glory. Imagine how much more glory He receives from a story of hope, purity, faithfulness, provision, and protection! Please don't ever again doubt or hesitate to share what God has done in your life. People need to hear that God not only pulls us out of the pit, but also chooses to protect some from ever falling into that filthy pit.

My heart is that you would consider the sheer power that your testimony has to offer and be reminded that Peter says in 1 Peter 3:15, *"Always be prepared to give an answer to everyone who asks you to give the reason for the hope that you have."* In Acts 4:20 the apostles say, *"for we cannot stop speaking about what we have seen and heard."* In 1 John 1:1, John says, *"That which was from the beginning, which we have heard, which we have seen with our eyes, which we have looked at and our hands have touched—this we proclaim concerning the Word of life."*

These passages speak of the need for and the power of personal testimonies. There is not much that can stand up to the power of personal testimony in the hands of a mighty God. People may wrestle with a teaching or practice of the church today, but few people will counter or refute what you have experienced first-hand. When articulated clearly, sincerely and humbly with courage and conviction, your testimony used in the hands of a loving God will change hearts, lives, cities, nations and the atmosphere around you!

In this book, I will be sharing what God has done in and through my life over the last few years. I hope that what I have written in this book will inspire and encourage you to consider your personal relationship with God and your testimony that you can share with others. What you have to say could really make a difference in someone's life. We give all glory to God as I leave you with this one very important thought and I would encourage you to write it down in your Bible.

"God will use your life experiences
BUT ONLY THROUGH HIS PERSPECTIVE!"

1

*T*he *O*ther *D*oor

*T*he movie, War Room, was one of the most incredible movies I have seen! My husband, Greg and I, went to see it together, and we openly wept right there in the theater because we both know that room intimately. I have met many Christians, especially intercessors that have a War Room, and this encourages me. They know it and they know it well! But there is a difference between the War Room and the room I have come to know as the Tameion Chamber.

God led me to my War Room many years ago and I still have journals packed full of prayer requests, scriptures, dreams, visions and many intimate conversations between myself, the Father, Jesus and the Holy Spirit. It has been a place where I have cried over my family, and the lost in my community. I have prayed the Word of God over myself, my family, my church, my city, my nation and our government. I have stood, I am standing, and will continue to stand firmly on the Word of God and the promises to every believer that are contained in its precious pages. I believe in the living, breathing, inspired Word of God. I believe it to be the most powerful, effective life changing TRUTH any person on this earth could ever encounter.

My War Room is the place that I have been given divine assignments. It is where I have learned how to pray and how to war. My War Room journals are packed full of pictures of family, friends, soldiers, saints and sinners. I cherish my prayer journals and hope that someday one of my family members will cherish them also.

Just as Greg and I saw in the movie, the Christian's War Room is a necessary and very real place that we can experience on a daily basis. As pastors, it is also a place of necessity, promise, provision and safety. As prayer warriors, our prayer walls and journals can and do fill up fast.

What I am going to share with you in this book, I would ask that you please hear my heart in that I am not undermining the importance of this very important place of prayer or the business done there. But I do want to caution every intercessor, every pastor and every praying believer on something I feel is of great importance in these last days and in these turbulent end times.

The truth is that our greatest enemy, Satan, doesn't mind if you go into your War Room, and at times he will even encourage you to do so.

Satan and his cohorts have a love/hate relationship with believers getting into their War Room. I know that statement might sound a little crazy, kind of like an oxymoron, but hang with me for just a moment.

The reason for this love/hate relationship with a believer's War Room is that Satan knows and understands that a true believer, one who carries the heart of God within them will eventually find their way into this War Room, and there's not much he can do about it. He knows that it's inevitable, so he has had to devise and orchestrate a plan for its eventual demise in the heart of the believer, and he knows exactly what he's doing. It is for this very reason that I am compelled to share my heart and my experience.

I have met and spoken to many Christians who "once had" a War Room. They lovingly recall how at one time in their life, they fervently prayed there often. They truly loved keeping up their prayer journals, they were encouraged in prayer and are quick to speak highly of the War Room they "once had." As I have pressed farther into the "once had," I have found a heartbreaking common denominator, and this common denominator has the enemy's handprints all over it.

Through the years I have continued to hear person after person talk about how they became discouraged, even disillusioned at times because of the experience of being attacked at every level of their life by discouragement, distractions, complacency, sickness, tragedy, etc. The list goes on and on. They are always quick to share with me how they really have tried being faithful and it just didn't work out for them. They often state that praying for others can be so overwhelming, especially because they do not see results fast enough, if ever. But, the most heartbreaking testimonies I have continued to hear is that they have given up and walked out of their War Rooms altogether, some never to return.

My heart of passion for this book is that we, as God's Beloved, the one He has promised will be the Bride of His Son, are and will continue to be called to hear from the heart of our Father God. At some point in our walk we will be given a mandate, a calling, a challenge along with the wisdom, promises and a strategy from the Lord on how to pray! He has given us this call to duty all throughout His Word, and with that call comes the ability through Him to carry it out.

But I want to stress that when we hear the call, stand up and walk into that War Room and shut the door, (Matthew 6:6), immediately the principalities, powers and rulers of this dark world are alarmed at the highest levels (Ephesians 6:12). We, as "Called Out Ones" will be targeted and an "assignment of destruction" will be placed upon our life with the hope that it will bring the destruction of not only our faith, but of this vitally important War Room.

We are in a time when the Church will be waking up from her slumber and becoming so aware of her need for more of God, for more of His presence and power in all its fullness. It is in these last days that we will see His Holy Spirit being poured out to ignite hunger for more of Him, and believers all over the world will be drawn away individually to a more intimate time alone with the Father. A time where the Bride will be prepared for what's to come with such a stirring in her spirit that it brings her to a place of surrender and repentance. A place that she becomes desperate for what only He can give and there will be nothing else that will satisfy.

As I see Christ's Bride waking up, I am even more aware that Satan's entire Kingdom of Darkness is now on high alert and taking notice. The Kingdom of Darkness has but one goal and that will be to kill, steal, lie, discourage and destroy you, your faith and anything you are believing for! Our enemy does not want us praying for others, or finding our way into the War Room, but the truth is that he will tolerate it. I do believe that he allows us a little time in our War Room, but just for a short season as he schemes and plans his strategy. His strategies for destruction will be a tailored fit just for you and I. He knows our weaknesses and will be subtle in using them against us. He has been studying us for a long time. Please make no mistake in understanding that Satan and his cohorts operate with hearts of pride, rebellion and jealousy toward us because we are God's beloved and He is jealous of how much God loves us. Satan will allow us to pray, but he most certainly doesn't want us to enter into an intimate relationship of prayer with our Father God, Jesus His Son and the Holy Spirit.

I am always reminded of a quote from David Wilkerson, "Make no mistake, these attacks are the result of Satan at one time losing his own intimacy with the Father. This is one reason why the devil continually tries to bring down God's saints. He wants to rob them of their rest, their intimacy, their hope of paradise with the Lord — in short, all the things he lost when he was cast out of heaven. Some Christians believe we shouldn't even mention Satan's name, that this would somehow glorify him. But the Bible makes clear that if we are taught about the enemy's devices, we have no reason to fear him. Indeed, we're told that in these last days, Satan has come on the earth with great wrath, so we had better know his strategy."[1]

I truly believe that hell's motto is, *They must be stopped!*" This "assignment of destruction" is put forth upon anyone who would dare to enter into their prayer closet, close the door behind them, kneel before the One True Lord their God, pray, repent for their sin, and cry out with love and passion for the lost. When we bow down in humility before the King of Kings and Lord of Lords, it's at this point that hell starts panicking! When you or I would dare to breathe one breath of prayer toward heaven, when we start calling on the Mighty Name of Jesus, the demons start trembling (James 2:19). If in any way we attempt to receive not only the revelation of prayer but the strength to conceive the seed of faith with it (Matthew 17), no matter how small, and if that faith is put into action along with our prayers, the alarms in hell get all the louder because something amazing is taking place. A believer is becoming a Warrior Bride.

---

1 https://worldchallenge.org/newsletter/2007/a-target-of-satans-env

Our adversary knows that ALL things are possible to those who truly believe. But that's not all! He is also terrified of the POWER that comes to an individual who is becoming a Warrior. Warriors are those who would enter this War Room humbly, willing and ready to learn. And man oh man, watch out if that Warrior also wants to add in a lifestyle of holiness, righteousness and fasting...well... hell is truly trembling at this point.

Unfortunately, most of the American church hasn't ever studied their opponent. They do not realize to what extent he will go to stop a believer who has been called to this level of prayer. As David Wilkerson stated, some are not even aware that there is an enemy.

Satan and his cohorts are very deceiving and highly skilled in their mission of destruction to anyone who even contemplates prayer. And if you are even a little bit serious, he and all his minions are out to distract, discourage and to eventually wear you out! (Daniel 7:25).

Though Satan defected from his position in Heaven, even abandoned and rebelled against the very God that created him, we must not forget that he was trained by God Himself. We must not forget that he held the highest position in the inner courts of heaven covering the glory of God. He held not only the highest position in God's throne room but the whole Kingdom for thousands if not millions of years. He chose rebellion and defected to the Kingdom of Darkness of which he now rules from his throne on this earth.

Being familiar with the intimate details and inner workings of God's throne room, and at one time also being part of the divine counsel,[2] he has had to come up with a plan to separate us from the God who loves us, and to stop the true Warrior Bride from being successful in learning to war.

His first hope is that we won't enter our War Rooms at all, but he knows that we will more than likely find our way to it. That is when his plans are put into place.

I personally call his destructive schemes Plan A and Plan B. There are many plans of the enemy to stop the Warrior Bride,

---

[2] Michael S. Heisner, "The Unseen Realm, Recovering the Supernatural Worldview of the Bible." Lexham Press, Bellingham, WA., 2015, p. 23.

and he has tailored them differently and specifically for each individual. I know I just said this, but please remember that we cannot forget his training! It should be no surprise to us that he would understand completely the inner workings of a personal War Room. He knows what God has called us to do and is terrified of the power and ability of the Warrior Bride to bring down his kingdom.

Plan A: This may sound like a contrast to the paragraphs above, but there are times the enemy actually loves to encourage us to enter our War Rooms, and that might shock some theologians. He loves for us to get busy praying so that we are completely covered and buried with so much "God stuff!" You know, the stuff that looks like God, sounds like God, acts like God, but is it really Him? Is it really God that has you covering every single need brought before you or that comes to your mind?

As a pastor's wife and intercessor there are so many requests, so many burdens, that we, that I, can easily get overburdened and overwhelmed if discernment is not used with each request brought before me. As I stated above, throughout the years, I have spoken with the men and women of God who are called to intercession. I have seen so many up and walk away from their prayer lives, their War Rooms, and all too many were not interested in going back. I have even walked away at times.

This bothered me greatly! I noticed that their stories all had a common denominator. They would seem to get discouraged, distracted, disheartened and overwhelmed! I truly believe that this is our enemy's Plan A! He knows you are going into battle and so he overwhelms!

Plan B: If we are persistent and Plan A doesn't work, he switches his tactics to the gift he was given in heaven! Clearly, we know from scripture that he rebelled against God and his gift is now distorted, so he operates through deception as an angel of light (2 Corinthians 11:14).

His job in heaven was to be a covering cherub for the glory of God.[3] He knows all too well about the importance of

15

being covered before a Holy God. We must never forget that even though his gift is now distorted, Satan was and still is a master at covering things up. I have always said, "He's a master coverer!" So how does this "covering" apply to a prayer life, a War Room?

This is how he works. If he *can't* discourage and overwhelm us about prayer, then he must make sure that he covers the walls of our War Rooms with requests, petitions, distractions and anything else he can come up with, because he knows that **there is another door.** He must make sure that we don't see it, or he is done! He must, at all cost, get our War Room walls covered and so filled up that we don't realize that there is another door inside our War Room. He must make sure that we don't EVER enter that door!

This is exactly why he will allow pastors, saints and intercessors to stay in the War Room for years and years, always covering the walls of our hearts with more and more things that "look like God, feel like God, act like God."

The door he doesn't want you to see is the door that leads you into your **Tameion Chamber.** *The War Room is like the outer court of the temple of our prayer life, and our Tameion Chamber is the inner court of our prayer life.*

The Bible talks in types and shadows, and the War Room of your prayer life would be as in the outer court of the temple in the Old Testament. The priests were called to duty, their ministry role ordained by God. The ministry that took place in the outer courts of the Temple was not only necessary, but meant life or death in the lives of God's chosen people. It was essential in linking God Himself to His sons and daughters here on earth because there was a veil that separated man from God. When Jesus died at the exact moment designed by God, the temple veil was torn. The tearing of the veil by God Himself symbolized the fact that mankind's separation from God had been removed by Jesus' supreme sacrifice at Calvary. Since Jesus was without blemish, without sin, and He kept the Law perfectly for us, His death was the propitiation or satisfaction of the wrath of God against humanity's sins. Isaiah 59:2 states, *"your iniquities [or sins] have separated you from your God; your*

---

[3] https://www.igniterevivalministries.com/written-bible-studies

sins have hidden his face from you, so that he will not hear you."
Since Jesus' once and for all sacrifice was given, we can now have access to the inner court that I call the Tameion Chamber.

We have now been called to be kings and priests. We must be faithful to continue the ministry that God has called us to, which is working in both the inner and outer courts of our lives. The ministries are different though. Said simply, the outer court of our prayer life always has to do with other people, situations or circumstances, and we must learn to discern the heart of God regarding each matter brought before us. We are called to do that.

Please understand that my heart is not to take away the importance of the War Room, the outer court work that we do! This War Room is a vital and greatly needed ministry of the church. But I truly believe that *the Tameion Chamber is the inner court, the place of intimacy between you and God.* It's the place that God works in you, your character, your heart, your mind, will and emotions. This is the place where the Holy Spirit and Father God raise you up and prepare you to go out into a dark, lost world victoriously.

When you find the door to your Tameion Chamber and go into that inner room, it's not going to be about other people. It's going to be about what He's doing in you. This is the secret place where God comes in and He does the work in us.

The Tameion Chamber, the place of intimacy with our Lord is foundational in us becoming the ready, watching, waiting Warrior Bride of Christ who is prepared for her Bridegroom's return.

John Paul Jackson, in his book, *"Seven Days Behind the Veil"* explains beautifully and simply what this "intimacy" will look like for each believer that would dare to enter into the deep places with God. He states, "The deeper, hidden levels of intimacy carry a secret that most people cannot bring themselves to touch, for in the touching, change occurs, and blood is let. These hidden levels of intimacy require that all barriers and every other protective countermeasure be removed and the most sensitive places of the soul be touched. It can be frightening. It can be painful to make this secret, solitary journey. No one can make it with us, and few will understand our embarking on it.

"If we want to grow closer to the Lord, it will cost us our identity, not just our name, not just our desires, but everything that makes us who we are. This is what holiness does to a human; it purges the temple before taking up residency. So if God is to draw close to us, whatever is not of Him must leave the vicinity, for darkness cannot stand His fire, and neither can a soul that is desperate to keep its identity.

"I'm not saying here that the desires of our hearts, or the works or our hands, are evil and need to be purged. Not at all. But the truth of the matter is that being in the Lord's presence is an all-consuming experience. It is much like standing in the middle of an active volcano, there is nothing in us that is not touched. Only that which is most like Him remains."[4]

[4] John Paul Jackson, "Seven Days Behind the Veil, Throne Room Meditations" Streams Publishing House, N. Sutton, NJ., 2005, p. 73-74.

2
The Warrior Bride

Jesus is soon coming back for His Bride, and I put to you that the Bride that He is returning for is not one that is decked out in the traditional garb of religion. He is returning for a Warrior Bride who is dressed in all of the garments and armor described in His Word. Being properly clothed according to God's standard and His Word is critically important, and as I share the visual of my wedding dress a little later, it may be quite shocking to you.

Writing about this dress has been a three-year process for me, as my Father God wanted to take me to a new level of relationship with Him. He wanted me to go deeper in my commitment to Him. Honestly, this had been a struggle for me until I became desperate for more of Him. That's when I saw the other door inside my War Room. He tenderly showed me the inner chamber of my spirit, my *Tameion Chamber.* I do believe that every believer has one if they are willing to go there.

In history, the Tameion Chamber was actually a real place, an inner room where the bride and groom would go and consummate the marriage. This is a physical representation of the spiritual intimacy and relationship that Father God, Jesus His Son, and the Holy Spirit desire to have with us. If you are truly the Bride of Christ, you either have been or will be in the Tameion Chamber at some point in your walk with Christ. And if you haven't been, I'm excited to introduce that to you.

Matthew 6:6 says, *"But thou, when thou prayest, enter into thy closet, and when thou hast shut thy door, pray to thy Father which is in secret; and thy Father which seeth in secret shall reward thee openly."* In studying out this scripture, the Greek word for closet is "tameion,"[5] or inner chamber, closet, secret room and storehouse. This secret, inner Tameion Chamber is not only a real physical place, but it is also a room within our spirit, a safe, deeper place of intimacy with our Father where He ministers to our deepest needs, reveals things hiding inside our

---

[5] https://www.blueletterbible.org/lang/lexicon/lexicon.cfm?t=kjv&strongs=g5009

heart and mind that need the touch and care of an Almighty God, and where He provides all the resources and spiritual blessings that we need in order to overcome. It is the place that we become prepared and properly dressed for every assignment He gives us.

In the first couple of years as I spent more and more time in my Tameion Chamber, I never once spoke to Jesus, and He never once spoke to me. It wasn't that I didn't have a relationship with Him; it's just that I didn't encounter Him in my Tameion Chamber. I had asked my Father God about this, continually questioning Him as a child. It was always the Father that I encountered. Down the road I learned that this was a very important factor for me.

That being said, let me note here that the Father, the Son and the Holy Spirit are all the same, but we, as His children, are all unique. That's why the Father has designed each and every Tameion Chamber according to the needs of that individual and their unique relationship with Him.

In order for you to understand the importance of God's role as Father in my Tameion Chamber, I'm going to give you a brief background of who I am. I was born to an alcoholic prostitute, and my father was just some man my mother serviced. To this day, I have no idea who he was. I was given up for adoption at the age of 2, but was in and out of that home from 12 to 15. Then I find myself pregnant at 15 and a drug addict. At 16, along comes another baby. I was unwed, a mess, and headed down the same road as my birth mother. I can truthfully say that I didn't have a really good experience with fathers, and I hated men at an early age. When I first became a Christian at the age of 23, my spiritual mom said, "I want you to go home and just climb up in your Father's lap and let Him hold you." Honestly, I wanted to vomit because I could not even comprehend that picture. It was disgusting to me.

Fast forward 27 years, and as I cautiously step inside my Tameion Chamber for the very first time, I am in awe and have come to learn that this is the wedding chamber where I have experienced my true, loving Father God in a very real way as He is the one preparing me to meet my groom. There is much refining of my character that needs to take place.

I went from being sickened at the thought of a father, to allowing a loving Father God to train, raise up, equip, mentor, prepare and dress me for His Son. This is what every little girl wants and dreams of, and it can happen for anyone. To this day, I go to my Tameion Chamber every single morning anticipating the loving arms of my Father God. What treasures will I find next in this amazing storehouse? What incredible lesson will I learn that will help others? What mysteries of His amazing Word will be revealed to me this day? What divine appointment is He setting me up for me?

Our Husband-to-be is looking for a Warrior Bride that He is able to send into the end-time world that is being revealed day by day. He's coming back for a Bride without spot or blemish, so what does that really look like? He's coming back for a Bride who will "make every effort" to get through the narrow gate spoken of in Matthew 7:13-14. *"Enter through the narrow gate. For wide is the gate and broad is the road that leads to destruction, and many enter through it. But small is the gate and narrow the road that leads to life, and only a few find it."*

In sharing this, I want to give you a different perspective of the Bride of Christ than you may already have or even previously envisioned. We need to understand that the wedding dress we are called to wear is that of a war bride. There is so much more to this dress than most know about and it can all be found in His precious Word. I'll talk about that in detail later, but first, let's make sure we understand the foundational truths of being wed to Christ as His Bride.

3
Bride VS. Fiancé

There is a whole church in America that loves being a fiancé of the Bridegroom rather than a Bride, and there is a huge difference between the two. The Bible is very clear that the true Bride will recognize the Bridegroom for who He is. They believe that the cost is well worth their own life and they will willingly take on His Name and identity. They exchange His life for their own as they lay down their life in love and surrender for His. But the fiancé will selfishly take the name for what they can get out of the relationship without surrendering themselves and becoming totally immersed in the Bridegroom.

A fiancé is one who has not yet taken the vow of total commitment. They are still checking out the goods and can break the commitment at any time without the stigma of being divorced. They can break off the relationship and walk away if they decide that it's just too hard. A fiancé isn't required to give up their secret sins, their addictions or their ungodly lifestyles. It doesn't require them to deal with their inner junk, bad attitudes, the sin in their life or the affairs they are having with the world. They want to be known as the fiancé of a King with a Kingdom and all the privileges that come with that. They want this "soon-to-be husband King" to lavish them with grace right where they're at, not requiring them to change, to leave behind all the things they love in this world. They will also make excuses when He presses them to pursue change from their image to His image. Yet they expect Him to bless them with riches beyond all they could hope or imagine!

There are too many of these uncommitted fiancés in our churches. Nowhere in the Word does it say that Christ is coming back for a fiancé. It says that He's coming back for a Bride, a spotless Bride clothed in His righteousness.

In Matthew Chapter 25, I believe that Jesus gives us a clear representation of the difference between a fiancé and a bride. Let me explain. He shares a parable of what the kingdom of heaven will look like when He comes to retrieve His Bride.

We must remember that the responsibility for us in this parable is twofold. It is the responsibility of the bridesmaids to prepare the bride to meet her groom, but we also, as a whole, make up the Bride that Jesus is returning for (1 Corinthians 12:18-20).

He explains that all the virgins took *"their"* lamps and went out to meet the bridegroom. This is a picture of us accepting His proposal or dowry gift, and now we are taking our gift, our lamps out into a dark world (Matthew 5:13-16). Why would we need lamps if it wasn't going to get dark?

Jesus clearly states that all ten of the virgins had lamps that were *"theirs."* This gift of lamps also represents a deposit of the Holy Spirit within us to assist us in the use of our spiritual gifts, strengths, talents, callings, fruit and abilities which are given to us for the preparation of the Bride. *"And in Him you were sealed with the promised Holy Spirit, having heard and believed the word of truth, the gospel of your salvation. The Spirit is the pledge of our inheritance until the redemption of those who are God's possession, the praise of His glory" (Ephesians 1:13-14).*

At one time, all ten virgins were at the same place spiritually. So what happened? They had all accepted the groom's proposal, they were all given a lamp, a power source outside of themselves for the journey. They all went out to meet him. So what had changed?

I believe that once they accepted the groom's proposal, they were left a virgin bride in waiting and in need of training. They didn't realize that not only had the groom gone away for a time, but they also now had to go on a journey of sanctification that would prepare them to not only meet their groom, but to become the bride of a king.

This is where the road gets narrow or wide for these virgin brides in waiting. It is at this point that she makes her choice of which road she will take. The road of the fool or the road of wise.

The scripture goes on to say that five of the virgins were foolish. The foolish virgins took their lamps but did not see the need to take any extra vessels or oil for their journey of salvation. They were interested in nothing more than what they had already received. They were happy and in love with the "idea" of being married to a king, nothing more, nothing less.

The wise virgins, however, not only took extra vessels, but sought out the needed extra oil to keep their lamps burning. The extra vessels filled with oil represent something in addition to and separate from the lamp. This takes a lot of work, and in the taking of the extra vessels, the wise virgins gave all diligence to make their calling and election sure (2 Peter 1:3-11).

During the waiting period and along the journey, the rules of engagement clearly laid out in the Word of God had to be explained to all the virgins. I do believe that the five foolish virgins, at this point, had a change of heart to their original commitment and found there to be a bit too much work in the preparation process. Unbeknownst to them, this is where they became fiancés and were no longer qualified to become the bride of a king.

The Bible says they all became drowsy and at midnight the cry of his return rang out! Please notice that the cry was before the groom actually arrived. They all had the same warning. They all went into lamp trimming mode. The foolish fiancés did have a small flame up to this point, but it was going out fast, and five out of the ten virgin brides would find themselves unprepared.

What does the oil represent, and why is it so important that we have more than enough? We all understand that the oil is what keeps that lamp burning brightly, but is there more? The Old Testament is full of wonderful symbolism and is our best guide as to the significance of the oil. All throughout scripture, oil symbolizes the divine influences, callings and mandates that come down on men and women appointed by God to their functions and callings here on earth. This could be anything from a prophet, king, queen, priest, shepherd boy or even a servant. All these offices are traced to the Spirit of the Lord, the third person of the Trinity, which we call the Holy Spirit, and He is given to help in the preparation process of the Bride. Jesus clearly stated that He must go back to the Father so that the Holy Spirit could come and convict the world of sin, righteousness and judgment and that He would teach us all things (John 14:26; John 16:7-8). There are many examples throughout scripture and if studied as a whole, it gives a

24

complete picture of this precious gift of "oil" that we are offered, and our continual need for a fresh supply.

One of my favorite Old Testament portions of scripture, which I believe bears closely with the text of Matthew 25 and these waiting virgins, is Zechariah 4:1-14. Zechariah saw in a vision a golden lamp-stand with seven lamps, and on either side of it an olive tree, from which oil flowed through golden pipes to feed the flame. The interpretation of the vision was given by the 'angel that talked with' the prophet as being, *"not by might nor by power, but by My Spirit, says the Lord."*

As I just mentioned, the Bible does state that, *"they all trimmed their lamps and the foolish ones said to the wise, 'Give us some of your oil; our lamps are going out'"* (Matthew 25:7-8). We must understand that it will not be enough to have burned at one time in the past! As the Bride of the King of Kings and Lord of Glory, we will be expected to be "BURNING BRIGHTLY" upon His arrival, and that can only be achieved by a continual flow of the "oil" filling our extra vessels. The Greek word for "lamp" in this portion of scripture is (G2985) "lampas" with its root in (G2989) which is "lampo." It is an active verb and means to beam, that is, radiate brilliancy; to give light and shine.[6]

The Church is expected to be His lampstand, both corporately and individually, with no exceptions to this rule. But the only way we can truly fulfill the calling and mandate placed upon us by our Groom and His Father is by our dependence on the continual supply of the Father's gift of the Holy Spirit which is the "oil" of His anointing and the baptism of His Holy Spirit. This is what will keep our lamps burning.

There is a path that we can follow through scripture that the listeners of Jesus' day understood because they had been instructed in the old things which He, Jesus, was bringing forth in a new perspective. This is why it is so vitally important that we get into the Old and New Testament and understand scripture as a whole. Jesus was drawing from the ancient treasure house of the Word of God, which He knew intimately. He knew that we would need the influence from Heaven that could only be bestowed upon us through the "oil," the only thing

---

[6] (G2985); (G2989) www.esword.net

that would feed our flame, light our lamps and keep us shining brightly until His return.

The difference between the ten virgins is that five of them had a heart of preparation for the groom's return and sought out the oil. This extra oil represented a power outside of themselves that only God could offer, and it helped them to carry out their callings to the Body and the Bride.

Alexander Maclaren was born and lived in the early 1800's and he wrote an exposition on Matthew Chapter 25 and the ten virgins called *"Dying Lamps."* He states, "How could a sleeping woman know whether her lamp was burning or not? How can a drowsy Christian tell whether his spiritual life is bright or not? To be unconscious of our approximation to this condition is, I am afraid, one of the surest signs that we are in it. I suppose that a paralyzed limb is quite comfortable. At any rate, paralysis of the spirit may be going on without our knowing anything about it. So, dear friends, do not put these poor words of mine away from you and say, 'Oh! they do not apply to me.'

"I am quite sure that the people to whom they do apply will be the last people to take them to themselves. And while I quite believe, that there are many of us who may feel and know that our lamps are not going out, sure I am that there are some of us whom everybody but themselves knows to be carrying a lamp that is so far gone out that it is smoking and stinking in the eyes and noses of the people that stand by. Be sure that nobody was more surprised than were the five foolish women when they opened their witless, sleepy eyes, and saw the state of things. So, dear friends, 'let your loins be girt about, and your lamps burning; and ye yourselves like unto men that wait for their Lord.'" [7]

Again, at first glance it does appear that all ten virgins are at the same spiritual place at the same time. They have all heard the cry and have been woken up at midnight. It is dark outside and they are all desperately trimming their lamps. The difference is that the wise had plenty and the foolish did not have enough.

---

[7] http://biblehub.com/library/maclaren/expositions_of_holy_scripture_b/dying_lamps.htm

Having many oil lamps in my home and using them for years, I am fully aware that your wick needs to be saturated to burn correctly. After the foolish virgins trimmed their lamps their oil supply was not sufficient and their lamps went dark. They were not prepared.

They did ask for oil from the wise virgins, but our salvation cannot be given away or bartered. The wise virgins did give them the advice to go and buy because I believe they bought from the Source themselves. (See Isaiah 55:1; Proverbs 23:23; Revelation 3:18).

Unfortunately, they could no longer buy. They didn't anticipate the cost or that there would be more required than just meeting Him at the altar. Jesus wants to know His Bride intimately. Only the true Brides who had counted the cost, who had gotten to know the Father of the Groom and the character and ways of the King intimately were the ones prepared. With their lamps full of oil, they are the ones invited into the wedding banquet. This is the marriage supper of the Lamb and of the Kingdom of God for all eternity (see Revelation 19:6-9).

Jesus is very clear and explains in the Book of Matthew that those who want to be admitted into the wedding must be attired in the proper wedding garments or they will be thrown out. *"But when the king came in to look over the dinner guests, he saw a man there who was not dressed in wedding clothes, and he said to him, 'Friend, how did you come in here without wedding clothes?' And the man was speechless. Then the king said to the servants, 'Bind him hand and foot, and throw him into the outer darkness; in that place there will be weeping and gnashing of teeth.' For many are called, but few are chosen"* (Matthew 22:11-14).

We need to wake up from our slumber while there is still time to fill our vessels with extra oil for the journey. We need to learn to trim our wicks properly. We need to get our houses in order, put on our wedding garments and rise up as the Bride of Christ, choosing no longer to be just a fiancé. Remember, this is a choice, your choice. Never enter into a vow quickly or with your eyes closed because you may wake up someday and be without oil, or worse, have no time left to get some.

However, with the above being said, I am encouraged and am seeing some vital signs of life within some of the Church, myself included. I see her stirring, waking up and beginning to respond to the real message of the Bridegroom and His love for her. But there is another problem for this Bride who is now stirring and I would like to quickly address it.

The Wise Virgin Will Need Discernment as

it plays a vital role in the success of our intimate relationship with the Father. If we want to avoid being foolish virgins, we cannot take the chance and lack true biblical discernment. There are not only many counterfeit grooms trying to steal away the waiting virgins of today, but there are waves of counterfeit teaching coming from the pulpits of the churches that these "brides-to-be" are attending.

Some have mistakenly defined spiritual discernment as a God-given awareness to detect evil or good spiritual presences or the ability to tell if a demon or an angel is in the room. While some people may possess this capability, it is not the true biblical meaning of *discernment.* Discernment comes through the *"training"* of our spiritual senses, and if you're not "training," you're not discerning.

Spiritual discernment ultimately has to do with wisdom and the ability to distinguish truth from error. Hebrews 5:14 says, *"But strong meat belongeth to them that are of full age, even those who by reason of use have their senses exercised to discern both good and evil."* (KJV). Please notice the word "use" in this scripture. In the NIV the word "use" is translated "constant use." This is the only time the Greek word "hexis" (G1838) is used in the entire Bible. The word, "hexis" means a condition, state or habit. So our spiritual "senses" should be constantly exercised and become a habit for us to be able to discern correctly.

We easily recognize the word "exercised" in this scripture as it is "gumnadzo" (G1128), which in the Greek means, "to practice or train naked." Yes, I said the word "naked!" It is interesting that Paul uses words here that he uses no where else in scripture. I believe that he is trying to emphatically emphasize a point to mature believers. Being "naked" is that we should have nothing hindering us.

28

But the main word I want us to understand here is the word "discern" (G1253). The Greek word is "diakrisis" and is from the root word "diakrino" (G1252). Its meaning is "properly, a thorough judgment, i.e. a discernment (conclusion) which distinguishes "look-alikes," i.e. things that appear to be the same. The Greek prefix "dia" at the beginning of each of these words helps us to understand the intensifying force of these words.[8]

I was a teller at a bank for many years. I still remember the day that I was working the Merchant Teller line and had been counting several thousands of dollars that were being deposited to this merchant's account. I immediately felt something different as I handled one of the twenty-dollar bills. I stopped and looked at it closely. It looked so much like a real twenty, I questioned my own judgment for just a moment. But I knew, I just knew something didn't feel right. Sure enough, I grabbed my manager and the twenty ended up being a counterfeit. I only knew this because I had handled the real, the genuine for so many years. I was trained and didn't even realize to what extent until that day.

True biblical discernment is not being able to tell the difference between good and evil like I always perceived. It really means being able to discern the look-a-likes. The Word clearly states that Satan presents himself as an angel of light. In Matthew 24:5, Jesus said that many will come in His name. He warned us that there would be look-a-likes, and it is imperative that as wise virgins we must be able to discern the truth from error that we are being taught.

Charles Spurgeon once said, "Discernment is not simply a matter of telling the difference between what is right and wrong; rather is is the difference between right and almost right."[9]

We must change our thinking in the area of discernment. It is not distinguishing bad and good. We know what's right and wrong. 1 John 4:1 admonishes us that we are to test every spirit to see whether it is from God, and that can only come through the knowledge of His Word. We must be diligent and knowledgeable in our studies of His Word like the Berean Jews

---

[8] "Discernment, Good or God" Pastor Greg Stoffel. www.igniterevival.org
[9] http://apologetics315.com/2013/02/charles-spurgeon-on-discernment/

of which the Bible says "*...were of more noble character than those in Thessalonica, for they received the message with great eagerness and examined the Scriptures every day to see if what Paul said was true*" (Acts 17:11). They were not argumentative, but investigative. They were eager, yet with earnestness they judged his words carefully to make sure he was not a look-a-like Jesus or false prophet.

True discernment means not only distinguishing the right from the wrong; it means distinguishing the primary from the secondary, the essential from the indifferent, and the permanent from the transient. And yes, it means distinguishing between the good and the better, and even the better and the best.

As Jesus' discernment penetrated to the deepest reaches of the heart, we, as the wise virgins are called to develop similar discernment. For the only worthwhile discernment we possess is that which we receive in intimacy with the Father, Jesus His Son, the Holy Spirit and His Word.

This can only be accomplished by a life of prayer, the study and reading of God's Word and being accountable to those God has placed over us. Yes, even our husbands. If you choose to let your mind, will, emotions or circumstances surrounding you control the atmosphere around you... God, Himself will stop you dead in your tracks to save you from yourself.

Our Father is very well aware that this life is a training ground for our future. We will be ruling and reigning with Him on the New Earth (Revelation 20:4-6). He knows the importance of learning to war correctly. We must protect ourselves from the enemy, and this is one reason we need to put our armor on daily. The earth is full of minefields and we are in the middle of a real battle. Different battles require different weapons, but **discernment is always necessary**! So how do we navigate this minefield? We train and we learn to discern!

The original intent of your life and your kingdom purpose will always be tampered with by the enemy. We can, in a moment, in the blink of an eye, get off course. Our actions and response as wise virgins should be set up to discern the right placement of our feet *before* we step on that mine. We need to have the ability to keep effective tabs on that mine *while* it is present around us, and to debrief after it explodes.

Discernment is learned and takes practice. Because of this, there will be times when we will get off course. When you find yourself at that crossroad, simply enter your Tameion Chamber, close the door behind you, humble yourself, repent and report back for duty. Stay teachable and be willing to take whatever disciplinary actions your Father deems necessary, for there are always clarifying and valuable lessons to be learned. (See Hebrews 12: 4-12)

In doing all this with a pure heart of perseverance, expect that the Father will teach and that the Spirit *will* lead. Move out carefully, thoughtfully, biblically, and prayerfully.

Discernment is not only necessary, but is vital to the winning of every battle we will face as wise virgins and women of warfare. As virgins of the Most High God, we are being trained at every level and we must be able to discern correctly with every encounter. True discernment is being able to recognize when discernment is lacking in the heart and mind of another believer, b*ut even more important is being honest with ourselves when that discernment is lacking within us.*

Like everything in the Kingdom of God, it takes diligence in order to develop true Biblical discernment. It is not an overnight thing, and our hearts must be willing to practice and train.

"For it is no small thing to enter the service of the King!"

4

A Counterfeit Bridegroom?

*Y*es. **There is a counterfeit bridegroom** who wants you to become his counterfeit bride. His name is Satan and he would love nothing more than for you to make vows and to covenant with him in marriage.

I believe I have encountered this counterfeit groom in my own life many times because he continually comes around to see if I am available. He waits and watches to see if I will grow tired and weary waiting for my King.

You see, I defected from the Kingdom of Darkness, which I used to serve fervently, and am now a part of the Kingdom of Light. Satan hates defectors. So this angel of light will try anything to look and act so much like the real Jesus that even the best of us can be misled, especially in the last days (see Matthew 24:24). Not until I started really digging into the Word of God myself, getting to know my Lord personally and intimately did I discover that I couldn't be so easily deceived.

We are told to test the spirits, *"Dear friends, do not believe every spirit, but test the spirits to see whether they are from God, because many false prophets have gone out into the world. This is how you can recognize the Spirit of God: Every spirit that acknowledges that Jesus Christ has come in the flesh is from God, but every spirit that does not acknowledge Jesus is not from God. This is the spirit of the antichrist, which you have heard is coming and even now is already in the world. You, dear children, are from God and have overcome them, because the one who is in you is greater than the one who is in the world"* (1 John 4:1-4).

I believe that most of the American Church believes in this look-a-like Jesus. There is so much deception, wrong teaching and wolves in sheep's clothing in the Church today that it is scary. Most base their beliefs about Jesus on what someone else tells them or by the sermon preached on Sunday. Your pastor may be anointed and can preach his heart out, but it is up to you personally to be responsible to KNOW the truth. To KNOW, discern and recognize the true from the false.

So ask yourself, "Am I really engaged to the Jesus of the Bible? And if so, how is it that I have gotten to KNOW Him? Do I know His Father, God? Do I know His character and personality? Have I treasured His love letter left to me until His return? Or, have I been engaged to a counterfeit groom, the one I have only heard others talk about but not really checked into myself?

Counterfeit Armor. As I will be talking to you later in depth about counterfeit armor, please keep in mind that Satan will continually be offering himself up as the counterfeit Jesus but he will also continuously offer you counterfeit garments, robes, a wedding dress, weapons and armor.

In 1 Samuel 17, David was offered the king's armor. We know that it didn't fit, but David could still have chosen to put it on. Think about that for just a minute. What if he had? His brothers, the Kings mighty warriors, and everybody present on the battlefield would have seen him wearing the king's armor, a position of honor, favor and importance. But David knew that what he was being offered wasn't from God. It wasn't how God had taught him to fight.

This is a vital and important truth as we become Warrior Brides. We need to be on high alert and watch out for that which we are offered. At some point we will be offered, even by those in high places, counterfeit armor that goes right along with a counterfeit anointing.

Everything that the Kingdom of God offers, the enemy counter offers. Please be aware that Satan will only offer look-a-like's, and if you're not prepared, you will be tempted to put it on. It will look really good and feel really good, but you must be able to discern the difference between the two, and it's not always easy because Satan will appeal to your flesh and pride.

Satan does have power, real power and can even do miracles, signs and wonders, and many have been and continue to be deceived, and are still operating in these look-a-like anointing's, gifting's, miracles, signs and wonders. Jesus has warned us blatantly of what will happen to those who have operated with the look-a-like powers offered them by the enemy. *"Many will say to me on that day, 'Lord, Lord, did we not prophesy in your name and in your name drive out demons and in your name perform many miracles?' Then I will tell them plainly, 'I never knew you. Away from me, you evildoers!'"* (Matthew 7:22).

We have to be real here! Satan has power, real life power! He is the ruler of this world and has a Kingdom set up in it. This Kingdom consists of Principalities, Powers, Rulers of Darkness, and Wicked spirits, what I call "The Big 4!" The Bible is very clear that they are seated in high places and are out to destroy, deceive and conquer the True Bride.

Many believers just bury their heads in the sand and don't want to ever mention his name let alone give Satan any credit for his counterfeit powers. But the truth is, you will always be tempted by, and be at war with the "Big 4." If you don't know how to discern, you can easily be tricked into accepting his offer, and through you he will prophecy, and through you he will heal the sick; and he will even allow you to cast out his own demons. You must know the difference. Is it God or is it counterfeit?

When Eve was in the garden, I don't believe that she chose the evil on purpose. The Bible is very clear that she was deceived. She chose what seemed good and what was pleasing to her eye, but she didn't discern the look-a-like from the truth. The only way we can know for sure that we are operating in Truth is to make sure that we are spending time getting to really know this amazing ALL powerful God through prayer and through His Word. His Name is YHWH (Yahweh) and He is all-powerful! His Word is powerful and His Kingdom is powerful. We are never to jump right into anything spiritual without much prayer and fasting. We need confirmation from the Word of God and we need the wisdom of God and the advice of Godly counsel.

5
The Bridegroom

Just as fathers used to arrange marriages for their daughters, as believers, our marriage to Jesus is being arranged by His Father, God. If you have fully committed your life to Christ, God His Father has orchestrated a divine heavenly arrangement and has chosen you to become the Bride of His Son, Jesus!

Throughout this chapter I'm going to let you in on the way my wonderfully created mind tends to think outside the box, and I pray it blesses you. I must admit, my precious husband, Greg, thinks I'm a little out there sometimes. I just gently reassure him that the reason I am this way is because I am brilliant and creative. Can I put a big LOL here??? I always ask him the question, "How many brilliant people have you really met?" He will always smile, look up to heaven and shake his head. He can't quite explain me, but I think he gets me after all these years and I am thankful for that!

I must admit that I have a little daydreamer within me and most who really know me can honestly say I am all over the place. I have to often explain that the filing cabinets that live in my mind and heart are a complete mess, but it's my mess, and it's beautiful to me.

The bottom line truth is, I love my Lord and Savior more than any words I could ever express. Through the last 30 years of walking with Him, I adore every scripture memorized, every lesson learned, my journey walked, rough or smooth, and every note written and tucked away in these filing cabinets. I may not always be able to find what I'm looking for, but the Holy Spirit, in His faithfulness, always seems to pull open just the right drawer at just the right time, and there it is. Just what I need to bless someone else. He keeps it all safely tucked away and available for when He wants to use me.

So here goes, let's jump out of the box, open a drawer and talk about the Bridegroom.

Let's explore a side of this mysterious amazing Man, One who has gone away for a little while but will be returning for us. If I am going to be ruling and reigning with Him in His Kingdom forever, I want to know everything I can about Him. His name is Jesus. Wouldn't you want to know this man intimately since you will be spending the rest of your eternal married life with Him? I would! This is a forever deal! No end to this marriage. It will be eternity upon eternity!

My next statement may be the most important statement in this whole book so I would ask you to take it very seriously, pondering the magnitude of the truth behind it. I'll even put it in bold letters. **You may only have this one opportunity to choose Him as your husband and the one opportunity is ONLY in this life, NOT THE NEXT.**

There won't be another chance at your funeral or a million years down the road. This must be a decision you make right here on this earth and in this life. Once your last breath is gone, there won't be another chance, and you can't change your mind. So again, I will ask you to take very seriously the vows and covenants you make to your Bridegroom and the preparation you put into yourself as the Bride of Christ.

We need to keep before us always, in our mind and written on the table of our hearts, the greatness of who He really is and who His Father God is. Yes, they are one. I believe in the Trinity, Father, Son and Holy Spirit. But they are also separate, and the greatness of their vast Kingdom is a reality.

Defending His Character. I have talked much about us being the Bride of Christ so now let's take a look at our Groom.

He has made some incredibly bold claims about Himself that most in this world completely disagree with. Over two thousand years ago He said some pretty outrageous things that continue to offend many even today.

Our Groom claims to have led a sinless life. The Bible is very clear that no one is without sin (1 John 1:8). So your Groom is either "a legend, a lunatic, a liar," or He is truly the Lord and Son of His Father, God.

36

He has also claimed to be the only way to God His Father (John 6:44; John 14:6). This is in direct conflict with what every other religion claims, so He is pretty much a lone ranger, and definitely in defiance of what others believe to be the truth. This claim alone can get a bit dangerous, especially today because our society, which has been labeled by many as the "melting pot" of world religions coming together, has influenced the American Church so very subtly that we are expected to accept and love everyone even if they don't agree with us. There is so much mixing in of other religions that I want to put this question before you. What if you come across a person who believes that your Groom is not the only way to God? Will you, as His Bride, be able to defend His character and stand behind that which He has claimed of Himself?

In John 1:1-5, and John 17:5, He further claims that He has shared the glory of God His Father from before the world was, and He also claims that He is in heaven and sitting at His Father's right hand (Colossians 3:1).

He claims that you, as His Bride, cannot come to Him unless you are fully obedient to His Father, and that you cannot know Him, Jesus, intimately unless it is through His Father. He continues to claim that you have to learn from His Father, and that He will be the One to teach you about His Son. All of this without ever seeing His Father. What??? How could that be???

"No one can come to Me unless the Father who sent Me draws him; and I will raise him up at the last day. It is written in the prophets, 'And they shall all be taught by God.' Therefore, everyone who has heard and learned from the Father comes to Me. Not that anyone has seen the Father, except He who is from God; He has seen the Father" (John 6:44-46).

No other religious leader such as Buddha, Confucius or Mohammad, has ever made these startling claims. Your Groom claims that He is the only way, and that you come to Him through His Father. End of story, that's it. No other options! If someone were to tell you He doesn't share the glory with God, and that you don't have to go through the Father to get to the Son, would you be able to defend your Groom's character?

Now it doesn't stop there. It gets even a little more radical. When Jesus, our Groom walked on this earth, He claimed to have the authority to forgive sins (Matthew 9:1-8; Mark 2:5; Mark 2:10; Luke 5:20-24; Luke 7:48-49; Acts 5:31). This infuriated everyone around Him in every city He entered. He also claimed to be a heavenly King (John 18:37). He claimed to be able to give everlasting life (John 10:27-29). And the real kicker is that He claimed that He would die and come back to life! (Matthew 12:39-40; 16:21; John 2:19-22; 10:17-18).

Those are some very bold statements and these are just a few scriptures. I think that if someone were walking around today making these same kinds of statements about themselves, they would get locked up and put away in 3B for a 5150.

That was over two thousand years ago, and so what happens when someone asks, "Where is He? He said He was coming back." Are you going to be able to defend His character? When somebody says, "I can't be forgiven." Can you defend His character and explain to them His ability to do so? Can you take them to and through His Word explaining His abilities, promises, authority and love for them also? We have to be able defend His character and to show them His great plan of redemption.

Now this claim takes His personality and character to a whole new level. We are talking serious stuff here. He claimed that He would return again to judge the world (John 5:22-30; Acts 10:42, 17:31; 2 Corinthians 5:10). He also claimed that along with His Father, He would determine eternal life or eternal death for every person (Revelation 20:11-15).

I pray that you are looking up the scriptures I've listed because I want you to really think on them for some time asking yourself these questions. "How do I really feel about making a vow of marriage to a man who is going to condemn someone that I love who has rejected Him to everlasting torment in hell? How am I going to feel knowing that this loved-one will be separated from me and from Him for eternity just because they did not believe Him?"

These are some pretty hard but real questions we should be asking ourselves. As you can see, I'm writing about this from one of those filing cabinets in my head. These are questions I have had to take a look at personally.

The real truth is that, "YES," He died on the cross for everyone, but there will be people that reject that death, and your Groom will be the one who determines the final outcome for those who reject Him. It really is their choice, but if they don't choose Him, your Groom, Jesus, will allow them to be separated from you and God His Father for eternity.

That's your Groom! These are His claims! Will you stand by His side on this earth, or will you shrink back because of embarrassment? Will you be able to support Him fully? Can and will you defend His character when necessary?

What if someone you love dearly, who has chosen freely not to believe in Him, condemns and ridicules you? Are you going to stand by your Man?

Your Groom has gone away and He has been gone for a very long time. He has left to prepare a place for you and has asked that you prepare yourself for Him. He has promised that He would return for you, and that while He is gone the comforter, the Holy Spirit would be with you (John 14). He even states in John 14:28-31, *"You heard that I said to you, 'I go away, and I will come to you.' If you loved Me, you would have rejoiced because I go to the Father, for the Father is greater than I. Now I have told you before it happens, so that when it happens, you may believe. I will not speak much more with you, for the ruler of the world is coming, and he has nothing in Me; but so that the world may know that I love the Father, I do exactly as the Father commanded Me. Get up, let us go from here."*

How do you feel about making a vow, a covenant of marriage to a Man who has left you in a country to fend for yourself? Yes, He has left His Promised Precious Holy Spirit with us, and I am ever so grateful and thankful for this. I'm not sure what your thoughts are about this world, but bottom line for me, it's tough down here!

The truth is that we have been left by our Groom in a country where we are foreigners and strangers, and He expects us to abstain from sinful desires that will war against our souls. He has asked us to live such good lives among the non-believers of this world that they may watch us in our actions with the hope that it will give God the glory on the day He visits us (1 Peter 2:11-12). Our Groom has asked that our lives be so good that when Father God visits a person here on earth with the offer of salvation, our good life may be the spiritual influence He uses to bring the unbeliever to repentance and belief in Jesus Christ His Son. Wow, what a responsibility!

He has told us boldly that this is not His Kingdom, and that He is not the one ruling this world. He has given us plenty of warning about the evil rulers and authorities, the powers of this dark world and the spiritual forces of evil that are patrolling the heavenly realms round about us (Ephesians 6:12).

He has left us for over two thousand years, as a Bride who is called and mandated to defend herself fervently. We have been asked to bring others back from the Kingdom of Darkness to His Kingdom of Light. He has asked us to believe that He will return.

Not only are we foreigners and strangers here, but He's left us in a land owned and occupied by our Groom's arch-enemy, Satan! This enemy wants you and I destroyed! He will do everything within his power to hunt us down, looking for every opportunity to take our children, our churches, our cities, our ministries, our finances and our nation. My husband has this saying that I have never forgotten. "The enemy will always use the ordinary to threaten the Set Apart!" It's those ordinary things in life that we don't expect to hit us, which are the very things that the enemy will use against us because we are "Set Apart."

Our enemy is vicious, but he is subtle. He is not ugly. He is beautiful as the Bible states, "*And no wonder, for Satan himself masquerades as an angel of light*" (2 Corinthians 11:14). He wants nothing more than to take you out so that you won't be a problem for him.

This enemy's sole purpose is to stain our white wedding dress, to sell us defective armor, and to offer us a counterfeit covering. We cannot go before the Father unless we are covered in the blood of His Son, Jesus! Satan's sole plan is to deceive us into thinking that we are covered correctly having on a white dress, the proper armor, etc. What he is going to offer is so close to the real thing, that unless you can discern the look-a-like, you will wake up someday, standing before the throne in great shock.

I do believe this is what happens in Matthew 7:21-23 and Matthew 24 and 25. Please take the time to read these passages seriously. Satan is a counterfeit and he knows exactly how to look like Jesus. He can even make your skin tingle. You must not only be in prayer and reading the Word daily, but you must be studying the Word daily to be able to discern this very real look-a-like. Please stop right now and ask the Father if you could possibly be wearing a counterfeit wedding dress. Ask Him right now about a counterfeit covering. He will be faithful to answer.

This is serious business and very real because your Groom is the most hated man that has ever walked the face of this earth. He has made many enemies and nothing has changed to this day. He's still the most hated man with the most enemies. He is despised and has been rejected by almost everyone around us. When He walked this earth He was accused of being demon possessed (Mark 2:22; John 7:20; John 8:48; John 10:20).

He knew how to provoke a reaction that would bring out the worst in people, and He still does to this day. I'll ask again, can you defend His character? His words at times were so hard and non-negotiable, that even His family and close followers finally had enough and thought He was crazy (Mark 3:21). It's no different today.

The scale of negative reaction to our Bridegroom has not changed much over two thousand years, and actually has continued to escalate in our day. It is nothing to see the hatred, killing and murder over someone's belief in Him on the nightly news.

We are in such times that we have to be so passionately in love with our Man and so committed to Him that we will be able to defend His character at any and every level necessary, even if it costs us our life. Again, I must stress that the only way we can accomplish this is that we make ourselves knowledgeable and familiar with His Word, the precious love letter He has left behind. We must **INTIMATELY KNOW** what and who we believe in **WITH NO COMPROMISE.**

No matter what this world may throw our way or say about our Man, we must be willing to say, "yes" to the wedding dress He has asked us to wear.

In John 15:18-25 Jesus told His disciples, *"If the world hates you, know that it hated Me, because it hated you. If you were of the world, the world would love you. But because you are not of this world, I have chosen you out of the world, therefore the world will hate you."*

When our Groom walked this earth, the hatred for Him became so intense that it led man to a deep desire to kill Him no matter what the cost. Don't even kid yourself; it's no different today for us, the Bride of Christ that He has left on this earth. The hatred for His ways, His Name and His Bride are truly evident. We see and hear the persecution that's happening to her all over the world. It's even starting to happen in our little realm right here.

Christians are losing their lives because they have said "yes" to this very special wedding dress. If you are truly willing to say yes to the dress, be prepared. You will have a target on your back immediately.

Just as the world hated Him, the world will hate you, His Bride-to-be. If you are not living a life that the world hates, if you're blending in to the things of this world and have what I call "sin mixing" in your life, which is sin mixed in with your Christianity, you need to do a check and recheck of your vows.

In Luke 12:53, He informs us that even families will be divided, *"father against son, and son against father, mother against daughter, and daughter against mother, mother-in-law against daughter-in-law and daughter-in-law against mother-in-law."*

One of my children just told me recently that the one thing he hates about me most is my passion and my love for Christ. That I'm sold out. Yes, this broke my heart and I shed tears so deeply that I could have filled jar after jar with them. It was a horrible, heartbreaking conversation. Now with that said, I'm believing for my son and his personal salvation, but I felt like he was trying to get me to deny my faith. That he was trying to get me to say, "You're my son and I need to put you first." I had to let my heart be broken, do my best to confirm my love for him, but without denying my love for my Lord.

Bottom line, I won't be bullied and I won't budge. My Jesus is number one over my husband, over my children and grandchildren. This is a hard road to walk sometimes, because I love my grandbabies. When I had this conversation with my son

42

it cut me to the core because I realized that the scripture above in Luke was coming true. I don't preach to my children; I just try my best to live out my faith and love them with no compromise.

And I'm living this scripture out right now. My Groom along with His Holy Spirit has prepared me and warned me that this was going to happen. It hurts terribly, yes, but I know where my true peace comes from. I understand the anointing and calling that God the Father has placed on my life and I have no doubt that He has raised me up to be a Warrior Bride. I know how to fight for my children, my grandchildren and any other person God chooses to put in my path.

The writings about our Groom in John Chapters 5-12 are jam-packed with explosive confrontations, hard-core power encounters, and cases of incredible controversy and conflict. I suggest that you read them. This King of ours seemed to have this impact wherever He walked on this earth. With each step He took, He would anger the religious people to the point of frenzy. They would do things like stir up the crowds against Him, spread vicious lies, and threaten to stone Him. At one point, they even took hold of Him and drug Him to the edge of a cliff intending to throw Him off! Yep, that really happened to our Groom. But the good news is that our Man carried Himself with such authority that He walked right through this hysterical crowd and went on His way. (Luke 4:28-30)

I giggle at times as I hear and see how He still causes great disturbances all over the world at just the mention of His Wonderful Name. I will usually tell myself, yep that's my King and He's coming back for me. This is also your Groom, your King and your future Husband. Are you willing and able to stand with Him as the days grow darker and evil continues to gain a foothold? Will you be able to defend His character when necessary?

We don't know when this battle we are in is going to get worse on account of His Name, or when it is going to end. The Bible is very clear that the days ahead will be as birthing pains and full of trouble (Matthew 24 and 25). We have no idea when He will return for us. He has NO idea of the day or hour that He's going to return (Matthew 24:36). He's waiting expectantly just as we are to hear His Father's command, "Go get Your Bride!"

6
The Love Letter

Your Groom has prepared you by leaving you His Love Letter, which is the Inspired Word of God. This Love Letter should also be viewed as your Supernatural War Manual. I am not kidding a bit about this! It's the real deal.

His Word is considered as not only more powerful than a double edged sword but a Guide Book that carries with it the responsibility of not only teaching us, but training and equipping us for every good work (2 Timothy 3:16-17). It's literally alive and active. *"For the Word of God is alive and active. Sharper than any double-edged sword. It penetrates even to the diving soul and spirit, joints and marrow; it judges the thoughts and attitudes of the heart"* (Hebrews 4:12).

Everything you will ever need is available to you in His Word. I'm so thankful and grateful that He loved us enough to leave us this treasure.

With this treasure of Truth containing everything we could ever need for this life and the battles we may face, we have a huge responsibility as His Bride. Acknowledging the Truth found in its pages brings a real problem to light and we must be willing to do something about it. In the past 20 years, my heart has ached for so many hurting, wounded, completely rendered ineffective Christians. When I have asked about their relationship with God, they either know next to nothing or very little of the truths and treasures hidden within the contents of His Word. And this is true for many even though they have sat in a church pew, some for 50 years or more! So in doing our part to fix this problem, my husband and I have set our hearts to train, equip, mentor, challenge and raise up an army of epic proportions.

Can you just imagine a repentant, surrendered and transformed Bride who is passionately in love with her God? These Christians are mesmerized by the idea that this is not about them, but all about HIM. They have said to themselves,

"Could it be that God possibly thinks the Bride should be about Him and not about us? Lord, we repent!"

I see this Bride rising up, transfixed by God's presence, His glory and His heart for the lost in their families and cities. They refuse to go anywhere unless His presence goes before them. *"Then Moses said to Him, "If Your presence does not go with us, do not lead us up from here"*(Exodus 33:15). They are worshipers with worn out knees, Warrior Brides who are not afraid to do battle in the heavenly realm for the souls of men. They are fire starters, flame-throwers, hope peddlers, grace givers, and they plant their seeds in fertile ground. They have been touched by the heart of the Almighty God. They are young and old. They are men, women and children who KNOW Him.

These precious ones know who they are in their God, and even more important, who God is in them. They know what they have been sent to do! They are sent to empower the poor, strengthen the weak, embrace the outcast, seek the lost and IGNITE REVIVAL in the hearts of men and women. They are called to take care of the widows, feed the hungry, heal the sick, raise the dead, cleanse those who have leprosy, and drive out demons. Freely they have received; freely they give (Matthew 10:8). They worship together, pray together, fast together, repent together and serve God together. They are in hot pursuit of God's presence, knowing He won't relent until He has all of them. Their cities will change because God has called them unto Himself to worship Him and Him only. Our vision is simple yet powerful.[10]

"But the hour is coming, and now is, when the true worshipers will worship the Father in spirit and truth; for the Father is seeking such to worship Him. God is Spirit, and those who worship Him must worship in spirit and truth" (John 4:23-24).

Because our Father God has left us with an arsenal of knowledge, we are bound and determined to find every bit of information contained within its pages, and to put it to good use to further the Kingdom of God. It's heartbreaking that so many in our American churches choose not to use His Word. Some never open its wonderful pages and search out its unlimited treasures. We can see this to be true by the fruit that has been

---

[10] www.igniterevival.org

left by the Church. There is some good fruit, but the rotten fruit is evidence that has been left along the way and has had the enemy and his cohorts running right over to it, picking it up and throwing it upon those already wounded and hurting within our churches. Violation after violation, compiling the deception and tainting the good Name of our Father God and His Son, Jesus.

To those of us who are standing firm, doing our best at keeping our hands clean and our hearts pure, it can be a tough job cleaning up these hurting, wounded souls (Psalm 24:4). Most of the wounded in our churches are in such bondage they don't even know they can be free. They have never heard it preached from the pulpit and would not even know where to look for the answers in the Word of God. They just stay wounded, rejected, offended and hurt, and yes, we do go through those times, but we should never be allowed to stay there. I have had to go through deliverance and healing myself for years. And again, I am so thankful that He doesn't show us everything about ourselves all at once.

God is a good, good Father. But we, as a Bride-to-be, need to rise up, get ourselves ready, put on our wedding gown, our royal garments and our armor. The church in America needs to learn to use her sword again. There have been way too many unnecessary casualties of this war and it breaks my heart. I am willing to do my part and I pray that you will join me.

7
The Final Challenge

*H*ow do you feel about making a vow and covenant to a King knowing that the only way He will take you with Him is if you fight for your life just to get through the narrow gate of His Kingdom? What I am about to say is no joke. It's not a fairytale. It is not taught much in our American churches, but it is very clear in God's Word. I want what I am about to say to sink in so deep that you will never forget it.

To be able to rule as the Bride of Christ alongside of Him, you are going to have to contend as with an adversary. This is the only way to get into His Kingdom.

A while back, my husband taught on Luke 13:24. We learned that as the Bride, we are to *"Strive to enter the narrow gate, for many, I say to you, will seek to enter and will not be able."*

The Greek word here for "strive" is agōnizomai.[11] It means to struggle, to compete or contend with an adversary. This speaks of a very intense struggle, and this verb is used in a continuing tense, as to "keep on striving." The Hebrew word for adversary is "satan."[12] An "adversary" is also one who will try "to oppose" or "thwart" anyone in his purpose or claims. "One who is turned against another or others with a design to oppose or resist them; a member of an opposing or hostile party; an opponent; an antagonist; an enemy; a foe."[13]

So you and I, the Bride of Christ, have a narrow gate that we have to get through and it is not easy. I want you to picture yourself in a wedding dress, garments and armor squeezing through a narrow gate with a sword in one hand and your shield in another all the while contending with an adversary. The meaning of this word implies an agonizing, intense, purposeful struggle. It is the same word used in 1 Corinthians 9:25 as an athlete battling to win a victory. It's also used in Colossians 4:12

---

[11] http://biblehub.com/lexicon/luke/13-24.htm
[12] http://biblehub.com/hebrew/7854.htm
[13] http://biblehub.com/topical/a/adversary.htm

of Epaphras laboring fervently, and in 1 Timothy 6:12, of the Christian who fights the good fight of faith.

Our journey as the Bride is not only a struggle; it's an all out battle. It is going to take extreme effort, and I do believe that there are those who know exactly what I am talking about. In this portion of scripture, there is a violence implied, and appropriately so because truly entering the Kingdom of God as His Bride is all about going into warfare.

So let's get this straight. Yes, your Groom Jesus was, and still is, the most loving Man to have ever walked the face of this earth. There is no man who has left a footprint on the heart of mankind such as He has. He was and still is the most gracious, compassionate, kind, gentle, humble Man you could ever hope to meet. So much so that He was willing to be beaten, bruised and spit upon, giving His life for you and for me, paying the ultimate price for your freedom and mine, giving us the true ability to walk in the presence of His Father God knowing that we are covered in His precious blood. Every time His Father sees us, He sees the blood of His Son, our Husband-to-be. He notices that we are worthy and loves us deeply.

Yes, He was also the most reviled, the most hated, the most attacked and the most rejected, not only back then, but still today. The Bible describes it perfectly in the following passage, *"He was despised and rejected by mankind, a man of suffering, and familiar with pain. Like one from whom people hide their faces he was despised, and we held him in low esteem. Surely he took up our pain and bore our suffering, yet we considered him punished by God, stricken by him, and afflicted. But he was pierced for our transgressions, he was crushed for our iniquities; the punishment that brought us peace was on him, and by his wounds we are healed. We all, like sheep, have gone astray, each of us has turned to our own way; and the Lord has laid on him the iniquity of us all. He was oppressed and afflicted, yet he did not open his mouth; he was led like a lamb to the slaughter, and as a sheep before its shearers is silent, so he did not open his mouth. By oppression and judgment, he was taken away. Yet who of his generation protested? For he was cut off from the land of the living; for the transgression of my people he was punished. He was assigned a grave with the wicked and with the rich in his death, though he had done no violence nor was any deceit in his mouth. Yet it was the Lᴏʀᴅ's will to crush him and cause him to suffer, and though the Lᴏʀᴅ makes his life an offering for sin, he will see his offspring and prolong his days, and the will of the Lᴏʀᴅ will prosper in his hand. After he has suffered, he will see the light of life and be satisfied; by his knowledge my righteous servant will justify many, and he will bear their iniquities. Therefore I will give him a portion among the great, and he will divide the spoils with the strong, because he poured out his life unto death, and was numbered with the transgressors. For he bore the sin of many, and made intercession for the transgressors"* (Isaiah 53:3-12).

You have to know ALL the good and the bad, and you must be able to defend His character with honor and dignity and the truth of who He really is.

What does a Bride do if her husband is sinless? She defends her husband. I have thought long and hard about this. I want you to think about this as you go through the rest of this book. Ask yourself, "Am I truly committed to this sinless Christ?" And please know that if you choose to be committed to Him in this way, because He is sinless, you will be attacked, you will be scorned, you will be hated at some point in your walk with Him. We cannot be friends with the world and be the Bride of a sinless Christ. It just does not work that way. You will have to choose one or the other. The Bible is clear that our Groom will spew us out of His mouth.

This is my dilemma as a pastor's wife. I see so many in the Church today, even in our own church, that have decided to wed themselves to a different bridegroom, the look-alike. This Church in America tends to desire a more appealing bridegroom. A more palatable bridegroom. One that won't offend their friends or family. Just this week, somebody that I have been raising up and training, told me that they could not have this battle going on, and they walked away.

Personally, after many years of studying the Word and much prayer in the secret place, I have determined to set my face as flint, and to stand by my Man. And I'm hoping that you will choose to do that as well.

Please hear me on this and listen to my heart. When we fully commit, the perks are phenomenal. We are really going to rule and reign with the King of Kings, the Lord of Glory. Have you ever read what He has in store for us??? I don't want you to be discouraged, I want you to be encouraged. But this relationship with God is not for the faint of heart. Please don't get me wrong, but I have to be very truthful and honest. This life is a battle. We are in a battle for our very lives, our very soul, and the lives of those we love are at stake. We have got to be in God's Word. We have got to KNOW Him.

As I spoke about earlier in this book. In Matthew 7:22-23 they said to Jesus, "'we prophesied in Your name. We cast out demons in Your name. We've done all these things.' Then Jesus said to them, 'I **never** knew you. Depart from Me.'" That word "knew" is ginōskō in the Greek,[14] and it's the Biblical Jewish idiom for sexual intercourse. We have to have that intimate of a relationship with God the Father and His Son, Jesus.

We have already discussed the importance of getting to know Father God because He is the ONLY way to the Son. He's the one responsible for this marriage set up. He's the One who sent His Son to fix the mess Adam and Eve got us into so He could be reunited with us. He's the One that wants to redeem us simply because He loves us.

*P*reparation.   We are getting ready to enter the Tameion Chamber. But we must not go on this journey alone. It is imperative that we be connected with others who are walking with us, and to be spiritually covered and protected. I am covered under my physical husband Greg, who is also my pastor, and I surround myself with women of God who are powerful and effective in God's Kingdom.

I have one woman of God in particular though, a precious spiritual mentor, sister, advisor and friend who is also my prayer partner. She is truly what I call a "Kingdom of Darkness Devastator!" I stay accountable to her at every level. Nancy Bowser is the author of many amazing books including *The Soul Redeemer* series and *Watchman Warrior Intercessory Prayer,* and I wholeheartedly encourage you to read them and to visit her website, Buried Treasure Unlimited.[15].

---

[14] http://biblehub.com/greek/1097.htm
[15] https://buriedtreasureunlimited.wordpress.com/

My heart is that you would decide to enter your own Tameion Chamber after reading this book. At the end of this book I have written a very important chapter on vows and covenants called, "Wedding Preparations," and I pray that you will read, ponder, consider and take its contents seriously.

Before you make any vows or covenants with this Almighty God, I suggest that you seriously consider the cost of following this Royal King and of taking His Name. I have found that I must defend my Man almost on a daily basis, and I want you to be able to do the same. But in order to do so, you must be firm in your commitment to Him. I want you to be a Bride, not a fiancé. When the pressure comes, fiancés can back out of the commitment, but a Bride is excited to put on her wedding dress for her Bridegroom and to stand with her Man.

"And I heard, as it were, the voice of a great multitude, as the sound of many waters and as the sound of mighty thunderings, saying, 'Alleluia! For the Lord God Omnipotent reigns! Let us be glad and rejoice and give Him glory, for the marriage of the Lamb has come, and His wife has made herself ready.' And to her it was granted to be arrayed in fine linen, clean and bright, for the fine linen is the righteous acts of the saints. Then he said to me, 'Write: Blessed are those who are called to the marriage supper of the Lamb!' And he said to me, 'These are the true sayings of God.' And I fell at his feet to worship him. But he said to me, 'See that you do not do that! I am your fellow servant, and of your brethren who have the testimony of Jesus. Worship God! For the testimony of Jesus is the spirit of prophecy.' Now I saw heaven opened, and behold, a white horse. And He who sat on him was called Faithful and True, and in righteousness He judges and makes war. His eyes were like a flame of fire, and on His head were many crowns. He had a name written that no one knew except Himself. He was clothed with a robe dipped in blood, and His name is called The Word of God. And the armies in heaven, clothed in fine linen, white and clean, followed Him on white horses. Now out of His mouth goes a sharp sword, that with it He should strike the nations. And He Himself will rule them with a rod of iron. He Himself treads the winepress of the fierceness and wrath of Almighty God. And He has on His robe and on His thigh a name written: KING OF KINGS AND LORD OF LORDS" (Revelation 19:6-16).

Yes, this is truly the One who will be returning for you and me. Personally, I cannot wait for that marriage supper of the Lamb, and my heart's desire is not only to be a healthy part of this Bride, but to help in the preparation process of getting her ready to meet her king.

I hope and pray that all of you will be there with me. This is serious business. The Church is asleep. Wake up! We need to wake up. We need to set our faces as flint and stand by our Man. He's amazing, it's all amazing!

8

The Tameion Chamber

It **is my heartfelt desire** that the things I share with you will stir your spirit and create a longing for a deeper relationship with the Father, Son and Holy Spirit within your innermost being.

As a watchman warrior, I know that the armor of God is vitally important, for no warrior would willingly step out into battle without being properly outfitted. In Ephesians 6:10-17, Paul teaches us about the armor of God, and on this particular morning, as I was in my War Room preparing to put on my armor, I was amazed as in the spirit realm, I saw another door, an inner chamber, and I felt the Lord compelling me to go through that door.

I had been through doors before, but they were so painful in the deeper personal work being done that I was afraid to open this one. When I finally did, my Father called me to join Him in what appeared to be a larger closet within my closet, and the Lord started a brand new process right there.

In the vision as I stepped inside, He showed me the deep inner chamber of my spirit, the place I have come to call my Tameion Chamber. In this place, He revealed even more of the garments of preparation that are found in His Word. The things the Lord showed me in the Spirit have become a part of my everyday prayer life and have impacted not only my relationship with Him, but also the way I see and respond to everything.

Father God had prepared this place so that He could dress me as the Bride of Christ, right there inside that Tameion Chamber.

The book *"Watchman Warrior, Intercessory Prayer"* gives a background for this concept. "In ancient times, a Tameion Chamber was an inner room like a room within a room, a place of complete privacy that was set apart for the most intimate times between a man and woman. There were no windows, and there was only one door.

"In the temple that Solomon built, the Holy of Holies was a room within a room, an innermost chamber that was the home of the Lord, Yahweh. A Tameion Chamber. We are now the temple of the Holy Spirit and He has prepared a place for us where we can go and meet with Him in that innermost place of our beings, our Tameion Chamber.

"Jesus mentions the Tameion Chamber in Matthew 6:6. *'But you, when you pray, enter your **closet** and when you have shut your door, pray to your Father who is in secret. And your Father who sees in secret will reward you openly'* (MEV). The Greek word for **closet** (G5009) in this verse is **tameion,** and it is defined as a secret or inner chamber and a storehouse.

"There are two things going on here; a secret place for intimacy with God within us, and a storehouse of resources within His Kingdom. God created each of us with a Tameion Chamber that houses our spirits, and as believers in Jesus, God's Spirit also lives in this secret chamber. Studying God's Word and hiding it in our hearts stores up spiritual, heavenly resources within our Tameion Chamber, for Jesus is the Living Word and in Him *'are hidden all the treasures of wisdom and knowledge'* (Colossians 2:3b)."[16]

Maybe at one time or another you have been in your Tameion Chamber. It's not an easy room to stay in because it can be very painful and difficult when the Father starts doing a deeper work. If I can just encourage you to press in so that you will go through the process, you will stand amazed at the incredible work that happens in your Tameion Chamber. Father God in all His perfection and in the fullness of all His wisdom will change you from the inside out. You will become a beautiful reflection of His Glory. My life has been radically changed as I have allowed My Father God to prepare me to meet His One and only Son.

It has become a customary part of my morning to return daily to meet with the Father in this intimate, secret chamber, and to get dressed as the Bride of Christ. The reality of the things in my Tameion Chamber and the ministry of the Holy Spirit that goes on in that secret place help prepare me for each days assignments and for the calling of God in my life.

---

[16] Nancy Bowser, *"Watchman Warrior, Intercessory Prayer,"* 2015, p. 56.

I am going to take you with me into my Tameion Chamber. I believe that the Lord has prepared a Tameion Chamber for everyone, although each will be different just as our personalities and relationships are different. However, I will share some of the basic treasures I have found, hoping that my own experience will encourage you. I pray that you too will begin to discover the treasures that are found throughout scripture, for since our relationship with Jesus is always growing, our Tameion Chambers will continue to be filled daily with new treasures that the Lord has prepared for us to use.

As I share, keep in mind that this is *my* Tameion Chamber. With that said, a lot of the things that are in my Tameion Chamber will be in yours as well, because everything that I've found in mine is backed up by the Word. But I expect that the Lord will show you things in yours apart from mine, and that He will minister to you in a very real, very personal way.

The truth that I share is for the benefit of all who are serious about going deeper in relationship with Christ. Remember, we must prepare for war every day, for there is an enemy whose desire is for our destruction and for the destruction of God's Kingdom. And in these last hours before our Lord returns for His Bride, Satan is taking his warfare to a whole new level. We must be prepared and take our relationship with Christ to a whole new level as well, for our protection and victory is found only in Him.

So please, come with me into my **Tameion Chamber** and allow the Holy Spirit to minister to you as the Father clothes us with the garments and armor He has asked us to wear. These garments and armor are the proper wedding attire. May we not be found dressed inappropriately on that day (Matthew 22:11-14).

9
*T*he *D*oor

As I prayed, I saw a door...

"Father, I feel You beckoning me to a door that I see in the spirit, and I am going to move toward it with expectation! What is behind that door, Lord? I am curious."

As I open the door, I realize that it is a closet. I step inside and am surprised at how much room there is! I quickly see many things and know that I have been led here by the Spirit of God.

I see a shelf with many items... A crown, beautiful bottles of different sizes and shapes. In the far corner I see a stand made of precious metal, maybe brass with armor on it. There is a beautiful, very comfortable looking red chair with a crystal bowl sitting where you would place your feet. I also see a beautifully carved wooden table next to the chair with a Bible and journal sitting on it. And then there are all those garments! They are hanging on a beautiful rack that looks like it's made of gold.

There are many treasures in this closet, and I know that I will be in here for a while. It is lit by some kind of light, yet there is no lamp. As I am gazing and looking around, I am suddenly stirred by the Spirit of my Father.

I hear Him say, *"Awake, awake, Put on thy strength, O Zion; Put on thy beautiful garments, O Jerusalem, the holy city;"* (Isaiah 52:1, JPS Tanakh).

Cleansing. As I move deeper inside the closet, I notice that there is a golden mirror on the left wall. Looking into the mirror, I am surprised to see myself naked.

"Father, I have come. I am here! I have stepped into this closet by faith and I see that I am standing before You, naked, but somehow I know that I am pure and clean. Lord, I do feel somewhat damp, as though I have just had a shower but I feel that there is more that needs to be done. Interesting. Before I came into this closet I was reading Your Word and I was in prayer.

"Oh, now it makes perfect sense! I have been sanctified by Your Word. I have washed myself in Your Word and have bathed myself in the precious blood of Jesus (John 17:17; John 15:3; 1 Corinthians 6:11; Ephesians 5:26; 1 Peter 1: 18-19). That explains it! I have just been washed and bathed; yet I know something is missing. What else is there Father?"

I sense My Father motion for me to take a seat in the beautiful red chair. I can feel His presence kneeling before me and I immediately know that He is going to wash my feet!

"Father, I am not sure how I feel about this."

As if He didn't notice my apprehension or hear my quiet plea, He calmly stands and reaches for one of the beautiful jars on the shelf. He pours the fragrant water into the glass bowl at my feet, and then gently places my feet into the bowl.

"NO Father! You can't wash my feet," I cry! "I should be washing Yours!"

He gently says to me, *"You do not realize now what I am doing, but in a moment you will understand."* I then hear Him say, *"Connie, unless I wash your feet daily from all that you have walked in and picked up in the world where I have sent you, you will have no part with me."* He went on, *"A person who has had a bath needs only to wash his feet, and then his whole body is clean. Connie, you are clean. Your salvation is secure.*

"Do you now understand what I have done for you? Connie, for so many years you have called me 'Teacher' and 'Lord' and rightly so, for that is what I am and what I have been to you. Now that I, Your Lord and Teacher have washed your feet, I am asking you to wash the feet of those I put before you each day. I do all of this as an example that you should do as I have done for you. I tell you the truth, no servant is greater than his master, nor is the messenger greater than the one who sent him. My precious daughter, now that you know these things, you will be blessed if you do them for others."

"Yes, Father, I understand and I recognize these very words. They are from Your Son Jesus!"

I immediately grab the big, beautiful Bible that is sitting on the table next to me, and I easily find the passage as I have read it so many times. "Yes, here it is! It's just as Jesus said in John 13:6-17.

"You are saying that I need to have my feet washed daily and that I am to do the same for others. In this I am doing more than allowing Your Son, Jesus just to be my Teacher! Jesus has now become my, Lord! His role in my life has changed!

"Father, I want my feet to be washed daily as I come into this closet, and I will be faithful to do the same for others no matter how that may look."

As I lift my feet out of the bowl, I can sense my Father smile. I feel the warmth of the Holy Spirit upon my feet and they are instantly dry! I walk over and look in the mirror. My washing is complete.

I also have the new understanding that I can come into this closet at any time with things upon my feet that I have picked up in the world that haven't been pleasing to my Lord. He will always be here, waiting and ready, to wash my feet.

Again, I am startled out of my pondering as I hear My Father speak to me, *"Connie, now it's time to put your garments on. You must get ready for your day!"*

10
*G*arment Of *S*alvation

I **turn away from the mirror** and walk over to the hanging garments. I run my hand gently over them. Wow, they are beautiful and all so different!

I continue looking over the many garments and feel that the Lord is giving me the choice of the first garment. I know that this is a very important choice and that I have to *choose* to put this garment on. I select one.

"Yes, Holy Spirit, this is the right garment, I can tell. It looks very costly and precious."

As I touch the garment, I think to myself, "I have never felt anything like this before. I can't imagine how much something like this would cost!"

I hear the Holy Spirit whisper in my ear, *"We cannot put or place a value on this garment, for its purchase price cannot be measured by your earthly understanding of wealth."*

"Yes, Holy Spirit, I understand and I *choose* to put this garment on!" I ask, "Father, what is this garment's name? Why did I have to choose it? The Holy Spirit told me it was costly. Is it the most expensive garment in my closet?"

"Yes, Connie," the Father answers. *"This is the most expensive garment in your closet. It cost Me greatly, but I paid the price just for you! This is your* **Garment of Salvation** *and I purchased this with the life of My Son, Jesus, just for you!"*

"Father, You know how much I love Your Son, Jesus!" I respond. I obediently place the costly garment over my head. It fits perfectly and is the most beautiful thing I have ever put on! Realizing the price that was paid for me, all I can do is cry and tremble as the precious Fear of the Lord seems to overwhelm me (Philippians 2:12).

But then, as I turn, I look and am in awe. I see myself in the beautiful golden mirror, dressed in my Garment of Salvation. I have no control over my tongue and the precious Word of my Father leaps out of my heart and I cry out loud, *"Happy is he whose transgression is forgiven, whose sin is pardoned"..."I will greatly rejoice in the LORD, My soul shall be joyful in my God; For He hath clothed me with the garments of salvation, He hath covered me with the robe of victory, As a bridegroom putteth on a priestly diadem, And as a bride adorneth herself with her jewels"* (Psalm 32:1; Isaiah 61:10 - JPS Tanakh).

11

*P*riestly *U*ndergarments

I turn back toward the beautiful rack of garments with expectation. "Lord, what are these garments? I can see that they belong together and I know I am supposed to put them on next."

"Connie, these are your **Priestly Undergarments.** *They will go underneath all the rest of your robes. In Exodus 28, I reveal the importance of these special garments that Aaron and the priests were to wear as they served me. Priestly garments were worn as a physical manifestation of a spiritual truth taking place, an outward sign of an inward condition."*

I sit down in my red chair and pick up my precious Bible. As I read Exodus 28, I realize that these priests had to be right with God and seen as holy and pure. **It wasn't about human perfection, but it was the state of their heart in their sincerity toward knowing God and in having righteous fear of Him. Because of the garments they were wearing, they were identified as worthy and as His own.** They were able to push through all of the interference and hindrances, and to reach God's heart with their prayer. And I realize that it is no different for me.

I hear my Father speak. *"You are My priest just as they were then. Connie, what does My Word say about this?"*

"Father, 1 Peter 2:9 comes to mind. *'But you are a chosen generation, a royal priesthood, a holy nation, His own special people, that you may proclaim the praises of Him who called you out of darkness into His marvelous light.'"*

I look over at the undergarments hanging on the rack as the Father continues.

"That's right, Connie. **These undergarments are to remind you that you are chosen to be set apart, to fulfill a holy calling of service to Me. You are no longer your own, but have been bought with a price. It is no longer you who live, but Christ who lives in you.**

"In the Old Testament, it was only the Levitical priests who were able to enter My presence as they had been set apart from birth for the purpose of serving Me in My presence. Their clothing was an outward sign of their calling to holiness, and the priests were only allowed in My presence as they were properly clothed.

"There were some who were not born into the office of priesthood, but who chose to become Nazarite priests by taking a vow of holiness, a vow of sanctification, of being set apart from the world.

"I so desperately wanted all of my children to be able to be near to Me in My holy place, and now, as you are in My Son, Jesus, that has been made possible. I see you as He is: holy, pure and righteous. He is the covering that hides your nakedness and human condition. As you choose to be set apart for Me through Jesus, it is My greatest desire for you to come boldly into My presence."

Words that I know so well begin flowing through my thoughts, and I turn the pages of my Bible until I come to them. *"...Christ Jesus our Lord, in whom we have boldness and access with confidence through faith in Him....Let us therefore come boldly to the throne of grace, that we may obtain mercy and find grace to help in time of need"* (Ephesians 3:11b-12; Hebrews 4:16).

The impact of my Father's words strikes my spirit in confirmation as the truth sinks in. I fall to my knees in awe of His great love and desire for me!

"Father, I feel so unworthy! But I know and choose to believe the truth that in Christ, my guilt and shame are removed."

The assuring words of Hebrews 10:21-22 come to mind. *"...and since we have a great priest over the house of God, let us draw near with a sincere heart in full assurance of faith, having our hearts sprinkled clean from an evil conscience and our bodies washed with pure water."*

"I choose to accept this calling based on the cleansing blood of the perfect Lamb and my faith in Him. I choose to be set apart for You. My life is Yours, Father. I will live to love and serve You, to be near to You."

"Connie, I accept you, your love and service. Now put on your priestly undergarments."

I lay my Bible on the table, and as I stand and obediently put them on, I can feel something happening within my spirit as I place each garment over my head. It's a strengthening, a covering and yet there is a spiritual weightiness to them that I cannot put my finger on.

"Connie, with these priestly garments come great responsibility. I have told you that you are to put on the FULL armor of God and these priestly garments are part of your armor as my daughter. These garments carry with them the anointing of **'Sincerity of Heart'** *and the* **'Fear of the Lord'"** (Colossians 3:22). *You will need to seek My heart and My wisdom daily, for to wear these garments without obedience would be very costly to you."*

He continues, *"Many of My children put these robes on daily but they are not obedient to Me or My ways and their hearts are not sincere. They have no fear of Me and wander after the things of this world rather than the things of My Kingdom! This does not please Me!*

"Connie, I will only be able to bless you in your obedience! **You must never forget that when you are wearing these robes, you represent Me!** *I have spoken to you very clearly through My Word.*

"Daughter, take My Word off the table and turn to Exodus 19:5-6. What does it say? I want to hear you speak it out loud!"

"Yes Father. It says, *'Now therefore, if you will indeed obey My voice and keep My covenant, you shall be My treasured possession among all peoples, for all the earth is Mine; and you shall be to Me a kingdom of priests and a holy nation.'"*

"Connie, do you see that I desire a priestly people to represent Me in your city?"

"Yes Father, I understand."

"My Word declares that, I, not only as your Father but also as your great 'I AM,' am not visible in the physical realm. (Exodus 33:20; Colossians 1:15). It is a great sin to pretend otherwise and to produce an image that is worshipped in My place (Deuteronomy 5:8-9). But because of My kindness and love toward you, I sent My one and only Son, Jesus, who WAS visible, to

represent Me. Yet many have and are still rejecting Me when they reject Him, and now that He is with Me at My right hand, I have chosen to elect you as one of My priestly representatives who can be seen, just as My Son was seen.

"You, Connie, as My priest, are visible. I have covered you in flesh and you are an ambassador to your city along with the others I have chosen that have been obedient. You must never forget that you are serving on behalf of Me, the Invisible, the Great 'I AM.' You are only one of many I have chosen and set apart. I have called others, but not all have been obedient to that call."

"Yes Father, I am humbled at even the thought of all that this entails, but I understand."

12

Robe Of Righteousness

"Father, I know which garment is next! It stands out so brightly!"

I have to close my eyes for a moment due to the brightness of this garment. My eyes become very watery, but somehow I can see more clearly. I can see that this garment is different. It is a robe with a belt attached to it, and I can't help but notice that the belt is even brighter than the garment!

I can feel a gentle warmth coming from the garment, and my spirit and my mouth at the same time cry out the rest of the scripture in Isaiah *"...and HE arrayed me with a robe of Righteousness, as a bridegroom adorns his head like a priest, and a bride adorns herself with her jewels!"* (Isaiah 61:10).

It is so bright that I am almost afraid to touch it. I am unfamiliar with this color of white and have never seen it in this earthly realm. I place my hand on the beautiful robe and my emotions are stirred at their deepest level and my heart immediately runs to His Word.

"Father, You have told me in 1 John 1:5-7, *'You are Light and in You there is no darkness at all!'"*

I ask cautiously, "Father, it seems to be made of light. Is it?"

"Connie, you know the scriptures well. What comes to your mind?"

"Well, Romans 13 verses 11 and 12 come to my mind."

"Go to it Child and read! What does it say?"

I feel Him so close to me and I read His Word out loud to Him. *"And do this, understanding the present time: The hour has already come for you to wake up from your slumber, because our salvation is nearer now than when we first believed. The night is nearly over; the day is almost here. So let us put aside the deeds of darkness and put on the armor of light."*

All of a sudden it makes perfect sense!

"Father, Your Word says in this portion of scripture that the day is near. Your Son is coming back soon. I understand that completely. I also know You are with me in this secret place and clearly You are teaching me the things You want me to know. This is my dressing room and You are having me to get ready for my day! You are the One who brought me in here...

"So let me get this straight. Your Word is telling me that my **Robe of Righteousness** is not just something that I put on for my pleasure. It is not just something that will get me through the pearly gates, although I do believe and understand that is part of it. This Robe of Righteousness has another vital purpose. **"The Robe of Righteousness is also for my protection in what you have called me to do!** Father, You are teaching me that this is a very, very important part of my armor!"

I ponder the thought for what seems like hours and the implications of this robe. This changes everything for me regarding spiritual warfare! I realize that this is a very strategic, very important garment in battling the enemy. I must be faithful to put it on daily.

I leave the bright garment for just a moment and grab the golden journal off its stand. I start writing down everything that I am being shown by my Father.

When I am done, I touch the robe again and lift it off the rack. I notice right away that it has been created to fit me perfectly, and I immediately drop to my knees. Right now, here in this Tameion Chamber, I feel led to make a covenant with my Father.

"I'm saying to You, my Abba Father, that I choose to put aside the deeds of darkness and to put on my Robe of Righteousness daily, faithfully!"

I stand and gaze at the robe. "This robe is so beautiful! Father, I know that this is Your light, Your righteousness, and that of your Son, Jesus. I will now joyfully put this robe on over my other garments."

"Wait!" commands my Father. *"I am the One to place this garment on you!"*

I quickly let go of the robe and obediently lift my hands in surrender.

Immediately I feel my Father placing His righteousness over me and it covers my whole body. I am again feeling strengthened deep inside. It's an inner strength and my heart sings out, *"Let us rejoice and exult and give Him the glory, for the marriage of the Lamb has come and His Bride has made herself ready; it was granted her to clothe herself with fine linen, bright and pure, for the fine linen is the righteous deeds of the saints..."* (Revelation 19:7-8).

Belt Of Righteousness. I stand before my mirror and notice a stunning bright belt attached to this robe. I see that they must go together. The robe is not complete without it. I ask, "Father, what is this belt?"

His reply comes immediately. *"This belt belongs to My Son Jesus, and because of what He accomplished on the cross, each one of My children have the opportunity to wear His **Belt of Righteousness**. This is what secures your Robe of Righteousness. It will always be a reminder to you of the work that He accomplished. So, yes, you wear a Robe of Righteousness, but when His Belt of Righteousness is added to the Robe, it becomes your 'Armor of Light!' It is only secure and powerful because of Him."* (Isaiah 11:5)

"My Armor of Light?"

13

Armor Of Light

"**Father, I am so in awe** of this revelation and heaven's mysteries. I remember reading about the Armor of Light in Your Word many times, and now I have so many questions. What does this Armor of Light do? And what is it for? How can light be armor? How can this beautiful Armor of Light protect and defend me?"

I know from experience that darkness has no choice but to flee in the presence of light. How much more so when a woman or man of God is wearing an Armor of Light?

Yes, now it is clear to me that my Robe of Righteousness is also my **Armor of Light**! I feel like a 4-year-old full of questions because my heart is filled with such wonder. I slowly turn to look into the beautiful mirror, and my wonder turns to amazement and awe at what I see standing before me. I can no longer see the Robe of Righteousness and the Belt of Righteousness as two separate pieces because they have become one and are something so beautiful that there are no words on this earth that could explain them.

As I awaken out of my place of wonder and fasten the bright belt tightly around my waist, I again hear my Father's voice. *"Connie, this weapon of Armor can only be activated as you put upon yourself the Robe of Righteousness and My Son's Belt of Righteousness. This will be one of the most important pieces of your armor, and you need to make sure you put it on daily.*

"You know that I have taught you to put off the things of darkness that will continually pull at your hope and trust in me. This darkness will be in relentless pursuit of you, wanting nothing less than your total destruction. This darkness wants to undermine My work in your life.

"As well as protecting you from things of this world that come against My Kingdom, your Armor of Light will protect you from your own inner struggles and fears. I know that there are times that you feel unworthy and are afraid. Please know daughter, that I am fully aware of each lie the enemy tries to

whisper in your ear and every darkened memory he tries to dig up and place within your mind hoping for your defeat. He wants you to come to a place within yourself that you question who I have made you to be.

"This Armor of Light that I am providing for you will be faithful to shine so specifically and in such a way as to protect you from these enemy-driven thought patterns. Your Armor of Light has been created specifically for you in such a fashion that it will enable you to face both your inner and outer fears. It will give you the courage and strength to respond appropriately to deadly thought patterns, situations, offences and any other thing that may be thrown your way."

"Yes, Father, I understand, but I still have more questions."

I immediately turn and walk over to my beautiful red chair and take a seat. I grab up His precious Book of Promises that is opened to the familiar passage in Romans 13 and I read it again.

"Yes, here it is! *'And do this, understanding the occasion. The hour has come for you to wake up from your slumber, for our salvation is nearer now than when we first believed. The night is nearly over; the day has drawn near. So let us lay aside the deeds of darkness and put on the armor of light. Let us behave decently, as in the daytime, not in carousing and drunkenness, not in sexual immorality and debauchery, not in dissension and jealousy. Instead, clothe yourselves with the Lord Jesus Christ, and make no provision for the desires of the flesh'* (Romans 13:11-14).

"Father, I see first and foremost that You command me to pick up these pieces of armor for a reason. You say that I am to 'wake up,' for the 'Night' is nearly over. You have asked me to 'lay aside' the deeds of darkness and to 'put on' these weapons of war because I will need them to prevail in every form of spiritual warfare.[17] Father, I can understand that it is imperative that I pay attention to Your Word in this portion of Scripture as the word 'armor' here in the Greek is the word 'hoplon,' and it is always in the plural, meaning 'weapons to wage war.' This implies that it is something very real and is very necessary. Not

---

[17] http://biblehub.com/greek/3696.htm

for myself alone but anyone else who would choose to put them on.

"Father, Your Word has taught me so much and I am grateful and thankful. You never lack in the area of preparing me for what is to come. I do understand that I have to *'put my trust in the light while I have it, in order that I may become a daughter of light'* (John 12:36). I need to be faithful to put on these very necessary weapons called my Armor of Light. This is so confirmed Father all through Your Word as I am also reminded that, *"if we walk in the Light as He Himself is in the Light, we have fellowship with one another, and the blood of Jesus His Son cleanses us from all sin"* (1 John 1:7).

"Father I can now clearly see the direct relationship between this Armor of Light and You being my defender as a God of Light! There are so many privileges that come with these weapons of warfare, and one of them is the freedom to enter the throne room and stand before You, My Lord. Am I correct in my assumption?"

"Yes daughter."

My heart is again filled with joy, and the room is filled with blinding light. I dance before my Father with all that I have in all of my brightness. With every move, I can hear King David's penned words of praise, *"The Lord is my light and my salvation; Whom shall I fear? The Lord is the defense of my life; Whom shall I dread. My adversaries and my enemies, they stumbled and fell. Though a host encamp against me, my heart will not fear; Though war arise against me, In spite of this I shall be confident. One thing I have asked from the Lord, that I shall seek: That I may dwell in the house of the Lord all the days of my life, to behold the beauty of the Lord and to meditate in His temple. For in the day of trouble He will conceal me in His tabernacle; In the secret place of His Tent He will hide me; He will lift me up on a rock"* (Psalm 27:1-5).

I have no idea how long or how many times I have danced before Him, but what I am fully assured of is this. When I draw near to Him, trusting that what He says is truth, He will be the glorious light that becomes part of my strong armor. May I also remember that His glory light will be my rear guard (Isaiah 58:8).

His precious promise to me is this. *"Righteousness and justice are the foundation of your throne; love and faithfulness go before you. Blessed are those who have learned to acclaim you, who walk in the light of your presence, LORD. They rejoice in your name all day long; they celebrate your righteousness. For you are their glory and strength, and by your favor you exalt our horn. Indeed, our shield belongs to the LORD, our king to the Holy One of Israel"* (Psalm 89:14-18).

14

Sash Of Faithfulness

"Connie, there is a golden sash laying on the shelf *above you. Take it down."*

I obediently reach up and take down the beautiful golden sash that is folded perfectly.

"Father, it's so beautiful! I also sense that it is powerful! What is in this material and why a sash?" I can feel my whole body shaking as I handle it! There is so much substance in this golden sash!

*"This sash that you hold in your hands belongs to My Son Jesus. It is His **Sash of Faithfulness**! Place it over your head, Child."*

I tremble as I slowly place the beautiful golden sash over my head. I can feel it falling over my mind, my eyes, my face, my heart, and then over my waist and down to my toes. I am overwhelmed and overtaken by this golden Sash of Faithfulness that belongs to my Lord!

"Child, now you are to take this sash into your hands and wrap it around your waist to bind the other garments together. This will mean to you that the Faithfulness of my Son, Jesus will be as girdle of faithfulness around your waist and will be the controlling and binding influence over your life. His Faithfulness will affect all of the garments you wear and will be a blessing over all of My purposes and actions for your life."

In obedience I do as my Father has asked, and as I wrap myself up in this beautiful, weighty sash, I am overwhelmed with a feeling that I can't quite put words too. All I know is that the Truth of who He really is, is becoming more real every moment.

I hear the Word of my Father resounding in my spirit. I can hear it clearly in my mind as I prepare my heart for what is happening.

"A shoot will come up from the stump of Jesse; from his roots a Branch will bear fruit. The Spirit of the Lord will rest on Him, the Spirit of wisdom and of understanding, the Spirit of

counsel and of power, the Spirit of knowledge and of the fear of the Lord and He will delight in the fear of the Lord. He will not judge by what He sees with His eyes, or decided by what He hears with His ears; but with righteousness He will judge with justice He will give decisions for the poor of the earth. He will strike the earth with the rod of His mouth; with the breath of His lips He will slay the wicked. Righteousness will be His belt and faithfulness the sash around His waist" (Isaiah 11:1-5).

Again, all I can do is drop to my knees in adoration and praise and I cry, *"You are faithful! O Lord, You are my God; I will exalt you and praise your name, for in perfect faithfulness you have done marvelous things, things planned long ago"* (Isaiah 25:1).

I know immediately, and it has been confirmed in the depths of my spirit, that it is only by His Son's faithfulness to the cross, and by no other means can my garments be secure. I have again readied myself for my soon coming King.

"Connie, open My Word and turn to Revelation 1. Read how John the Beloved described My Son. What did he notice My Son Jesus wearing?"

"I see it Father, it's a Golden Sash!"

"Yes, Connie, a Golden Sash! One that He still wears just for you today. My Son was never unprepared as He walked among men on the earth, so I will not have you unprepared. He always stood ready for His service to Me and I expect the same from you. To this very day, as He sits at My right hand, He continues in His ministry as your great High Priest.

"Daughter, it is good for you to understand, and I want you to make it clear to others, that He has not ceased to fulfill this very important ministry of love, especially for you and anyone else I would choose for Him. This ministry is set in place and will forever be part of the safeguard I have set up for you. Until His return for you and the rest of His Bride, He will live to make intercession for you. Your soon coming King, My Beloved Son Jesus, never sleeps, nor does He slumber, and He never takes His ministry for granted. His Golden Sash is never to be taken off as though His ministry for you has ended. He continues in it faithfully and diligently carrying out this vital ministry on behalf of those I have given Him. As His

Father, I am the one who has placed this golden sash tightly around His waist.

"As His Father, I declare to you, His superiority over this safekeeping ministry that I have called Him too. As His Father, I declare to you, the royalty and magnificence that He holds is from Me as He carries the highest honor held within all My Kingdoms. As His Father, I declare to you, the dignity and worth, the majesty and loftiness of His Name. His Name is above every name, and the glory of His reward will never be matched, even throughout eternity. He no longer cries from the dust of an earthly realm, but He makes intercession on your behalf with the authority of not only a King, but as a High Priest.

"Connie, this is what your Golden Sash represents and I want you to share it with others. Because of the ministry of your King, you are safely kept in the intercession of your Redeemer."

"Father, your Son, Jesus has always been my greatest example, and just knowing that He keeps His sash secured just for me, binds my heart to His. Just as He is faithful, I must be faithful to not unbind my sash.

"Father, You have expressed your heart to me on many occasions and said through your Word that this is the time to wake up, be sober, be alert, always watching for your Son's return. You have asked me to keep my oil lamp full and burning. This golden sash will help in the keeping of my character in order with Yours. I also understand that it can keep me safe from the earthly temptations.

"As I bind Your Word upon my heart, I bind this sash around my waist. This is my season of service and warfare, and I must teach others what you have taught me. More than any other time in history, it is relevant that I bind the Truth of who Your Son Jesus is more tightly around me. I know that I am to adorn myself with His Faithfulness.

"Father, He was faithful even unto death on a cross and my heart can hardly bear the thought of that day. My need is great for the truth of this new revelation."

15
Garment Of Praise

As I ponder the wonderful work that was done for me I finally gain my composure and remember where I am! I am in my Tameion Chamber! Yes, this is my inner closet of prayer, my secret place! It is much different than my outer closet. I am so excited and I love being in this inner chamber!

"What's next Father?" I ask in joy and expectation. "I know I need to finish getting ready for my day!"

"You must also choose daily to put your next garment on," I hear my Father say.

I reply, "Yes, Father, I understand," and I slowly reach for the next beautiful garment that catches my eye. As I take it off the golden rack I notice that it has a beautiful fragrance.

Again, His Word becomes the meditation of my heart and I remember having read His promises many times. *"...You have loved righteousness and hated wickedness; Therefore God, Your God, has anointed You With the oil of joy above Your fellows. All Your garments are fragrant with myrrh and aloes and cassia..."* (Psalm 45:7-8).

As with the other garments, the material of this garment is foreign to my touch. It's unlike anything I have ever felt before. I also notice that its colors are unlike anything I have seen on this earth with my physical eyes. It changes colors with any movement, and it is much different than the bright, white light of the other garments. It is similar to my Robe of Righteousness, yet completely different in so many ways.

"Lord, this garment seems to be made of light as the others but it's a colorful light. And yes, Father, I choose to put this beautiful and fragrant garment on today and everyday hereafter!"

As I slip this garment over my head, the fragrance and colors are overwhelming and I realize that this garment is overtaking my spirit! It is bringing all the other garments and robes that I have placed upon my body together and I feel them all becoming one garment. Looking down, I see its beauty.

I slowly turn toward the golden mirror in anticipation of what I will see. As I look at myself, my spirit is overcome from a well deep within me. I can feel something rising, coming forth and erupting from this deep place within my soul! All I can do is cry out with praise.

"My Father, I now truly know who You are! You are the Lord Most High, the Lord of Glory! *'Praise the LORD. Praise God in His sanctuary; praise Him in His mighty heavens. Praise Him for His acts of power; praise Him for His surpassing greatness. Praise Him with the sounding of the trumpet, praise Him with the harp and lyre, praise Him with timbrel and dancing, praise Him with the strings and pipe, praise Him with the clash of cymbals, praise Him with resounding cymbals. Let everything that has breath praise the LORD. Praise the LORD'"* (Psalm 150).

It's confirmed in my spirit by the Holy Spirit! I have been given something so precious, my very own **Garment of Praise!**

"Father, through this garment You will become more real to me. Your depths cannot be reached! My praise for You will never cease! Even in eternity there will be no end in my pursuit of You and Your pursuit of Me! We will love each other for all eternity! Thank You my Father! This garment is more beautiful than I could have ever imagined! You know how much I love to praise You. I will put it on every day!"

"Connie, your Garment of Praise will never wear out, nor will its colors ever fade. If you choose, you will always have a new song in your heart, and your eyes will experience life through the colors of heaven. I have created you to praise Me with your whole being. I will never grow tired or become complacent in your praise, and this is My promise to you! Your praise brings Me close! Your praise brings Me pleasure and I can do great and mighty things with a heart that is filled with praise. You will also be wearing this garment in my presence in heaven. It's yours for eternity!"

"I stand before You humbled and with a thankful and praise-filled heart, my Lord and my God!"

"Connie, there is one more thing I want you to understand about this Garment of Praise. It is one of the most valuable and important weapons you have in your entire wardrobe as an

intercessor. It must be worn by you daily and used for the many assignments I have for you here on this earth."

"But Lord, a Garment of Praise used for assignments? I'm not sure I understand. I don't really see how this can be a weapon. I do know that it helps to push back the spirit of Heaviness. Is there more?"

"Yes, Child! This garment is to be used to defeat the many and very specific enemies that come against My children. Especially, the spirit of Heaviness! These same enemies have troubled you since you were a child, and there is one in particular that I want you to defeat with your Weapon of Praise!"

"I'm listening Father. You have my full attention!"

"You have been seeking My heart for many years about this unrelenting spirit in your life that has been so contrary to My plans for you. I am now giving you the weapon you will need to defeat this spirit.

"For as the days grow darker on the earth and My return is closer than it's ever been, this spirit grows stronger. It is in full operation in many of those around you and will try and overtake you and My other sons and daughters. You will need to know how to defeat this spirit and teach others to do the same.

"Connie, you know My Word. What does it say about the Garment of Praise? What is it for?"

The Spirit of *Heaviness,* *Amalek.* I take a seat in the big red chair, reach for the beautiful Bible, and turn to the familiar passage of Isaiah 61:3. "*To appoint unto them that mourn in Zion, To give unto them a garland for ashes, The oil of joy for mourning, The mantle of praise for the* **spirit of Heaviness***; That they might be called terebinths of righteousness, The planting of the LORD, wherein He might glory*" (JPS Tanakh).

"Lord, this spirit that has troubled me is the spirit of Heaviness!"

"Yes, Connie, that is one of its names, but only one. It has many names and presents itself in many ways. I also want you to look up Exodus 17 and read about the Children of Israel and the enemy they had to fight because of their spirit of Rebellion."

As I turn to Exodus 17, I also grab the beautiful journal. I can sense the Holy Spirit getting ready to teach me something that I need to remember as an intercessor.

As I am reading in Exodus 17, verses 12-16 jump out at me. *"But Moses' hands were heavy; and they took a stone, and put it under him, and he sat thereon; and Aaron and Hur stayed up his hands, the one on the one side, and the other on the other side; and his hands were steady until the going down of the sun. And Joshua discomfited Amalek and his people with the edge of the sword. And the LORD said unto Moses: 'Write this for a memorial in the book, and rehearse it in the ears of Joshua: for I will utterly blot out the remembrance of Amalek from under heaven. And Moses built an altar, and called the name of it Adonai-Nissi. And he said: 'The hand upon the throne of the LORD:* **the LORD will have war with Amalek from generation to generation'"** (JPS Tanakh, author's emphasis).

I ponder this portion of scripture in Exodus and the full implication of why this garment is so vitally important as a weapon of spiritual warfare begins to set in. I hear the Spirit direct me to read about King Saul, Samuel the prophet, and the king of the Amalekites in 1 Samuel 15.

I open the Bible and begin to read. King Saul was fighting against Agag, king of the Amalekites. The Amalekites had aligned themselves with Egypt's king, Pharaoh, and they hated God's chosen people.

I stop and consider a new thought. "Father, the roots of destruction in this king of the Amalekites go way back in history and are also far reaching into the future! I know from my past studies that Amalek (father of the Amalekite nation) was the grandson of Esau (Genesis 36:12; 1 Chronicles 1:36), and Esau was a man who despised his birthright, which would have been the precious 'Promised Land!' This descendant of Esau, King Amalek, was the first King to attack the Children of Israel right after they had miraculously crossed over the Red Sea on their way to the Promised Land."

I close my eyes and lean my head against the softness of my red chair as I reflect on Amalek's influence down through the generations. Moving one thousand years forward in history, past the time of King Saul, the Book of Esther tells of another descendant of Amalek. Haman was a wicked man who hated the Jewish people so much that he passionately and fervently tried to plan their destruction. The spirit of Amalek had been passed down generationally and was operating in and through him. I know the story of how Esther, Mordecai and the Children of Israel were only able to defeat the wicked Haman through fasting and prayer and spiritual warfare.

I shake my head in sorrow when I realize that all the hatred against the Jews at that time came about because King Saul had disobeyed God so many years before.

I open my eyes and turn back to the beautiful pages in my Bible. 1 Samuel 15 tells this story that I have read many times, but I am now seeing it through a whole new perspective.

Shortly after Israel became a unified Kingdom under the reign of King Saul, the prophet Samuel told Saul to gather his troops and to totally wipe out Agag, the King of Amalek, the people of his city, and even every animal. God had ordered that anything with the breath of life in it must die! It was very clear to Saul exactly what he needed to do in obedience to God.

King Saul started out in obedience and assembled his army. He went to war and was able to overtake his enemy. At first, he appeared victorious over the king of Amalek by virtually destroying the nation. But...there is always a "But!"

In true form and faithful to his character, the real enemy shows up. King Saul was tempted with pride, rebellion, greed, and even pity for Agag, the king of the Amalekites.

"Father, I can see the smallest of sin finding its way into the heart of King Saul! And then he disobeyed You, God, in a big way and it cost him his anointing and his throne, and so much more! He did not listen to You when You specifically instructed him to destroy King Agag. You told King Saul through the Prophet Samuel to *'go and smite Amalek, and utterly destroy all that they have, and spare them not; but slay both man and woman, infant and suckling, ox and sheep, camel and ass'* (1 Samuel 15:3).

"And in 1 Samuel 15:8-9 Your Word says that Saul went against the Word of the Lord. *'He took Agag the king of the Amalekites alive....King Saul spared Agag and the best of the sheep, and of the oxen, even the young of the second birth, and the lambs, and all that was good, and would not utterly destroy them; but everything that was of no account and feeble, that they destroyed utterly'* (JPS Tanakh).

"Father, King Saul only obeyed half of what You told him. How many times have I done that? And at what cost to my anointing and testimony? By having mercy on the king of Amalek, Saul went against the specific directive You gave him, which was to destroy Amalek! Father, You are never pleased by partial obedience!

"In 1 Samuel Chapter 15, Your precious Word says that the prophet Samuel rose early the very next morning, came to Saul and informed him that God was angered by his taking King Agag alive. He was also angered that he had taken the best of his sheep and his cattle for spoils! Samuel informed King Saul that God was angry with him for not fulfilling the direct commandment to utterly destroy the king of Amalek.

"Saul lied and denied the charges the prophet was bringing against him! Oh Lord, how many times have I tried to make excuses and even lied to you in my rebellion? My heart is breaking as I read this chapter in your Word. There are so many lessons to be learned here. A whole book could be written on just the 15th Chapter of 1 Samuel. At least King Saul soon realized his disobedience and he admitted his rebellion against You. Unfortunately it was too late. Samuel immediately ordered King Saul to have King Agag brought before him. Samuel killed Agag, the king of Amalek on the spot!

"At this point I can't help but think that King Saul's disobedience had everything to do with the battle that had to be fought a thousand years later with Haman who was an Agagite, and most likely a descendent of this awful King Agag, king of the Amalekites! The Amalekites have been long-time enemies of the children of God. God had ordered King Saul to destroy the Amalekites centuries earlier for a reason! (1 Samuel 15:3). Saul failed to obey God's mandate and his disobedience led not only to the loss of his kingdom and his anointing, but to the mortal danger that the Jews were faced with even over a thousand years later as a result of Haman's hatred for them.

"Father, it seems to me that all the descendants of Amalek in one way or another have purposed in their hearts to annihilate Your children. Not just to wound them or capture them or to keep them in bondage, but to destroy them.

"There are great lessons for me to learn here. Father, thank you for showing me about this grandson of Esau named Amalek. I believe that You are showing me that the spirit of Amalek is still in operation today. Satan still hates the children of God and wants nothing more than to destroy me as I am on my way to the 'Promised Land.' I need to pay close attention to this passage of scripture and what it is that You want me to learn. One thing I know You are teaching me. **This spirit will be defeated through my full obedience to You and also through intercession and praise."**

As I pull my heart and my mind back to the scripture in Isaiah, all of a sudden I can see this spirit of Heaviness for what it really is. It is something that Moses seemed to experience while he was interceding for the battle against Amalek on behalf of the Children of Israel. Even though they had to fight this battle because of their own rebellion, God still raised up a man named Moses, an intercessor, to pray them through the battle to victory.

When Moses lifted his hands, Israel prevailed. But when Moses' arms grew heavy and he could no longer hold them toward heaven, the enemy would prevail. Hands lifted toward heaven represent praise! And that is exactly what Moses was doing!

"Father, You are showing me that Moses' lifted arms were a sign of praise, surrender, humility and worship! He was putting on his Garment of Praise for the battle at hand with this wicked King Amalek.

"I have a feeling that the spirit of Heaviness and this spirit that was within Amalek are in cahoots and operating together still today. And it looks like intercession, praise, lifted hands and unity all play a part in defeating him.

"Father, as I continue to study, I am convinced that this same awful spirit does exist today. **Your Spirit has taught me that spiritual warfare is won within the confines of one's own heart.** It is an enemy that I must be willing to defeat in my own life on behalf of my future generations and for the body of Christ. Satan and his cohorts are a fierce opposition, always waiting to way-lay and assault me, my family, my church and the children of God. It is waiting to ambush, ensnare and destroy the lives of those around me. We each have a part to play in the larger picture of the body of Christ, and I know I have a part to play here, especially for those whom I have been interceding for. My personal victories will always benefit the whole body, so I need to understand this spirit and overcome.

"Father, You vowed to fight the Amalekites from generation to generation. Am I correct in these assumptions that I have made?"

"Connie, I want you to study Amalek; what he represents and the meaning of his name in Hebrew. You must be familiar with all aspects of this very real enemy!"

So I begin this journey right here in the big red chair inside my Tameion Chamber.

As I study out the Hebrew meaning and traditions of King Amalek, I find that he represents pure evil. The Hebrew name עמלק Amalek begins with the Hebrew letter ע Ayin, which symbolizes the "eye." The second letter מ Mem, means "water, chaos, blood." The third letter ל Lamed means "to shepherd, lead, goad control, move toward" and ק Qof which means "revolution, condense and time."

"Father, this spirit of Amalek represents 'the evil eye of doubt and pride.' I also see him representing chaos, blood, control and moving toward a revolution! A revolution against your chosen people! When I remove the Ayin from 'Amalek,' I am left with malak. This is a verb that means 'to chop off' or to sever.

"So Father, am I understanding this correctly? Amalek can represent spiritual blindness, and one of his duties or functions is to chop off, pull out or even sever our spiritual eyes. And doubt! He causes doubt! The Bible's history is clear. You called the Israelites to go to Mount Sinai. You wanted to present Your plan, Your purpose, Your Word and Your mandate to Your beloved people. And as they were going in obedience to You, Amalek played dirty. He went behind them and struck the Children of Israel 'from the rear!' Amalek ambushed the weak and feeble as they were on their way to meet with God! He struck his deadly blow when they were faint and weary.

82

"The inner workings of the enemy of our soul are clear and undeniable to me. Amalek's timing and attack on God's people was no coincidence. This would cause them to doubt and that is why You wanted the Amalekites destroyed.

"And he has caused me to doubt! Especially in those times when I'm weak or tired and feel that spirit of Heaviness coming upon me. Father, it is no different today, is it?"

I consider how many times I have been on my way to receive my call, my mandate, my Word and instructions from the Lord and then find myself ambushed from behind. My personal victory in this battle against the spirit of Heaviness and the spirit of Amalek will come through my faithfulness in wearing my garment of praise daily.

"Father, you have given me Your Word as an instruction manual. This wicked King Amalek represented a nation that actually existed, but I rest assured that this Bible You have placed in my hands is no mere history book. Beyond its writings and histories of past events, it can and will furnish me with the insights and weapons that can and will encourage my present callings and service to God. I need to make sure that I teach others to do the same.

"You taught me long ago that I am to always look at the character of the people that You chose to name in Your beloved Book, whether good or bad. I am also to learn these things because this may describe a character trait I need to see within myself, good or bad.

"Father, this character of Amalek stood in direct opposition to the plans and purposes You had for the Children of Israel. The actions of Amalek were in blatant defiance of the very foundations of what You wanted to do in and through Your people. It's no different for me!

"In Deuteronomy 25:17-19, You told the Israelites, *'Remember what Amalek did unto thee by the way as ye came forth out of Egypt; how he met thee by the way, and smote the hindmost of thee, all that were enfeebled in thy rear, when thou wast faint and weary; and he feared not God. Therefore it shall be, when the LORD thy God hath given thee rest from all thine enemies round about, in the land which the LORD thy God giveth thee for an inheritance to possess it, that thou shalt blot out the*

remembrance of Amalek from under heaven; thou shalt not forget'
(JPS Tanakh).

"If You told them that they must remember what Amalek did and how he operated then, You must be telling me the same. You didn't want them to forget the hideous attack by Amalek because their battle with the spirit of Amalek would be ongoing and would affect future generations if they were not obedient and able to defeat it.

"And what truly stands out to me and is most important, is that Amalek did not fear You, the God of Israel! That is pride and arrogance.

"While this battle was raging, Moses, Aaron and Hur went to the top of the mountain to intercede on behalf of the battle with Amalek. When the spirit of Heaviness came upon Moses, with a heart of unity and a oneness of spirit, Aaron and Hur stood in the gap and helped to lift the humbled, surrendered heart and hands of their leader, brother and friend in the Lord.

"Father, I see this picture clearly. If I need help I can call upon other prayer warriors, intercessors and watchman, and they can call upon me. Together we can get the job done.

"You declared in Exodus 17:16 that Moses' hands were on Your throne and that You, God, will be at war with Amalek for all generations. You hate arrogance. But Moses was a man of humility, surrender and praise, and through his intercession with clean hands and a pure heart, the battle against Amalek was won that day.

"Father, You have not called us to sit back and do nothing. This is Your call to action! Just as Moses' surrendered and lifted hands were as 'a hand laid upon the throne of heaven,' so can my hands and my intercessor sister's hands be 'a hand laid upon the throne of heaven' as we come to You with clean hands and a pure heart as well.

"Bottom line. **Praise, humility and surrender can and will win the battle and defeat this enemy, which today represents spiritual blindness.** Through praise and with our garments of praise, together we can continue to fight this spirit of Heaviness, this spirit of Amalek."

"Connie, continue to read the end of Chapter 17 and tell me what stands out to you."

84

"Well, Your newly-revealed name in this portion of scripture is **Yahweh-Nissi.** You are my War Banner, the 'standard' that leads me as a watchmen, warrior and intercessor. Apart from Your leading, all warfare that I choose to enter into will be my flesh and should be avoided. Only You, God, are capable of determining what truly righteous warfare is! Only You, God, will tell the others and me where, when and how to proceed with the battle. **And if I will stay under the submission of the 'Lord my Banner,' this enemy will be defeated through my 'Garment of Praise.' Lord, You will war on my behalf if I will but praise You!**

"Father, this is a call to me! There is an ongoing spiritual battle that will have to be fought in my life. I must determine that I will not just sit by and passively accept this spirit of Heaviness called Amalek! I will no longer ignore or tolerate it in my life! I must be willing to call this spirit out by name and expose it!

"Father, by giving me my personal Garment of Praise You are giving me the authority and power over the spirit of Heaviness who works in operation with the spirit of Amalek! (Ephesians 5:11; Luke 10:19)

"You have promised me that the weapons of my warfare have divine power to destroy any enemy strongholds (2 Corinthians 10:4). Not only am I protected by the Armor of God, but also by the 'weapons of light' according to Romans 13:12 and Ephesians 6: 11-18."

As I lay the precious Word of God back down on its resting place, I stand. The memory of His Word in my heart cries out from my mouth to my God, *"And in Thy mercy cut off mine enemies, And destroy all them that harass my soul; For I am Thy servant"* (Psalm 143:12).

16
Crown of Beauty

Immediately, a bright flash of light catches my attention and I notice my armor over in the corner on a sturdy brass stand. I know its mine; I recognize it! I have put it on daily for many years. As I walk a little closer and examine it, it's confirmed! "Yep, it is mine for sure!" I can even see some of the dents that have come from past battles.

I hear myself talking out loud again, "Wow, it's been cleaned and shined up! Thank you Lord!"

As I walk over to my armor and prepare to put it on, my Father says, *"Wait, there is another garment that you need to put on before your armor."*

"Yes, Lord, what is it? I see other garments hanging on the golden rack, but Your Spirit told me that it's not the time to put them on, so I assumed it was time for my armor. Father, please help me. I want to be obedient to Your Holy Spirit."

I feel a big smile come from my Father and hear Him say, *"Look upon the shelf."*

I turn and see the most beautiful golden crown. Sitting beside it are several other crowns made from materials I am not familiar with that are more beautiful than I could ever imagine. But the crown of gold is extremely different. It stands out among the others and I know something life changing is about to happen.

"Ok Father, is this the one?"

He answers, *"Yes, Connie, this is your **Crown of Beauty**. Please take it off the shelf."*

As I reach up for the beautiful crown, it isn't at all what I expect! It is actually made of some kind of tangible, thick cloth. It is transparent gold, but it has many colors. And it is adorned with precious stones that resemble all the colors of a rainbow. I explain to the Lord that I still don't understand exactly what to do with this Crown of Beauty.

I hear Him say, *"Connie you know how to study your Bible in Hebrew. I want you to sit down in your chair again and take the Bible off the table. This is why I have placed it there for you. I know how much you love and cherish My Word and you must always reference it. This will always be My confirmation to you, and I will teach you through My Word. I want you to look up the word 'crown' and the word 'beauty' in Hebrew according to Isaiah 61:3, 62:3. These are scriptures you know well."*

With this new crown in my hands I move quickly and take a seat in my red chair. In great expectation, I grab my Bible and look up the meaning of these two amazing words in Hebrew. I immediately see that this beautiful 'Crown' that I am holding is in fact, my **wedding veil!** I'm in awe as I study out the Hebrew word for "beauty" which is (H6286) "pĕ'er" peh-ayr'; an embellishment, fancy headdress, a tiara, a turban, beauty, ornament. The beautiful Hebrew word for "Crown" is from (H5849) "at·ä·rä'" at-aw-raw' meaning a crown, a royal diadem.

I set my precious Bible down and take a moment to let that thought sink in. With both hands I pull the beautiful crown close to my heart. I hear myself speaking the scriptures I know so well *"...to bestow on them a **crown of beauty** instead of ashes, the oil of joy instead of mourning, and a garment of praise instead of a spirit of despair. They will be called oaks of righteousness, a planting of the LORD for the display of His splendor...Thou shalt also be a **crown of beauty** in the hand of the LORD, And a royal diadem in the open hand of thy God"* (Isaiah 61:3; 62:3 NIV, JPS Tanakh, author's emphasis).

I begin to understand that this "**wedding veil crown**" is something my Father wants me to place upon my head daily underneath my Helmet of Salvation. I hear the Holy Spirit speaking to me.

*"Connie, this veil is made to cover your eyes for a very specific purpose. **As you gaze through it, you will see everything from the perspective of being the Bride of Christ including the way you view yourself. It will influence your perception and will have the same effect on others when they look at you!** They will see you as the Bride of your Father's Son, Jesus."*

"Yes, Holy Spirit, I understand, and I choose to wear this Crown of Beauty." I gently place it over my head and as it falls, I can feel it covering my eyes, my ears and my neck.

Excitement begins to build deep inside me as I continue to study these two amazing words in my precious Bible! The Holy Spirit gently reminds me that just as a bride prepares herself for her wedding day, as the Bride of Christ, by studying His Word I am preparing myself for my wedding day with Jesus, my Bridegroom.

My heart begins to pound in response as I ponder the Hebrew meaning of the word, "beauty." **This "beauty" is an attribute of God Himself and also represents His Glory!**

I am breathless as the implication of this truth hits me. "Father, You are perfection! Your beauty will always naturally flow from Your perfection, and now You have adorned me with Your perfect attribute of beauty! This is amazing! I have no words to express how I'm feeling right now.

"Father, Your beauty is perfect and desirable and nothing is lacking within Your beauty. Am I understanding this correctly? You are the perfection of everything desirable! Father, there are so many that don't desire You, Your beauty, Your Word or to even be a part of Your Church. If I am honest before You, I have not always desired Your beauty; and I most certainly have not understood it as something that is perfect. I must admit, I have not been a good reflection of You to others, and definitely not Your attribute of 'beauty!' This must have greatly grieved your heart."

"Yes, Connie, My heart would be that my Church would be willing to put on My Crown of Beauty which represents My attribute of beauty in all its perfection. There have been those who have found this gift and they know its power and influence upon others.

"This is why Satan has worked so hard to present beauty in the deceitful way he does. Not all, but many of My Church have no idea that they are wearing a false crown of beauty and are wedding themselves to Satan himself. Most who claim to be Christians do not display My attributes of beauty and they look no different than the world. This is exactly why most of the world wants nothing to do with My Church. Very few who claim to be My children really walk in or desire My true attributes. And there are even less who have put on My true bridal veil.

"Because Satan is the ruler of this world for now, he has set up everything in this world to be pleasing to the eye. The world and the Church see a false beauty that is desirable to their flesh and they have taken it upon themselves as a crown of beauty. Just look how Satan has used fashion and Hollywood to set the standards for beauty! Connie, not only have you bought into this deception over the years, but you yourself have worn the false crown of beauty that Satan has offered.

"Daughter, you have studied your enemy well and know that he was one of My most beautiful creations. Did I not say of him, 'Thus saith the Lord GOD: Thou seal most accurate, full of wisdom, and perfect in beauty...'

"Your enemy knows exactly what he is doing in distorting My attribute of beauty! **He is deceiving many in My Church to take his counterfeit crown of beauty and place it upon themselves (Ezekiel 28:12) so that what they are seeing through the false veil is not My perspective, but Satan's.**

"Connie, what I am showing you here today should put the pieces together for you. **You must understand the importance of what it is to wear My Crown of Beauty. This means that you have pledged yourself fully to be wed to my Son, Jesus, and you must see yourself as He sees you,** *for you will act according to what you believe.*

"I so love you and want you to understand the truth of this precious gift I am giving you today. Connie, when others encounter you, and you are found wearing My true attribute of beauty, it is only then that My Word will accomplish that which it is set out to do, and only then can it prosper! (Isaiah 55:11). That, My daughter, is when you will have something that others will greatly desire. Do you understand Child?"

"Yes, Father, I have never seen this until this day, and now my eyes have been opened to the truth. You have warned me in Your Word that I should not let anyone deceive me into forfeiting my crown or reward. This is exactly what the enemy has tried to do; to steal my Crown of Beauty which is my wedding veil that carries with it one of Your most powerful attributes, Your Beauty. 2 John 1:7-8 now makes so much sense. *'For many deceivers have gone out into the world, those who do not acknowledge Jesus Christ as coming in the flesh. This is the deceiver and the antichrist. Watch yourselves, that you do not lose what we have accomplished, but that you may receive a full reward.'*

"Oh Father, please forgive me. My heart is grieved that I have grieved your heart. For so many years I have accepted unto myself this counterfeit crown of beauty. I have tried to be like the rest of the world even when it comes to the things of God and the Church. I now know that this area of counterfeit beauty is something that truly grieves You and Your Holy Spirit. It is in complete contradiction of how You would have me to live. Your Word is clear that You hate wickedness! And when we, as Your Church put on the enemy's counterfeit crown of beauty, it is nothing short of readying ourselves as the bride of Satan instead of the Bride of Christ, Jesus, Your Son.

"Father, these are harsh words for me to even be speaking out loud to myself, but I know they are truth and I know I must confess my sin before You and ask that You forgive me. You have been so patient with me in my blindness, Father, and for this I thank You. But now that I see my sin, I take full responsibility for it, and I choose to forsake it!

"I know Your Word well, and it says in Genesis 6:5-6, *'Then the Lord saw that the wickedness of man was great in the earth, and that every intent of the thoughts of his heart was only evil continually. And the Lord was sorry that He had made man on the earth, and He was grieved in His heart.'* And You also have said in Ephesians 4:30-32, *'And do not grieve the Holy Spirit of God, by whom you were sealed for the day of redemption. Let all bitterness, wrath, anger, clamor, and evil speaking be put away from you, with all malice. And be kind to one another, tenderhearted, forgiving one another, even as God in Christ forgave you.'"*

I find myself compelled to kneel in front of my chair before my Father. My mind is flooded with thoughts of all the times I have come before Him to confess my sin. I know with confidence that He loves me greatly and that every tear I cry, He is catching, even now.

"Father, I kneel before You this day as my King, my Maker and the Judge of all of creation. I lift up Your Name, YHWH, and that of Your Son, Jesus. I ask You to forgive me for listening to the voice of the enemy and for accepting the counterfeit bridal veil that he offered me. I cast down that counterfeit crown and any and all sins committed with it to the feet of Jesus for judgment. With praise and thanksgiving, I am grateful for the free gift of Your love and the grace of Your redemption. This is my promise and it is for all who turn to You through the precious blood of Your Son, Jesus.

"Lord, my heart's desire is to place upon my head your Crown of Beauty, and I look forward to the day of my wedding to Your Son. I also desire to be a blessing to those to whom You would send me to, and to be a mighty witness and testimony of Your beauty, grace and goodness to those that cross my path. Most of all, I pray that I may forever bring You joy and never again grieve Your heart. Amen."

As I stand, my first thought is that I am thankful that I was able to throw that counterfeit crown to the feet of Jesus and that it is now under His feet. Someday I will be throwing good crowns at His feet in worship to Him (Revelation 4:10). But for now I am grateful that I can take my sin and my shame and lay it at His feet. I turn and gaze into my beautiful mirror and I see before me a young woman who has the true attribute of Godly beauty, and she is wearing a royal crown on her head. It is hard to recognize myself through my tears. I sense the presence of my God standing next to me catching each and every one that falls. They are tears of joy because I know I am loved and forgiven.

"Father, King David comes to my mind as he was a man after Your heart. I now better understand the heart of this king that loved You so much. He wrote of Your beauty and his desire for it in Psalm 27:4. I know this scripture by heart, but until today I didn't really understand it. *One thing I have asked from the LORD, that I shall seek: That I may dwell in the house of the LORD all the days of my life, to behold the beauty of the LORD and to meditate in His temple.'*

As I ponder the Crown of Beauty, King David, and all the other scriptures that are flooding through my soul, I hear the Holy Spirit speaking to me.

"Connie, every day as you place this Crown of Beauty, this bridal veil over your head, you must remember that a crown is placed on your head, not in your hands. This is figurative for you

being 'under the Lord's protection.' You will be kept in HIS hand, not in yours. All His true saints are kept in the palm of His hand and in this truth you must trust, rely on and abide in. Yet at the same time, you must believe and not doubt that you are a 'Crown of Beauty' to Him just as much as He is the 'King of Glory' to you (Deut. 33:3; Revelation 6:2; 19:12).

"You must never forget the crown that adorned your Bridegroom. He was rewarded with a crown of thorns knowing that someday you would wear this Crown of Beauty with the promise of your love, devotion and marital commitment to Him. Never forget that His brow was bloodied that your brow would be adorned just for Him.

"Connie, your Father God delights fully in Himself and in all His children that reflect His true attributes and character. You are most beautiful as God's daughter and are now ready to be wed to His Son. As the days on this earth grow darker, you must be faithful and respond quickly to My promptings and teachings. You must continually exhibit a conduct in your life that is most pleasing to Him. You can and will be a living, breathing manifestation of His beauty to a lost and dying world, and they will be attracted to the message of hope you have to offer them. This is My promise to you, Child. You will be most blessed when you delight yourself in all that pleases your Father.

"You have learned well today, Connie, and I want you to look upon your shelf and tell me what you see."

My heart leaps with joy! "Oh Precious Spirit! I see many crowns and they are all so beautiful. I have read about these in Your Word, and here they are, right in my Tameion Chamber! They are the imperishable crown, the crown of rejoicing, the crown of righteousness, the crown of glory, and the crown of life." (2 Timothy 4:8; 1 Corinthians 9:25-27; James 1:12; Revelation 2:10; 1 Peter 5:2-4; 1 Thessalonians 2:19; Philippians 3:12-14; Revelation 2:7; 2:11; 2:17; 2:26; 3:5; 3:12; 3:21; 21:7; Isaiah 62:3)

"Connie, the rewards of heaven will be yours someday and your Father has promised them to you and to those who are faithful."

"Thank you Holy Spirit!" After a moment of reflection, I ask, "Father, am I now ready for my armor?"

17

*T*he *A*roma Of *C*hrist

"*M*y beautiful daughter," He replies. *"Be patient! The business of your day will come all too quickly. I want your victories and accomplishments for this day to be greater! You must dress appropriately and properly because I have many assignments that I need you to be prepared for; and there is an enemy that will look for any area of your spirit, soul and body that is not covered. I want you to learn this well, for this is to be something that you do each and every day. Now, look again upon your shelf!"*

"Yes, Father. I see two beautiful bottles and there are other things, but I am not sure exactly what they are."

He says, *"For now, take that bottle to the left and pick it up."*

"Yes, Father. It is beautiful and I have never seen anything like this before. I know it's not glass, but I can see through it."

"You are right," the Father answers. *"It is not glass. It is pure gold just like my streets in heaven. Now go ahead and open it!"*

"It's perfume! Oh Father, it's the most beautiful scent I have ever smelled!"

My heart is overwhelmed and overtaken by this first encounter of the **Aroma of Christ.** I earnestly take the perfume and lavish it on myself. The smell of the fragrance overtakes my senses, and then my mind, my will and my emotions. It brings me to my knees and I am compelled to lay face down for quite some time. Tears from someplace deep inside pour out of me onto the floor of this precious room, for it has been my deepest desire that my life would be a sweet aroma to my Father and my Most High God!

I am not sure how long I lay there, and only after I feel the Holy Spirit complete the task at hand in me, am I able to slowly sit up and look in front of me. I can see myself in the beautiful golden mirror. Again, my heart cries out from the wells of scripture deep within me. *"... The fragrance of your perfume is intoxicating; your name is perfume poured out. No wonder young women adore you"* (Song of Songs 1:3, Holman).

I am compelled to say out loud, "Right now in my Tameion Chamber, I call upon the name of Jesus and I ask that this perfume continue to cover me in its sweet aroma all the days of my life! Father, you have called me to a great thing! This perfume, this aroma, is the aroma of Christ, Your one and only Son, and it's not only for the saved, but also for the lost."

His Word again fills my heart and mind. *"...For I am now the aroma of Christ to God for those who are being saved and those who are perishing..."* (2 Corinthians 2:15).

"Connie, the fragrance of My Son that you now wear, is uniquely your own. It represents what has been done in your life and is something that will affect the lives of those around you. But most importantly it reaches My throne. I long to smell the aroma of My Son upon you and upon those He has redeemed."

Then I heard Him gently speaking to me again, *"Now it is time to put your armor on."*

My eyes are still damp from the powerful experience of the moment before. How does one even put into words that they have not only encountered the aroma of Christ, but have covered themselves in it? I begin to realize that this powerful and potent fragrance is not only covering me now, but the sweet aroma has filled the closet and everything in it!

18

Belt Of Truth

As I gather myself, my thoughts and my composure, I walk over to the corner where my armor is. I gently and lovingly touch my breastplate. My heart is forever grateful that I learned to put this armor on daily as a young Christian. I know full well how it has protected me throughout the years, and that by putting it on each day, I have learned how to prepare myself for the battle (Ephesians 6:10-20).

But today it is different. This closet is different. I have learned about and read of these other garments, robes, sash's and fragrances for many years. I have always believed they existed because His Word is truth and life; however, I have never encountered them in such a personal way or entered into a spiritual closet like this one. I have had many spiritual journeys with my Father, but this one tops them all.

As I ready myself for my armor, I see my **Belt of Truth** sitting on the shelf above the stand that holds the armor. I realize that this piece is more important now than it ever has been. It has a new purpose. It will be holding all of my new garments in place. My Belt of Truth is the most beautiful belt I have ever seen. It is adorned with jewels, and I assume that it is made of gold. There are also places on this belt that hold all kinds of different weapons of different sizes.

Tucked away inside my Belt of Truth are all of the precious *Gifts of the Spirit* and all of my *Fruit of the Spirit.* I learned long ago that along with each gift there comes a fruit that must accompany that gift. [18] I also learned that we can and should operate in all the gifts, not just one, and that these can never be separated from my Belt of Truth, but must always operate together in unity, and always be readily available to be used as my Father commands.

It has not been easy learning to use my gifts and the fruit at the same time. Our flesh is not naturally wired to operate in

---

[18] Teaching Available on CD: "The Fruits of Your Spiritual Gifts" by Pastor Connie Stoffel. Order at www.igniterevival.org

the gifts let alone the fruit of the Spirit. We must become spiritually skilled in using them both properly.

I'm reminded of our Sunday service last week. At the end of the service my heart was burning with a "Word of Encouragement" for someone in that service. This gift came to me as my husband was finishing up his sermon, and then we went into a worship song. I could feel this word bubbling up and it was all I could do to not run up and tug on his shirt, but I waited. Then I saw myself running up to him and taking the microphone out of his hand, but again, I waited.

I kept asking, "Father, is it time?" I could hear nothing, and that brook that was bubbling inside me was now acting more like a volcano. My spirit felt ready to explode.

Years before, I would have run up and tugged on my husband's shirt or grabbed the microphone out of his hand and blurted out the word. But I have learned that every time one of my gifts surface, I must pray and that there must be at least one fruit that accompanies that gift. In this particular case, the fruit was "Patience!" I didn't get the go ahead from my Father and the service was being closed. I prayed again, "I hear nothing Father, have I missed it?"

We were then dismissed, and as I turned, I heard my Father's voice say, *"Now. She's the one!"* I looked and saw a member of our congregation crying. I knew immediately that I was to go to her with the specific word that had been given to me. This Word of Encouragement was meant specifically for her and if I would not have exercised the fruit of Patience, I would have blurted out the word to the whole church and I would have missed the opportunity of truly ministering to this precious woman.

As I turn my attention back onto my Belt of Truth, I notice right away that its size and weight has become bigger. It looks very heavy as if it comes with a responsibility that must be weighed out each time it is placed around my waist. I do believe that this is why so many believers don't want to put this belt on. **It is full of responsibility!** As I lift the beautiful belt off the shelf, I find that I have no problem picking it up. It looks strong, heavy and durable, and I confidently place it around my waist as I have done for so many years.

19

Breastplate Of Righteousness

I reach for my *Breastplate of Righteousness*, but pausing for just a moment, I step back as I am always in awe of its beauty! It's as if I am seeing it for the first time, every time!

As I approach it, I gently touch my Breastplate and my mind can only ask the same two questions as always. How could this God love me so much that He would prepare me as a Bride for His Son? And, how could He, the Holy One, the One True God who created the heavens and the earth be so mindful to prepare such a beautiful piece of armor for me to wear?

I have learned much in my Tameion Chamber and know that I am different and stronger in many ways. But the smallest of His ways and His mysteries will never cease to amaze me. I will now be wearing many very important garments under this beautiful Breastplate of Righteousness that has His Great and Mighty Name written all over it. I stop and wonder how I survived all of these years without really knowing how to apply the garments and robes.

"Father, this really does change everything for me! I am going to have to tell the world of my discovery of this amazing place and all that you have prepared for each one who would enter into their own Tameion Chamber.

"I now have my Robe of Salvation, my Priestly Undergarments and my Garment of Praise. I am also wearing my Robe of Righteousness and Your Son's Belt of Righteousness, which I now understand create my Armor of Light! And over these I have the greatest of honors, to stand before You with Your Son, Jesus' Sash of Faithfulness covering me from head to toe. Wow!"

Again, I turn to the beautiful golden mirror provided for me and I can't hold back my tears. They are tears of joy and thanksgiving. They are tears of hope and tears of gratefulness. I know what comes next as I turn my attention back to my beautiful Breastplate of Righteousness.

"Father, I love this essential piece of my armor. It has protected my spiritual and physical heart and vital organs for so many years, and it is just so beautiful." I reach out to put it on over all my new garments and I hear my Father's voice.

"Wait Child, sit with me for a moment!"

"Yes, Father, it's always my pleasure to be with You!" I take a seat in my beautiful red chair. "Father, do I need my journal to write about what You are going to tell me?"

"Yes Connie, you can write this down." I sense Him smile as I grab everything I need from off the table next to the chair.

"I know My ways at times seem so contrary to the way your mind works, and I know there is so much that you want to know and don't understand. You are always full of questions and I am always full of answers, am I not?"

"Yes, Father, you always have an answer for my relentless questions. I do have to wait at times though, and that's not easy!"

"Child, I'm just glad that you have been and are still willing to learn from Me, and it has been My honor as your Father to dress you and teach you in Righteousness! It has affected everything around you, especially how you see yourself.

"I must admit that it took a bit of work on the part of My Holy Spirit to get you to throw off your filthy robes and to accept the ones that I have offered you. But you have done it, and you are now wearing not only your Breastplate of Righteousness, but your robes as well.

"My Precious One, may I share with you, your story?"

"Yes, of course Father. You have my full attention!"

"After you were found by Me in the depths of the sea of sin, you walked into My Kingdom and your repentant heart meant business, and I knew it! The enemy also knew you were the real deal, alive again, and that it was I who had found you. He knew I would be training you up in righteousness and that you would be prepared to become the Bride of My Son, Jesus.

"The enemy also knew that you would be called on to expose the things you knew and had experienced in the Kingdom of Darkness. He understood it to be true of My Character, that I would be the One to raise you up to be even greater in My

Kingdom than you yourself could have ever imagined. Have you found this to be true Child?"

"Yes, Father, I most certainly have! I would never have dreamed that I could become the woman I see here in this secret place today. I know I was such a mess when You found me, and now it seems as though I am so separate from who that young woman was. I know it is only through Your love that I am who I am today."

I feel so grateful and I can feel the tears welling up. I know He can sense the gratitude of my heart but I must say it out loud. "Thank you Father for all You have done for me. I could never pay the debt I owe for my sin, but I know that my Redeemer lives and that my debt has been paid in full for me with the life and blood of Your Son, Jesus. I accept His gift."

"My Precious Child, I love to give you gifts, and when you first came to Me, I had no other option than to offer you the gift of your beautiful breastplate. It was imperative that you learn to wear it right away.

"I knew that you had defected from the enemy's camp and that he would have stopped at nothing to kill you, for the enemy hates those who defect. If you hadn't been so involved in the Kingdom of Darkness, you wouldn't have been such a threat to the enemy.

"Connie, Satan hates the Ones I save. He despises those whom I breathe My breath of life into, those who give full allegiance to My Kingdom, serving Me with humility and true repentance such as you have done at every turn! He hates those such as yourself that have the boldness to share the truth of what I can do with a life that looks like a shipwreck, that has sat at the bottom of the sea for a thousand years with no hope of resurrection, no hope of someone ever finding that sunken ship.

"As I have had to bring you up from the bottom of the sea of sin and shame, I have set your feet firmly on The Rock of My Salvation. It has taken years for the cleaning and restoration process to become real in you. I have also had to clean off all the years of silt and sand, guilt and shame, the barnacles over your heart and scales over your eyes. They have all had to go!

"The day you approached My throne, your life resembled not only a sunken ship, but an abandoned one. Not only have I had

to bring you up from the deep, but I have had to remove the anchor that held you down at the bottom. I have had to bring you back to the land of the living and have had to breathe the breath of life within you so that you could live once again.

"Connie, I gave you breath when I first gave you life, but through your choices it seemed as though I had lost you to the Father of Lies forever. I gave you the freedom of choice of which you chose for yourself a path of destruction for many years. It could have cost you an eternity away from Me.

"But in My Great Mercy, I searched desperately one more time looking for the one My heart loved! The one I knew by name, My treasured possession, You! With My Great Knowledge of the planet I created, I searched for you in every dark crevice. With My Great Hand and My Outstretched Arm, I reached down to the deepest depths and found you there, at the bottom of the sea of sin, dead.

"My Precious One, did you know the depth that I would go to retrieve that which I love?"

With my heart nearly bursting in love for my God, I respond, "Father, I didn't understand back then the lengths to which you would go. But I know now, and I also know that if you would do if for me, then You would do it for anyone."

"Connie, you could not see when you were young because of the circumstances into which you were born. But I was fully aware of the hidden treasure that was buried within you. I am the One who put it there, deep inside your spirit, from the moment of your conception."

"Father, my mother was an alcoholic and a prostitute! I simply cannot understand Your mysteries at times."

"I know daughter, but continue to trust Me. This treasure was what the enemy of your soul was after. He wanted to steal what I had placed away deep within your spirit for My plans and purposes. If Satan could not steal your hidden treasure, he was going to make sure that you were destroyed and hidden where I could not find you. He wanted nothing more than to use you up, and then discard you as trash! He wanted to make sure you were lost to the depths of eternal hell forever. But I know how to find that which is lost, and to fix that which is broken, and I have always had a plan!"

"Yes, Father I do believe in Your plan, and I am so excited to be apart of it! And I will share that plan as long as you give me breath on this earth. I know I have purpose and that my story is not ending anytime soon. I am Your Precious Treasure and the work of Your hands, no matter what the circumstances were in the beginning!

"Father, I believed for so long that broken things are despised, thrown out and worthless. I viewed myself as rejected and damaged goods, but Your Word says differently." I quickly turn to the familiar passage and read it out loud to my Father. *"The Lord is close to the broken-hearted and saves those who are crushed in spirit"* (Psalm 34:18).

I set my Bible and journal down and kneel before my Father. "Here I am, Your very Precious Treasure. What is it that You would have me to do? I am so grateful and thankful and willing to follow You anywhere You ask me to go."

"Stand and look at your Breastplate of Righteousness! Do you see the jewels I have placed within it? Do you see the rubies, diamonds, emeralds, sapphires and every precious stone? Do you see the workmanship, the gold, the silver? Now, look at your other pieces of armor! Look closely at your Sword of the Spirit, your Shield of Faith, your Belt of Truth, your Spear, and all the other weapons I have given you here in our Tameion Chamber. Do you see the beauty and worth in them?"

I stand and look lovingly at all that is before me. "Yes, Father, I am in awe of their beauty, and their value to me is beyond earthly measure. Only You would know how many times I have lost myself in just the wonder and beauty of them. They are truly one of Heavens greatest mysteries."

"My Precious One, you are one of Heavens Mysteries, and all of these weapons are a reflection of the treasures I have placed deep within your spirit. They represent your character, who I created you to be. Someday you will lay your weapons down, no longer needing to fight the battle because I am going to win this war. But now it is time! Put on your Breastplate of Righteousness and let Me look at you!"

I am not a bit surprised to find that as I put this breastplate on over my new garments that it fits me perfectly.

20

Shoes Of Peace

I **take a seat again** in the beautiful, red, comfortable chair that my Father has provided for me in my closet. ***My boots*** are right there. I put them on and lace them up. I notice the spikes on the bottom of my shoes. I have never questioned spikes on the bottom of my war boots; I have simply put them on each day. Since I am in this new secret place, I ask my Father, "Why spikes?"

He answers simply, *"They are there so that you will stay put during the battle! Your feet won't ever slip out from underneath you as long as you have your boots on."*

"Thank you, Father! You explained it perfectly!"

I hear the Holy Spirit whisper in my ear the Word of the Lord that I have read so many times. *"Your steps have held to His paths, and your feet have not slipped. If you keep the law of your God in your heart, your feet will not slip. Always ask of your Father, 'Show me your ways, Lord, teach me your paths,' and He will be faithful and instruct you in the way of wisdom and lead you along straight paths. When you walk, your steps will not be hampered; when you run, you will not stumble."* (Psalm 17:5; 37:31; Psalm 25:4; Proverb 4:11-12)

Again I can hear my Father speaking. *"Connie, when you follow Me in the paths that are specifically designed for you, then you have My promise that I will always lead you in the way you should go. When you walk, your steps will not be hindered, and when you run, you will not stumble. Put your boots on daily and never forget that in following the call of My Spirit, you will never get lost. The right path will be clear to you.*

"Now, I am going to leave you with one of the most important assignments I have given to those of My children who choose to trust and obey Me.

"Connie, in order to walk in peace, you must be willing to go to war! This is a spiritual principal that I laid out before the creation of the world. If you are not willing to live by this principal, the enemy will capture you, and you will walk and live in

bondage. Your walk is everything to all who are watching, and there can be no room for compromise of any kind. Your obedience in mandatory!

"The opposite of peace is fear. If you are in bondage to the enemy, you are fearful of him. When you are fearful, you are unable to step out into anything that requires faith and that leads to your freedom and victory. When you wear your shoes of peace in faithfulness to Me, then you will be able to face your enemy boldly because you will have no fear of him. You will be secure in who you belong to, and you will have peace no matter the circumstance or battle you face.

"And Daughter, don't ever forget that you will always be offered a false peace from the enemy that leads to bondage."

I am immediately reminded of the many scripture passages that confirm my Father's words in the Book of Isaiah. I quickly grab my beautiful Bible and read the familiar passages in Isaiah 36:13-20.

Yes, it is confirmed! When the king of Assyria tried to invade Jerusalem, he sent his general to intimidate King Hezekiah, to weaken his faith in God. It is clear that the enemy was offering false peace to the people so that he could enslave them. *"Do not listen to Hezekiah, for thus says the king of Assyria: 'Make your peace with me and come out to me, and eat every one of his vine and every one of his fig tree, and drink every one the waters of his own cistern, until I come and take you away to a land like your own land, a land of corn and new wine, a land of bread and vineyards"* (Isaiah 36:16-17).

The enemy will always offer me a false peace if he can just get me to take off my war boots and serve him in his kingdom.

"Father, I ask You to give me the same heart as that of King Hezekiah!"

I will do my best to do everything my Father and His Precious Holy Spirit have taught me. I still remember my days of bondage, and they were terrible. I turn again to His promise that I have stood on for many years. It states in Isaiah 36:8-10, *"And a highway will be there; it will be called the Way of Holiness; it will be for those who walk on that Way. The unclean will not journey on it; wicked fools will not go about on it. No lion will be there, nor any ravenous beast; they will not be found there. But only the redeemed will walk there, and those the LORD has rescued will return. They will enter Zion with singing; everlasting joy will crown their heads. Gladness and joy will overtake them, and sorrow and sighing will flee away."*

I stand again looking down at my feet, admiring my war boots. I am simply thankful for them.

21
Helmet Of Salvation

$\mathcal{N}$ow it's time for me to put on my **Helmet of Salvation**. Obediently, I place it securely on my head and think about the many years that I have done the same. But today it's very different. I am now wearing my Crown of Beauty, my bridal veil, under my Helmet of Salvation.

This is incredible! By wearing my Helmet of Salvation, **I am arming myself with the mind of Christ** (1 Peter 4:1; Ephesians 6:13). I have new eyes to see today! Eyes that are not only looking through a bridal veil but also eyes that see each and every person I encounter through the shed blood of Jesus Christ.

I stand gazing into the beautiful golden mirror. "Father, this is Your mirror. You have placed it in this closet just for me. I see only what you allow me to see and I only hear only what You want me to hear. I love what You have done in me Father."

"Connie, there will soon come a day where the military armor you are wearing will no longer be needed. You will beat your sword into a plowshare and your spear into a pruning hook (Isaiah 2:4), but for now my love, you must proclaim among the nations, for I have spoken: Prepare for war! Rouse the warriors! Let all the fighting men draw near and attack. Beat your plowshares into swords and your pruning hooks into spears. Let the weak say I am strong. Come quickly all you nations from every side and assemble there. Bring down your warriors Oh Lord" (Joel 3: 9-13).

22

Hidden Manna

I **suddenly realize** that inside my Tameion Chamber, I am unaware of time and that I am unconcerned about it. However, I also realize that I am beginning to feel rather weak.

"Father," I whisper as I sit down in my red chair. "I love what You are doing in me and what You are teaching me. But I suddenly feel weak and tired. I'm not sure that I can continue this adventure with You."

I am aware of my Father's gentle voice. *"My Precious Child, do you not understand that I have provisions available for your every need as you are in My service? Look once again upon the shelf."*

I stand on my tiptoes reaching over the top of the shelf where my eyes cannot see, and I touch something firm and small. I take hold of it in my hand and pull it down.

It is a small wooden box, red in color and etched with beautifully carved letters. I recognize the language as Hebrew although I am unfamiliar with the words.

"Father, it's beautiful! What does it say? And what is the meaning of this box?"

"Daughter, sit down and open it."

I obey, and as I spring the latch and open the lid, I am delighted by the aroma of fresh baked bread, and I suddenly know what this is!

"Father, it's manna isn't it?"

I hear my Father's joyful laugh as He answers. *"Connie, do you remember what My Son said to the disciples when they brought food to Him as He was ministering to the woman at the well?"*

"Yes I do. He said, *'I have food to eat that you know nothing about.' Then his disciples said to each other, 'Could someone have brought him food?' 'My food,' said Jesus, 'is to do the will of him who sent me and to finish his work.'* That's John 4:32-34."

"Daughter, the food that My Son was speaking of is

spiritual food. He mentions it again in Revelation 2:17. Open My Word and read it."

I set the manna box on the table and turn to the scripture in my Bible. *"To the one who is victorious, I will give some of the hidden manna."*

Now it's my turn to laugh at Father's sense of humor as I remember that the box of manna was hidden on the shelf. "Father, thank You for this **Hidden Manna**, Your spiritual food. May I eat a piece of it?"

I feel my Father's approval and I carefully take a piece of this spiritual bread from the box and place it in my mouth. Immediately I feel strength pouring into my body, soul and spirit. I feel as though I have been strengthened with might in my inner being, just as Paul prayed in Ephesians 3:16.

I fall to my knees in adoration, for I realize that I have just been strengthened through Holy Communion with Jesus, my Savior and Lord.

"Father, thank You for this awesome Kingdom resource. I will be sure to carry it with me at all times so that no matter where I am, I will always have the strength to be obedient to You, to do Your will and to fulfill Your plan and purposes."

"Connie," my Father said, *"you asked what the words on the box said. Look them up."*

I opened my Hebrew dictionary, and I soon realized that the words were scripture. *"I have food to eat that you know nothing about...My food, is to do the will of him who sent me and to finish his work."*

23

*S*pear

I turn, and there, mounted on the wall next to the empty armor stand, are my "Shield of Faith" and my *Spear.* I gently touch them and many memories of victory flood my mind.

As I take my spear from its secured mount on the wall of my Tameion Chamber, I can't help but remember that this weapon was given to me in addition to my Sword, and it comes with a beautiful promise. I had to earn the right to use this weapon and understand that it has a very important place in the battle between the Kingdom of Darkness and the Kingdom of Light.

I have been cautioned many times by the Holy Spirit to only use this weapon as My Father God directs, or I could have a mess on my hands. Unfortunately, I have come to realize the hard way that there is nothing more dangerous to the Kingdom of God than one of His own children yielding, fighting and tossing around weapons they really know nothing about, or using them for selfish purposes rather than for the Kingdom of God.

In using this powerful weapon against the Kingdom of Darkness, discernment is not only necessary, but is vital to the winning of every battle. As a child of the Most High God, I must be able to discern correctly. Part of this discernment is being able to recognize when that discernment is lacking in the heart and mind of another believer, but even more important is being honest with myself when that discernment is lacking within me.

I run my fingers along the staff of my spear as I contemplate what one of my favorite authors, Francis Frangipane, said about discernment. "Spiritual discernment is the grace to see into the unseen. It is a gift of the Spirit to perceive the realm of the spirit. Its purpose is to understand the nature of that which is veiled. However, the first veil that must be removed is the veil over our own hearts. For the capacity to see into that which is in another's heart comes from Christ revealing that which is in our own hearts. Before He reveals the sin of another, Jesus demands we grasp our own deep need of His mercy. Thus, out of the grace that we have received, we can compassionately minister grace to others. We will know thoroughly that the true gift of discernment is not a faculty of our minds." [19]

How many times have I looked back to see not only myself but God's own children turning on each other, or even worse, causing major damage to the body of Christ because we are not seeing things through the spiritual realm of spiritual discernment.

I think about the important lesson I learned about spiritual warfare and the weapons that God entrusts to us. We must understand exactly what these weapons of warfare represent and who their main target should be. Different battles require different weapons, but discernment is always necessary. We must understand and strive to know when and how to properly use our weapons of war.

"Father, I remember the day that You revealed this particular weapon to me. As I was reading your precious Word, I found myself in 2 Samuel 23. I was moved to tears at the thought that the following verses were King David's last words. I felt Your Spirit prompting me to pay special attention to the details of what King David was saying.

I remember our conversation that day...."

..."*Father, the first portion of this scripture says,* '*Now these be the last words of David. David the son of Jesse said, and the man who was raised up on high, the anointed of the God of Jacob, and the sweet psalmist of Israel, said, The Spirit of the Lord spake by me, and his word was in my tongue. The God of Israel said, the Rock of Israel spake to me, He that ruleth over men must be just, ruling in the fear of God. And he shall be as the light of the morning, when the sun riseth, even a morning without clouds; as the tender grass springing out of the earth by clear shining after rain. Although my house be not so with God; yet he hath made with me an everlasting covenant, ordered in all things, and sure: for this is all my salvation, and all my desire, although he make it*

---

[19] The Three Battlegrounds, Francis Frangipane, Arrow Publications, Inc., Cedar Rapids, IA, 1995, p. 74.

not to grow. **But the sons of Belial shall be all of them as thorns thrust away, because they cannot be taken with hands: But the man that shall touch them must be fenced with iron and the staff of a spear;** *and they shall be utterly burned with fire in the same place'* (2 Samuel 23:1-7 KJV, author's emphasis).

"Father, the first thing that comes to my mind is the awareness of a pattern in David's life. His actions stayed consistent and his heart knew You intimately. I have come to fully appreciate that King David understood the principle, the practices and details of war probably better than anyone. But most importantly, David understood the principle of war and how to defeat the enemy with a heart that followed hard after God. I know this is truly important to You Father."

As I continued to study this chapter, I noticed specifically verse 6 where David gives an important piece of information on how to defeat a particular enemy called the "sons of Belial." David stated that *".... the sons of Belial shall be all of them as thorns thrust away, because they cannot be taken with hands.'"* He goes on to let us know, *"But the man who touches them must be armed with iron and the shaft of a spear."*

So as I pondered the warning and instructions from King David to "anyone who touches them," I decided to look up the Hebrew meaning of the word "touches" in 2 Samuel 23:6, and I allowed the Holy Spirit to teach and instruct me as He has done so faithfully throughout the years. I was quite surprised at what I found.

"Father, I see clearly the meaning of this word 'touches!' It's very different than I have understood it. This word means to 'beat, to bring down, violently, to strike, punish, defeat, destroy, this enemy!' This is talking about a violent 'touch' that defeats the enemy![20]

"But there's a catch! Things aren't always as they appear! David clearly states that *'they cannot be taken with hands.'* So if I am to 'touch' and defeat this enemy, verse 7 states that I must be *'....armed with Iron and a shaft of a spear.'* Wow!

---

[20] Bible Hub, Strong's Concordance, H5060, *"Touch,"* http://biblehub.com/hebrew/5060.htm

"Father I know that the sons of Belial still exist today. Paul clearly spoke of the sons of Belial in 2 Corinthians 6:15. *'What harmony is there between Christ and Belial? Or what does a believer have in common with an unbeliever?'*

"I feel that I have encountered these spirits on many occasions and I have not always been sure of how I am to deal with them. At times, I feel they have been unrelenting in trying to get close to me, and at times have caused great harm to myself and Your church."

*"Yes Connie, this spirit is in full operation when there is an unequal yoke between believers and unbelievers. You know this well as it also goes by the name of an 'ungodly soul tie.' My Spirit has taught you much about this. In using this **'iron and shaft of a spear'** you will experience greater success in the breaking of any ungodly soul ties. Learning to use this weapon correctly will be a vital weapon of defeat that you can use for deliverance purposes not only for yourself, but for others as well. This is why it is so important to avoid and to keep at a distance any ungodly relationships or associations that could cause evil spirits to be transferred. If Belial cannot directly control you, he will influence you through any other ungodly association he can find."*

"Father, help me to understand. It seems as if this spear has a two-fold purpose. It provides protection from Belial as I use it as a type of boundary so that the enemy can't get close enough to connect with me. I see myself holding it in front of me with the tip of the spear pointing toward the enemy to keep them at bay. And then I see it as a weapon of warfare that I am to use to spear the enemy and to sever all ungodly soul ties with them."

*"Yes, Connie, This 'spear' will be imperative for you and others, and will protect you from Belial's control, and will assist you in being delivered from his control when you find that you have been bound to him in some way. This is why you must obey My Word which says, **'Be not unequally yoked together with unbelievers.'** These sons of Belial are planted in my churches and are also known to Me as 'tares.' and they will grow right next to you, the 'wheat.'*

"I want you to understand this enemy, how he and his sons operate and infiltrate My Church. This is why I am now giving you

your new weapon and I will teach you how to use this valuable weapon correctly.

"Connie, the sons of Belial continue to be a real problem for my watchmen, warriors and intercessors. They have caused many casualties in the Kingdom of God.

"Belial is one of the most wicked and vile spirits in the kingdom of darkness and it will try to defeat you at any cost. His children are sold out to him and you need to realize that you are dealing with demonic spirits that have a goal. They are driven, dedicated and diligent! They are highly trained to go after a specific anointing. Their goal is to corrupt and destroy My Kingdom and those I have anointed in any way they can. They have made a contract with their father Satan, to obey and serve him in exchange for the prize they so desire, the destruction of the saints, especially my watchman, warriors and intercessors! You are not dealing with lower ranking spirits here, but a very real opponent.

"When My Spirit breathed on David at the end of his life to pen these very specific instructions regarding the sons of Belial, I meant business! I did this so that you and others would learn how to deal with these very demonically driven evil people who mostly operate within My churches. It is no different today than it was with Hophni and Phinehas, the sons of Eli, and how they operated in vile sin, perversion and wickedness in My House. This angered me greatly.

"David also dealt with sons of Belial all his life, and when he stated in 2 Samuel 23:6 that, 'The sons of Belial shall be all of them as thorns thrust away because they cannot be taken with hands,' he was making a statement under My direction so as to instruct others. This is vitally important. You must always remember that when you are dealing with sons of Belial you are dealing with those who are sons of Satan.

"Connie, as King David warned, I do not want you to make the mistake of getting too close to people around you that carry this dangerous spirit. They can be very deceptive and they will try and draw you in close. The closer you get to them, the more dangerous they are to you. If you stay alert and sober, you will always be able to recognize them! Remember My Word to you, 'You and your sons are not to drink wine or other fermented

drink whenever you go into the tent of meeting, or you will die. This is a lasting ordinance for the generations to come so that you can distinguish between the holy and the common, between the unclean and the clean, and so you can teach the Israelites all the decrees the Lord has given them through Moses' (Leviticus 10:9-11).

"They will be the ones who continue to be yoked to demons. They will be the ones who bear no good fruit! *You will recognize them as thorns because they are something that will cause distress, pain, torment, confusion, adversity and irritation especially to those who carry My anointing. They will be full of difficulties and controversial points and this is why you must be sure to be alert, awake and sober minded at all times. It is important that you recognize them first, for they can and will instantly recognize you, your anointing and my Spirit, operating in and through you. My Watchmen, Warriors and Intercessors are always an immediate target.*

"These thorny enemies cannot be defeated in battle by hand, nor can you win them with love and compassion, for they belong to the evil one and are committed to his service. Their agenda must be blocked and their destruction stopped. They must be held back and put in their place with the tip of your iron spear. Nothing less will do. You must realize that they are truly enemies and persecutors of My Kingdom of Righteousness."

"Father, I remember reading about these kind of people in a commentary which said, 'They are no different than those prickly, thorny plants which are twisted together, whose spires point in every direction, and which are so sharp and strong that they cannot be touched or approached without danger; but hard instruments and violent means must be taken to destroy or uproot them.'" [21]

"Connie, in the end, I will remove and destroy all who are opposed to My Kingdom. There will come a day when they are thrown into the fire and burned, but until that day you must always be watchful of those around you that operate in this spirit. They operate on behalf of the kingdom of darkness and are on a

---

[21] Bible Hub, Jamieson-Fausset-Brown Bible Commentary on 2 Samuel 23, http://biblehub.com/commentaries/jfb/2_samuel/23.htm

mission to destroy you and your fellow watchmen, warriors and intercessors.

"Most of My children don't realize that you can't fight these sons of Belial on a physical level. You must fight them according to the rules of engagement I have laid out in heaven. David speaks the truth of what he had to learn the hard way in verse 7, **'the man that shall [absolutely] touch them must be filled (fenced in) with iron [full of the strength of the Lord] and the staff (this wood represents the cross) of a spear....'"**

....*A*s my reminiscing comes to an end, I am overcome with awe for my Father who has been so faithful to teach and train me. I carefully set my spear against the wall and fall to the floor, bowing down to My Lord in worship. Surrender is my heart's cry, for I understand the importance of this weapon and the seriousness of its purpose.

"Father, I give You my heart! The only way I can effectively use this weapon is to have my own heart exchanged for Yours. I know that You have given me a 'new heart,' but sometimes I operate from the old one. This must not be! When I hold onto things like unforgiveness I operate from the old heart. And my old heart attracts Belial and his children! Please forgive me for this! I hate this unforgiving spirit and I willingly choose to crucify it and surrender it up to You. Please take it from me. I want to be a woman after Your own heart like David was! I want to be able to destroy this vile enemy, not only for myself, but for others as well. Please help me!"

"Connie, my beloved daughter. I know your heart. It is done as you have asked. I am so very pleased with you, for surrender at this level seems difficult in the beginning, but it will lead you to great victory!

"Now stand up my Warrior Bride, pick up your 'iron and staff of a spear' and hold it in your right hand. I want you to notice the weight it carries and the distance it will put between you and your enemy. Rather than you being close enough to put a hand on these sons of Belial, you will need the distance of this spear between you. This is My protection. Sometimes that distance is physical and sometimes it is spiritual. You will always have to discern correctly according to each confrontation, which you are able to do when you operate from My heart.

"There is something I always want you to remember. When you hold this spear in your hand, it will always come with a promise, the same promise I gave Ezekiel. **'And you, son of man, do not be afraid of them or their words. Do not be afraid, though briers and thorns are all around you and you live among scorpions. Do not be afraid of what they say or be terrified by them, though they are a rebellious people'** (Ezekiel 2:6).

"This promise to Ezekiel and the verse in 2 Samuel compares the sons of Belial to 'thorns that cannot be handled.' So remember that when you deal with Belial and his sons, you must be fenced-in with your iron and the staff of your spear which is also a reference to putting on the whole armor of God. In dressing properly you will always have My promise that you need not be afraid.

"Connie, I am raising up watchmen, warriors and intercessors to come against this spirit in the last days. The sons of Belial have been around since the great war of rebellion in heaven and yet they are an end-time destroying spirit assigned to corrupt the earth and wear out the saints. But rest assured that I am raising up an end time army to combat them, of which you are a part."

"Father, I am honored to have received this weapon and the promise that goes with it! I am so thankful for Your Word and David's instructions on how to fight and overcome the sons of Belial. Just as David overcame, I will overcome and teach others to do the same. I will use my spear with great discernment, no longer handling this awful spirit with my natural hands but rather with '...iron and the staff of a spear.'

"Father, I thank You that with all Your gifts, weapons and wisdom, there always comes a promise. As your watchman, warrior and intercessor, I will stand on that promise, teaching others to do the same."

24
Garments Of Love And Humility

With my spear in my hands, I look up at my Shield still mounted on the wall, and I hear my Father's voice.

"Wait My Child. There are two more garments you need to put on. These garments are to be a covering over your armor. You must never leave this room without them. You must never forget to put them on."

Once again I lean my spear against the wall and move closer to the golden rack. I can see all the other garments clearly.

"What is it Father? Which garments am I to wear over my armor, and how exactly is that going to look?" My eyes move to the very far right and then to the left of the golden rack. I pause, wait and listen for the Holy Spirit and my Father to speak.

"All of them must be worn by you!" He says. *"They must be the garments that cover and protect all the other garments, robes, armor and weapons you are wearing."*

I identify two, well worn but **extremely beautiful** garments, the **Garment of Love** and the **Garment of Humility**.

"Father, I know these garments! I have worn them off and on throughout the years. These are the robes You gave me when I first came to know You, and I admit I have had to work hard at wearing them. You have put them before me many times, and on many occasions You have asked me to clothe myself with these robes of compassion, kindness, gentleness and patience.

"Father, You know I have struggled with these robes in the past, but now You have presented them in a whole new way. I admit that today I am able to see them with new eyes and a new heart. Seeing them here in my Tameion Chamber, they look brand new and stand out to me. They are more beautiful than I could have ever imagined, and I don't know how I could have ever gone even one day without them."

I feel in my spirit that there is a difference between knowing about these garments and robes, and then actually putting them on, wearing them daily and using them for their destined purpose.

I realize now the importance of "putting on" these outer garments daily. I realize the importance of getting dressed with a purpose. If this is not done correctly, others or myself could be in danger, and it could be costly to the Kingdom work being done through me.

This one thing I am now assured of. The Garment of Love and the Garment of Humility must cover my other garments, robes, my armor and even the weapons that are attached to my Belt of Truth! **Every move I make, every battle I encounter, every fruit I offer, and every weapon I draw, must go through love and humility**.

His precious Word again comes out of my mouth. *"Therefore, as God's chosen daughter, I am holy and dearly loved, I have clothed myself with compassion, kindness, humility, gentleness and patience"* (Colossians 3:12).

"Father, Your Word is very clear that my beauty should not come from outward adornment. Rather, it should be that of my inner self, the unfading beauty of a gentle and quiet spirit, which is of great worth in Your sight" (1 Peter 3: 3-4).

I secure the beautiful garments by placing them over my shoulders and am reminded again that everything I set my hands to do must go through love and humility.

I turn, stand and look in the mirror, and there I am, His Daughter, ready to be wed to His Son!

25
Oil Of My Anointing

I hear my Father's gentle voice. *"Connie, look back upon the shelf and take hold of the jar that you see there. This is My gift to you."*

I cautiously reach for the beautiful jar and am happy to hold it in my hands. It's made of some kind of pearl and has precious stones all over it. I carefully examine the beautiful jar and allow my fingers to touch each of the beautiful gems. I ask myself how I could possibly be holding something so beautiful in my hands!

I then speak softly to my Father, "This is for me? Really? What shall I do with it Father? It's so beautiful!"

*"I want you to take the lid off and look inside. Its contents are very rare and only come from the realm of My Heavenly Kingdom. Precious One, I am giving you the **Oil of My Anointing** and this will be greatly needed as the days grow closer to My Son's return. Connie, will you accept this gift and the responsibility that comes with it?*

"Daughter, I want you to choose to take this gift because once you take it, you will need to maintain it through prayer and fasting and the study of My Word. You must also walk in obedience to My Holy Spirit and the convictions that He will bring alongside this gift to compliment its power.

"Because this gift has My power and My authority flowing through it, you must always be awake, on high alert and sober in mind. The Kingdom of Darkness will stop at nothing to bring defilement to this Oil of My Anointing. You must always look to Me to have your jar replenished."

As I open the lid and look inside, I see what appears to be a golden, yet clear liquid oil, and the beautiful aroma begins to fill the room.

"Father, the smell is beautiful, breathtaking and unique, not something I am familiar with here on earth. I have no words to explain it. And yes, Father, I accept this gift and I will cherish it."

"Lift the jar above your head Child, I want you to pour out this oil all over you. Let it run down, over your veil and over your armor and garments. I want you to cover yourself with this oil. You must never leave this closet without it. Understand that there will always be a fresh supply, but only found in here, through Me."

I lift my arms, hold it over my head and pour! I can feel it covering me, overwhelming me, strengthening me and giving me new sense of direction. I feel it is tied somehow to my Garment of Humility.

"Yes Father, I promise that I will never leave this closet without it!"

After covering myself with the precious oil I feel as though I am preparing myself for something. I feel the oil touch my feet and I turn to look in the golden mirror. I just stand in awe of the woman He has created me to be, and I get lost in the wonder of it all. I look intently into the mirror and I can no longer see that 15-year-old teenage mother who was so angry at the God she has come to love. I can no longer see the drug addict that had a heart bent on destruction and filled with rage, bitterness and hatred toward men and Christians. As I am lost for a moment in trying to find the past memories I feel that there is a washing away of sorts. So much has happened and is still happening in this closet. I am again gently startled by His voice.

"Daughter, I have more that I want to share with you regarding My Oil of Anointing upon your life."

I quickly turn around and pay close attention to each word He speaks.

"I have already stated the most important thing regarding this anointing, but I want to say it again. I must be the only One you come to for this very rare and precious gift! This is not something you can get from anyone else, and any anointing offered to you outside of Me will be a counterfeit.

"There is a difference in this Oil of My Anointing that I have asked you to place upon yourself and the anointing oil that I have given you to place upon others for prayer. I have asked you to place this upon yourself today as a part of the preparation for your wedding day. Go to My Word Child, so that I may show you something."

119

Again, covered in this precious smelling oil, I walk over and settle myself in the comfortable red chair that my Father has provided for me. I pick up my precious Bible, and as I have done many other times, I pull it close to my heart and hold it so tight that I feel it becoming a part of me. I realize immediately that my Bible and my chair are also getting covered with the oil I just poured upon myself. I wrap my arms a little tighter around His Word, holding it closely in anticipation of what I am about to read. While doing this, I am a bit startled, something is happening!

I say out loud, "Father, the oil! What's happening?"

I can feel the oil that I just poured all over myself becoming warm and going beneath my skin. It feels very much like a soft blanket just taken out of the dryer. I am being covered completely inside and out by something new, and I just want to be still, allowing the warm waves to overtake me. I am so overwhelmed with love for My Father God! I feel compelled to stand, and taking my Bible, I walk over and kneel before the presence of my Father.

With my Bible held tightly to my chest and my face to the ground, I can feel His deep love for me as I lay there still at His feet. I could be happy in this place and position of humility for the rest of my life, and I do not want this moment to ever end.

"Precious One, sit up and open My Word to 2 Corinthians 1:18 and read it out loud to me."

"Yes, Father."

I compose myself, sit on the floor and open my Bible. I continue to feel the warm waves of oil coming in over me even stronger. I quickly turn to the scripture He has asked me to read and I speak it out loud to Him. *"Now it is God who makes both us and you stand firm in Christ. He anointed us, set His seal of ownership on us, and put His Spirit in our hearts as a deposit, guaranteeing what is to come."*

I hear myself say, "Father, this is what you are doing! You are anointing me with Your Holy Spirit and putting Your "Seal of Ownership" upon me! My future with you is being guaranteed!"

"Yes Beautiful One, this Oil of My Anointing placed upon you confirms and expresses the sanctifying influence of My Holy Spirit upon you. This anointing will work in and through you for

the benefit of not only yourself, but others. I have called you to walk on this earth with purpose. You are to walk in the office of a priest, an intercessor, a prayer warrior and a pastors' wife. I would ask that you always be open and ready to receive a new position and the training that will come with it. You will always know when I have called you to serve Me in a different office according to the season you are walking through. All this is but preparation for your guaranteed position in my Heavenly Kingdom. You are being prepared to rule and reign as My Son's Bride.

"You need to know that you have an anointing that is individually yours, and that this anointing abides and lives in you through the fullness of who I Am.

"You have accepted My gift with a pure heart and humility. From this day on, you are called to walk faithfully with this anointing on you. One of the most important functions of this anointing is that it will help you and those you encounter to overcome the world.

"Connie, I want you to teach others that when I call My children into the ministry to serve Me, I anoint them with supernatural power and ability to carry out the functions of that office. It is no different with you, and you need to teach others that it is no different with them.

"My anointing will give you the boldness to speak that which I am speaking through you. As this anointing is upon you, through it, you will carry My power, which will destroy the yokes of bondage that keep My children captive. Just as I anointed the hem of My Son, Jesus' garment and He was able to heal a woman of her infirmity, I am anointing you. Even as I anointed the shadow of Peter so that anyone who stepped into his shadow and walked away whole, I am anointing you. As I anointed the Apostle Paul's handkerchief so that demons would come out of people, I am anointing you."

"Connie, you know these are actual events that happened in the lives of real people just like you, and I need your faith to understand the greatness and reality of who I AM! The life giving power that flows through My anointing is attainable if you will but only believe. May I remind you my precious one, that My anointing was so strong on the prophet Elisha that even when he *was dead and buried, My Israelite children threw a dead man into his grave and as soon as the dead man's body touched the bones of My servant Elisha the dead man got up and walked out of that grave fully alive!*

"Daughter, My anointing is real! My Power is real! It's for you, and I want you to raise up an army of warriors who believe in Me and are willing to walk in My anointing! You must continue to enter your Tameion Chamber, shutting the door behind you and teaching others to do the same. You must stay in My Protective Presence and continue to read My Word to understand the mystery of My ways. It's only through these truths that you may continue to obtain the pure Oil of My Anointing.

Connie, in the past you have been guilty and have attempted to stand in a ministry anointing and office that was not appointed by Me. Not only is this dangerous for you personally, but if you attempt to ever walk in a calling that I have not called you too, it can bring great harm to the body of Christ. You have done your share of damage to others. You know exactly what I am talking about. Child, I need you to repent for this!

"It breaks My Father's heart when you have to learn the hard way, and I know the examples that have been demonstrated for you weren't always good, but now you understand. You have learned great lessons, and I would ask you to never forget, Child, that the distinction comes when you are not able to perform the duties in a manner consistent with the humility and love that I require to be present in My servants.

"I know you are familiar with what you have learned from Aaron and Miriam's story, but I want you to read again in Numbers Chapter 12. Pay close attention as you read and always be mindful of this lesson.

"I only have one question for you to answer when you are done reading. What do I say about My Servant, Moses?"

"Oh Father, I have never noticed this about Moses! Your Word says, *"Now Moses was a very humble man, more humble than anyone else on the face of the earth."*

I close my Bible, lay it at my Father's feet and put my face to the ground.

"Father, I do repent before You and ask that You would forgive my folly in wanting to be something you have not called me to be. I am so sorry for the damage I have caused to Your Kingdom work, and I thank You for a work of restoration on my behalf. I thank you that You are a God of second chances. I thank You that I am able to humble myself before You and know that the precious blood of Your Son Jesus puts me in a position to receive all that You have for me. I would never be able to achieve any kind of anointing on my own, and I want to thank You for the lessons learned here in my secret place with You. You are a good, good Father, full of mercies that I cannot even begin to comprehend. I want to be humble, just as Moses was humble. Father, I ask for an extra measure of humility to be poured upon my life to go along with the Oil of Your Anointing! This I ask in the precious and powerful Name above every Name, the Name of Your Son, Jesus, AMEN!"

As I stand, I somehow feel lighter than ever, and I have that very familiar feeling of awe mixed with excitement and hope. Not just hope for myself, but hope for others.

26

*E*ye *S*alve *A*nd *S*piritual *S*pectacles

"*My* **Beautiful Watchman Warrior Princess Intercessor Bride,** *I would like to give you a gift. It is on the shelf. Go ahead and take it down."*

"Father, the gift is amazing and beautiful! A white box with a red bow! Are you sure it's for me?"

"Yes, this is the gift that your fellow intercessor, Mae, said you would be receiving from Me. Go ahead Child, open it and look inside!"

"Lord, I have never seen spectacles like these before!"

"Connie, take them out of the box and place them over your eyes."

I quickly and obediently place them over my eyes.

He continued, *"I am giving you the ability to see all people as being under the shed sacrifice of the blood of My Son Jesus. He has died for all, and His forgiveness encompasses all. I am also giving you the ability to tell them the good news of My Son Jesus. I need you to freely forgive everyone you encounter just as much as you have freely loved them. Your love and your forgiveness toward others go hand in hand, for those to whom you extend My forgiveness will be able to experience it themselves. My love cannot operate without forgiveness.*

"Connie, I have provided a very important place on your Belt of Truth for your new spectacles. You are to keep your spectacles close at all times safely tucked away when you are not wearing them. You are to take them out of your Belt of Truth each and every morning as you read My Word. There is a reason for this. As you walk with Me, your vision of love and forgiveness and my plan for the lost will grow, and your vision will change. Only My truth can give you the new lenses needed for your journey. And it is imperative that you let Me be the one to clean and change your lenses."

"Yes, Father, I completely understand. I will take great care of this precious gift of **Spiritual Spectacles**! I will keep and use them faithfully so that I see others the way that You see them. I especially look forward to my vision growing in Your care knowing that where there is not vision, Your people perish (Proverbs 29:18). This I understand.

"Father, I have kept Your Word hidden in my heart and it confirms that I must be able to forgive. *'Therefore, as God's chosen people, holy and dearly loved, clothe yourselves with compassion, kindness, humility gentleness and patience. Bear with each other and forgive whatever grievances you may have against one another. Forgive as the Lord forgave you. And over all these virtues put on love which binds them all together in unity'* (Colossians 3:12-14).

"Father, I stand in awe of my gift. When my dear friend Mae told me I would be receiving a gift from You, I had no idea what this gift would be, but I couldn't be more honored to receive it."

My heart is overwhelmed as I take the spectacles off my eyes and examine them closely. I have never seen anything like these spectacles in this earthly realm. I quickly tuck them away in my beautiful Belt of Truth and they fit perfect!

"Thank you Father."

I hear My Father say, *"Look deeper into the box, Child."*

I look again and see a very small, round glass jar.

"What is this, Father?" I ask.

"Your eyes are also very important, even more important than your vision, for they are windows to your soul. Others may see into your heart through your eyes, but I am concerned with what you see as you look out of them. There are images that you will be unable to block from your view. There will be things that you witness either knowingly or unknowingly, that if ignored, can be an open window for the enemy to enter. He will begin to torment your mind by replaying the scenes, or he will use them to plant ungodly thoughts inside your mind.

"When applied to your eyes, this salve will remove unclean images, put a seal upon them, and bring healing from any damage of ungodly sights. And then you will be able to see clearly. You must apply the salve I am providing you daily, before you put on your spectacles. This salve will help to protect you."

"Father, I have heard of this before, but I haven't really understood it."

"Go to My Word, Connie, and look for yourself."

In Matthew 6:22 I find that, *"The eye is the lamp of the body. If your eyes are healthy, your whole body will be full of light."* And Revelation 18:3 says, *"I counsel you to buy from me gold refined in the fire, so you can become rich; and white clothes to wear, so you can cover your shameful nakedness; and salve to put on your eyes, so you can see."*

I begin to understand that the salve I am to put upon my eyes each day will help me to remember to guard what I see. And when I cannot, I can trust the Father to protect me through the choice I have made to align myself with His righteousness. I am also reminded that ungodly images can cause damage, and I suddenly understand that this **Eye Salve** will remove unclean images and bring healing to the eyes of my soul and spirit.

The old hymn, *"There Is A Balm In Gilead"* comes to mind. I know that it is based on Jeremiah 8:22 and the amazing, healing properties of that special balm are offered to every believer. I can almost hear angels singing,

"Sometimes I feel discouraged and think my work's in vain,
But then the Holy Spirit revives my soul again.
There is a balm in Gilead to make the wounded whole;
There is a balm in Gilead to heal the sin sick soul."

It's at this moment that I make a covenant with my God to bind around my heart the law of forgiveness, and to place upon my eyes each and every day the healing balm. I realize in His asking this of me, that He will be the One that gives me the ability to forgive no matter what the offence, for His Word is clear that I must love my enemies and treat those who do me wrong with kindness (Matthew 5:44). He is able, so I am able.

I pick up the beautiful box that was holding my very special gift and admire even the beauty of the box. I reach up and touch my nose and act as if I'm adjusting my spectacles properly, and giggle at myself. But all giggling set aside, I am grateful and thankful for this precious gift. Yes, it is confirmed in my spirit! Through obedience as I view others through these spiritual lenses, I will see them in a new and different light. I will be seeing others with My Father's eyes.

27
Shield Of Faith

My attention is now turned to my *Shield of Faith* that is mounted so valiantly on the wall next to where my spear had been. In reminiscence, before I *take up* this well used piece of battle armor, I can't help but quote the very familiar portion of scripture out loud knowing that His Word is Truth and that it is also my promise of protection... *"Above all, taking the shield of faith with which you will be able to quench all the fiery darts of the wicked one"* (Ephesians 6:16 NIV).

As I have done on numerous occasions, I pause for just a moment, and with a heart of thankfulness, I intently inspect every dent, and every scar that is on my Shield of Faith. As I do almost daily, I lovingly and carefully inspect the repairs I have made in the past, and I see that there are repairs that are needed even now.

I learned many years ago that if my Shield of Faith or any other part of my armor became damaged in battle in any way, my spiritual survival would depend upon my ability to fix the damage. As an intercessor and warrior, my Shield of Faith must be maintained on a regular basis. I must never enter a battle with a damaged shield. This would be too costly. I must always direct my attention to the repairs of my armor as part of my pre-war or battle engagement preparations, which my husband Greg lovingly refers to as "preventative maintenance." And it must be repaired immediately after any warfare.

As I prepare to *take up* my Shield of Faith, I feel the Words of my Father welling up from the deepest part of me. Sensing His presence, I feel led to speak His Truth out loud as a confirmation of His additional promises to me.

"Father I understand that...*'without faith it is impossible to please You, because anyone who comes to You must believe that You exist and that You reward those who earnestly seek You'"* (Hebrews 11:6 NIV).

Again, I am reminded of how He protects me, and I stand in awe as I think of how many hundreds, if not thousands of times I have had to *take up* and use this Shield of Faith. I am also grateful for all the times the Holy Spirit has asked me straight out, *"Connie, are there any holes in your Shield of Faith? When are you going to repair that? Do you understand that you are in the enemy's camp and he is coming for you? Girl, you better wake up and pay attention!"*

"Father, I am so thankful that Your Holy Spirit taught me long ago that the measure of my faith should be in response to Your proven Truth, and You are 'Truth!' I have learned that the level of my faith will be the level of my victories over the kingdom of darkness.

"Father You have shared with me Your heart and have cautioned me many times to exercise diligence in care with respect to my Shield of Faith. There is great danger in letting it become dry and brittle. I have seen too many Christians running around with dry, brittle, cracked and heavily damaged Shields of Faith that do not protect them from the darts of the evil one. I must, as a believer, take great care to protect mine and be faithful to teach others to do the same.

"You have taught me that my shield is to be used for many different kinds of warfare, but it's really all about my faith in You! I have to be diligent to protect my faith! What I believe about You should always line up with Your Word of Truth! As an intercessor, it is through the level of my faith in Your Truth that the kingdoms of darkness can be subdued and my promises will be obtained."

As I stand looking at this amazing piece of armor, I hear His gentle voice, *"Connie, I want you to do something a little different today, and I want you to see your Shield of Faith with a whole new spiritual perspective.*

"Daughter, your shield is normally used as a defensive weapon and will continue to be that. Yet, if your Shield of Faith carries with it My anointing, it is transformed and can be used for much more.

"There are two key points I want you to learn here today, and these things I admonish you to remember before you walk out of this closet each day. The first is that the enemy will always go after your anointing. The second is that he will always attack your faith.

"This is an area that your adversary and his minions are well trained in. Satan has attacked My children in this area from the very beginning. Your enemy will be relentless in trying to get you and the rest of My children to put your faith in something or someone other than Me. Connie, you must never let this happen.

"In this Tameion Chamber, this secret place, I have provided you with a jar of oil, and yes, you have already covered yourself with it. But, I also want you to make sure that you daily anoint your Shield of Faith and every other garment, robe, or weapon with it. The oil of My anointing will keep your shield, weapons and wardrobe soft, supple and moldable to My plans and purposes for you. This anointing will be able to quench each and every fiery dart the enemy throws at you.

"Child, go to My Word and read Isaiah 21:5."

I again turn and take a seat in my beautiful red chair and pick up the precious Sword.

"Yes Father, I can see right here that You had the Prophet Isaiah instruct the soldiers to 'anoint their shields' in preparation for battle. You taught me that the shields were made of wood and leather, and this would be why it was so important for the soldiers to keep their shields oiled. In fact it was so important, that they carried a bottle or jar of olive oil attached to their belt. This oil was imperative to keeping the shield in good condition and would help them from becoming dry and brittle which would cause them to catch fire all too easily."

"Connie, many of My children have faith, but it's not anointed faith. Since this oil represents My Holy Spirit and His anointing, it is something that My children need desperately to understand. My Holy Spirit and His anointing are something you should never be without, especially when it comes to your Shields of Faith. This is also the same oil that you will need to keep your lamp lit while waiting for the return of My Son Jesus. This truth stands firm according to My Word in Matthew 25. Unfortunately, there will be so many that will be caught without enough oil for their lamps."

"Father, I do remember the specific morning that I was in my Tameion Chamber, and You had me study out this shield.

"I learned that the Roman military had a very effective tactic that they used against their enemies, and they did this through the use of their large shields that were shaped like doors. It was called the testudo, or 'tortoise,' formation. When their enemy began to fire flaming arrows or any other deadly weapon into the air, these brave soldiers would immediately gather together in close ranks and form into a rectangular shape. The soldiers on the outside were trained to stand together and use their shields to create a wall around the perimeter of the soldiers in the middle. Those on the inside would then raise their shields over their heads protecting all the other soldiers from any oncoming fiery darts. They understood unity.

"I am so thankful that You have taught me to look into Your Word, to press in, tearing it apart as I ponder, pray and study. I remember clearly the Greek word for shield is thyreós. It means a gate or door (or "door-shaped"). Thyreós was a 'full-body' ancient Roman shield that looked like a full sized oblong door and was large enough to provide full protection from attack. The Shield (thyreós) of Faith refers to God's inner working of faith as something that protects the whole believer and is capable of covering their whole person during spiritual warfare. It's interesting that this Greek word is found only in Ephesians 6:16.[22]

"Father, I just wish at times Your Church could understand this very important principle because the result of this kind of teamwork is nothing short of a powerful and formidable human tank that can be moved onto the spiritual battlefield."

Immediately I am reminded of His Word in Ephesians 4:11-16. *"And He Himself gave some to be apostles, some prophets, some evangelists, and some pastors and teachers, for the equipping of the saints for the work of ministry, for the edifying of the body of Christ, till we all come to the **unity of the faith** and of the knowledge of the Son of God, to a perfect man, to the measure of the stature of the fullness of Christ; that we should no longer be children, tossed to and fro and carried about with every wind of doctrine, by the trickery of men, in the cunning craftiness of deceitful plotting, but, speaking the truth in love, may grow up in all things into Him who is the head—Christ—from whom the*

[22] Bible Hub, Strong's Concordance, G2375, *"Shield,"*
http://biblehub.com/greek/2375.htm

*whole body, joined and **knit together** by what every joint supplies, according to the effective working by which every part does its share, causes growth of the body for the edifying of itself in love."*

"Father, we as Your Church could learn great lessons from the Roman armies, just as Paul did. He knew that when the Roman army bravely joined their shields together, they became an almost unstoppable force. It is no different for us today. If we, as Your Church, would just join our Shields of Faith bravely together we could accomplish much for You. If we could just be faithful to strengthen each other with our faith, build each other up, support our fellow laborers by serving the body through humility and grace, losing our pride and recognizing that we are all on the same team, we could be just like those armies, an unstoppable force able to take on any challenge that the enemy brings our way."

"Connie, you must always remember that as you fight the good fight as a watchman, warrior and intercessor, it is not simply just your battle. This is the battle that I have called all My children to fight all over the world. Never forget that there are those that are battling right beside you in the spiritual realm. I know at times you and your sister warriors may feel very alone, but never forget I have an army that I have set apart for Myself. Just as I have instructed you, I am instructing them, encouraging them and assuring them, that if they are to win, they must be unified. This can only be when they acknowledge Me, My Son, My Holy Spirit and My Word with their Shields of Faith lifted toward heaven together in unity. I will continue to encourage them that they are to stand side by side with others in My body, that they must continue in contending earnestly and as one for 'our common salvation...the faith which was once for all delivered to the saints'" (Jude 1:3).

"Father, thank You for encouraging me in all that I have learned about my precious and very important, Shield of Faith. I now understand that it is designed to be linked in unity with other intercessors, watchmen and warriors. There is great protection that comes with unity.

"Father, this Shield of Faith serves as double protection for me as well as for the unified body of Christ as we engage in the battle. You have already given me my garments, robes, helmet, belt of truth, breastplate, sword and my war boots. All in all, those items could be enough, but I know now that my Shield of Faith has been provided as additional depth of protection. **My Shield of Faith hides me as Your warrior in the secret place and serves as a *'door of protection'* that not only myself but others can hide behind.**

"I have this promise from You and I stand on Your Word in faith that... *'The Lord Himself is my shield'* (Psalm 7:10 -13; Zechariah 12:8). You will always be faithful in providing for my protection by continuing to impart Your spoken Word of faith to me. I can stand firm knowing that this Truth will always extinguish the flames and will take the fire out of the arrows of my enemy (Romans 10:17).

"Father, through Your Holy Spirit teaching me in this secret place, I, your student have been listening! When Satan starts in to attack my values and beliefs, I am able to recognize that his voice is in contradiction to Your Word. Knowing the difference between the two will allow me to stand and to keep on standing. As Your Word says, *'Be on your guard; stand firm in the faith; be courageous; be strong. Do everything in love'* (1 Corinthians 16: 13-14).

"You have also taught me that my Shield of Faith will deflect the enemy. Satan is relentless and always looking for an opportunity to hurl his fiery darts of offence, doubt, fear and anxiety in my direction. If I lay my shield down, there is no doubt that I will be hit.

"And I have learned that my Shield of Faith is the first line of defense. This is the first thing that I put up when the arrows are flying. This is what will stand out the biggest and the brightest in the heat of battle, especially when we as watchman, warriors and intercessors unite, link up arm in arm, put our shields together and take over enemy territory. The rest of our armor is there to take some beating from the enemy, but it is not what we really want to be using to absorb every onslaught the enemy throws at us.

"Father, I have never forgotten a pastor once saying that, 'You do not, not even for a moment, go into battle intentionally blocking everything with your head.' There is great wisdom in this quote."

As I sit and ponder all I have been taught, my mind goes to the very familiar portion of scripture... *"Then Jesus said to him, 'Away with you, Satan! For it is written, 'You shall worship the Lord your God, and Him only you shall serve.' Then the devil left Him, and behold, angels came and ministered to Him'* (Matthew 4:10-11).

The realization comes to me that my Shield of Faith is a weapon as well as a defensive piece of armor. It can incapacitate and render my enemy ineffective! As Jesus was being tempted by Satan, it was His Shield of Faith, the Word of His Father God that repelled Satan for a season. My Shield of Faith in my God as demonstrated by Christ, will shut the mouth of my adversary.

"Father, thank You for my shield!"

"Daughter, you have learned well. **Take Up** *your Shield of Faith and remember to use it wisely."*

I lovingly and carefully remove the shield from its wall mount, and pick up my spear as well thinking that it is time for me to start my day.

28

Sword Of The Spirit

As **I prepare to leave** my very special intimate inner chamber, I walk over to where my precious **Bible** is laying on the beautiful table right next to my big red chair. I look at the chair and then again at the Bible and ponder all the hours and precious memories and lessons learned right there in that comfortable chair. I lean my shield and spear against the table, reach down to pick up my Bible and gently look through the worn and marked up pages.

I tightly embrace God's Word, holding it close to my heart. How I love this precious "Love Letter" written so personally to me. I am moved to tears at how I have had to grow through the years and I know now that my confidence is in whom my Father has called me to be. There is no doubt that His Word has taken its rightful place as the number one authority in my life. Pausing, I turn around and look into the beautiful mirror and kneel as my tears pour forth from a heart that can't find the appropriate words. I know my Father is next to me and I can feel the gentle touch of His hand catching every tear that is falling down my face.

"Father, as I hold Your **Word of Truth** in my hands, I am forever grateful and thankful that You have entrusted me with this powerful weapon of truth. I simply want to thank You. I have come to know You so intimately through this precious book of promises that was penned so long ago. I wish I had the words to express my love for You. If I were to pen everything I have learned, all of its instructions, promises, mandates and purposes, it would take me an eternity to list them all. Your Word is never ending, and the depths of it no man shall ever find. Its pages have been faithful to bring me peace, comfort, guidance and strength, and yet I have gained learning, discernment and wisdom. It carries within its pages all the answers I need for life, health and hope for my future."

I get up from the place I am kneeling, and as I pull His Word away from my heart, I hold it securely in my hands and I immediately notice how it transforms into a **double edged Sword**. This is the **Sword of the Spirit** that I have come to rely on as a watchman, warrior, and intercessor. I trust this Sword with my life. It has been my most sufficient weapon, never failing me during the battle. When the battle becomes greater than I could ever imagine, I find my feet standing firm and my hand bound to my Sword. I always have the promise just as Eleazar, one of David's Mighty Men did in 2 Samuel 23, that my Father will be the one to bring about a great victory. *"....and He* (Eleazar) *stood firm, and smote the Philistines until his hand was weary, and his hand did cleave unto the sword; and the LORD wrought a great victory that day; and the people returned after him only to strip the slain"* (JPS Tanakh).

As I lift my Sword toward Heaven my heart cries out in praise... *"For the word of God is alive and active. Sharper than any double-edged sword, it penetrates even to dividing soul and spirit, joints and marrow; it judges the thoughts and attitudes of the heart"* (Hebrews 4:12, NIV).

"Father, this is Your all-powerful Sword! It belongs to You, the Living God, and it is able to cut through every offense the enemy raises against me, even down to the very division of bone and marrow. As Your servant, when my Sword is wielded, nothing will be able to withstand the ability of this weapon, as it will cut straight to the core of every battle allowing the truth of the battle to be uncovered. As a warrior in Your army, it will always be my responsibility and duty to use this weapon to discern the truth and then to follow it.

"Father, Your Spirit has also taught me that when Your Word shows me something wrong within myself, I can use this spiritual weapon to 'surgically' remove any sin, rebellion, disobedience, wrong thinking patterns and spiritual strongholds that are contrary to Your plans for my life (2 Corinthians 10:4-5). My Sword has been uniquely designed for both defensive and offensive purposes of the battle.

"Just as Your Son Jesus used Your Word to counter Satan's attacks, I must also learn to live *'by every word that proceeds from the mouth of God'* (Matthew 4:4; 7, 10).

"As You have been the One to place this weapon in my hands, I am fully committed to placing my confidence in its power to defeat the enemy. I have no doubt as to its ability and reliability. I promise to continue to protect this Sword and will take great care to use it responsibly. Your Spirit has taught me that if I will only trust in and rely upon this Sword and the completed work of Your Son Jesus, they will not fail me during the heat of any battle Satan brings my way.

"Father, this is the very first weapon that You gave to me. It is the first weapon that You give to each of Your children when we enlist in your army. If only we are but willing, your Holy Spirit will teach us everything we need to know about how to use this weapon. I am grateful for the training I have received."

As I get a good grip on my Sword, I notice that I have become *intimately familiar with this weapon* after years of constant use. My heart rejoices in this because it means that I have become *intimately familiar with my God.*

I am immediately reminded by the Holy Spirit, that for years before I had to ever come near to any of the real battlefields, He taught me how to defeat a thousand imaginary enemies. I would practice each day by reading and memorizing His Word, and I was becoming familiar with the great men and women, the warriors of old. Now after years of fighting the real battles, I not only know this weapon well, but have also become familiar with the weight of my very own Sword. In any given battle, I have learned how much force is needed to cut down the enemies I encounter. I have thrived under His faithful training as He taught me how to use this weapon both defensively and offensively.

I am jolted out of my thoughts, of all the years of training, of wars past, of amazing victories and even some defeats, and of battles yet to be fought as I hear my Father speaking over me the Royal Wedding Song found in Psalm 45: 1-6.

"Connie, mighty warrior, strap your sword to your side. In your majesty and splendor, ride triumphantly in the cause of truth, humility, and justice. May your right hand show you awe-inspiring acts. May your arrows pierce the hearts of the King's enemies; and may the peoples fall under you. Your throne, God, is forever and ever; the scepter of Your kingdom is a scepter of justice."

Once again, I find myself on my knees, and as I stand, I place my Sword in its place of prominence secured to my Belt of

Truth. I confess His Word back to Him, reminding Him of His promises to me. *"But he who endures to the end shall be saved.... What then shall we say to these things? If God is for us, who can be against us?"* (Matthew 24:13; Romans 8:31, NASB).

I will continue to fight for my King knowing that I have put all my hope into the end of His story. I will continue to stand on both of these powerful and sure promises declared in His Word. If I remain faithful to my Father, and as my feet stay firmly planted in His Word, there is no doubt that I will make it to the end. I will be saved. My Father's promises are secured and backed up by all of heaven itself. He said it, and I believe it! Just as He told Isaiah, He has told me, *"Indeed I have spoken it; I will also bring it to pass. I have purposed it; I will also do it"* (Isaiah 46:11).

29

*R*od Of *A*uthority

*B*efore I leave my Tameion Chamber, I must check my equipment. My Sword is tucked into my Belt, and I reach for my Spear that is designed to defeat Belial along with my Shield of Faith, knowing that the battle truly belongs to my God.

I reach for the door and notice that there, leaning against the wall next to the door, is my **Rod of Authority**. I dare not leave without this vital tool and weapon.

My Rod of Authority is a sign of the authority that Jesus has given to me, recognizable by everyone, including the enemy. I call to mind the words of my Savior in Luke 10:19, *"I have given you authority to trample on snakes and scorpions and to overcome all the power of the enemy; nothing will harm you."*

I have learned that this Rod of Authority carries the anointing of the Holy Spirit for ruling with Kingdom authority in the spiritual realm, and in carrying out supernatural miracles. In God's Word, the rod is also a staff that can be used as a weapon or club, a tool like a walking stick, and as an instrument aiding in the rescue of God's people. It can also be used in discipline or correction.

My mind turns to the lesson I learned from Ezekiel 20:37, that the rod was used in making covenants. *"I will make you pass under the rod, and I will bring you into the bond of the covenant."*

I remember that I have chosen to make covenant with my Father, and once again, as I handle the smooth, wooden Rod of Authority, I remember that its authority comes through the power of the accomplishment of Jesus the Son as His blood was shed on the wooden cross, a type of rod. I am overcome with humility as I contemplate the price that was paid so that I could handle this Rod of Authority in service of my King.

"Father, I choose to rededicate and pledge myself to You for Your service, to recommit my vows. I choose to pass under the rod of Your authority and to enter into covenant with the You. I will stand firm in my faith. I will use the authority that

Christ has given me. I will accept His discipline and correction. I will use this rod as a weapon and a tool."

As I pick up the Rod of Authority, a smile touches my lips as Biblical scenes pass before my eyes. I picture Moses with his Rod of Authority, striking the Red Sea and watching it part in Exodus 4:17. Then I think of his anger as he struck the rock with his rod and water came pouring out; and while this miracle quenched the thirst of people, because the rod was used wrongly, Moses was disciplined by God (Exodus 17:9). I think of David the shepherd boy and Jesus the Good Shepherd, tending their sheep with their rod and staff (Psalm 23:4).

"Father, You have guided and directed me many times with Your rod and staff, and I have found that they have comforted as well as disciplined me (Proverbs 13:24). Thank You for this tool and weapon. May I be found as faithful in using my Rod of Authority and never forget that its power is from You as I walk in Your will."

30

Counterfeit Armor And Stolen Robes

My Father's voice is speaking yet once again.

"Connie, before you leave this secret, inner chamber, there are a couple very important things that I need you to clearly understand."

I turn expectantly toward my Father.

"Connie, the enemy will show up daily and you will be offered a counterfeit wardrobe. You must be able to tell the difference between the garments, robes, armor and weapons that I have prepared for you, from the counterfeits offered by the enemy! This is a very hard lesson that many of my watchmen, warriors and intercessors have had to learn.

"Your wardrobe must be chosen by Me each and every day. The weapons I place into your hands will depend on the battle you will be facing, and I am the only One who knows this. By staying close to Me, reading My Word, praying in the Spirit, listening to the Spirit, and being obedient, you will have no problem being ready for the battle. Seek Me daily in your Tameion Chamber."

"Yes Lord, I understand. I can and will recognize the armor You give because I am so familiar with You, its designer! You and You alone are the designer of my garments, my weapons of war, and You are the preparer of my battle plans. I understand that I must only receive these things from Your hand."

"Yes Connie, this is correct."

"Father, You have created them with me in mind and with the greatest of care knowing me so intimately. Only You understand the battles that I will face along the way. My heart, my mind, my will and my emotions need to pay the greatest of attention to Your details."

"Yes, Child, you must give extra attention to My 'Belt of Truth!' This will always be the first counterfeit piece of armor you will be offered. You know full well that the enemy of your soul, Satan, is the father of lies (John 8:44).

"Connie, so many of My children today try to put on armor that either belongs to someone else or that I have not called them to wear. This can be deadly! In doing this they bring great harm to themselves and even other believers because they don't know how to properly use these weapons.

"They have not spent time with Me, and this is what is needed for them to be taught and trained, but they don't want to take the time to learn! Because of this, there is always a mess that I am having to clean up for My children. I have had to clean up your messes many times and this does not please Me. Connie, I need you to learn these lessons deeply."

I hear Him sigh before He continues. "There is always a heart that gets broken or an offense that is taken. But even worse, there is a soul that will slip into the arms of hell when My Church is not praying, fighting, warring and getting dressed in their proper armor. I am very specific in My Word about this.

"Because many of My children either pay no attention or want to be something that they are not called to be, the enemy will use this strategy to distract them. Even worse, My children end up fighting a war that I have not called them to fight; a war they are not trained for; and even wars that they have brought on themselves because of a lack of self-control.

"Many of My children have fallen away from the faith because they are trying to 'put on the king's armor' like David did, instead of using the tools I am asking them to use. Only by staying in My Word, staying in prayer and relationship with Me, will you be able to know the difference.

"Connie, I know you have read the story of David and Goliath many times, but Child, I want you to go to My Word again. It will always be for your instruction and training. I spoke it into existence and wrote it on the tablets of men's hearts so that they could pen My instructions to you. As an intercessor, watchman, warrior, you will always find the training, tools, armor, weapons and words you will need to defeat your enemies in My Word, and you will always be in training, continually learning how to defend the weak, encourage the hopeless and to destroy the enemy. But it is your choice, and wearing the correct armor will make all the difference!"

I lean my Spear, Shield and Rod against the wall, and then retrieve my Sword from my Belt of Truth. As I sit down in my big, beautiful, red chair, the Holy Spirit whispers in my ear, *"I want you to read 1 Samuel 17."*

I stop and ponder verses 38-39. *"Then Saul clothed David with his garments and put a bronze helmet on his head, and he clothed him with armor. David girded his sword over his armor and tried to walk, for he had not tested them. So David said to Saul, 'I cannot go with these, for I have not tested them." And David took them off"* (1 Samuel 17:38-39 NASB).

"Father, I don't believe the issue was as much that David couldn't use the armor he was offered, but that it hadn't been tested. David had not been trained in wearing the king's armor, nor had he been able to test *or try* it. If this armor had been what was needed to kill the giant, wouldn't God have done it through whom the armor belonged, King Saul?

"Father, I think it was inappropriate and foolish for King Saul to offer his armor to someone that could not use it. But, in looking back, I can see the many times I have had someone spiritually over me who invited me into their tent and asked me to put on their armor. They even asked me to fight in their battle, their way. And I have done the same to others. There have been times I did try to put on someone else's armor because I wanted to be just like them or I just wanted to feel like I fit in.

"Father, You are well aware of all the times I have put on robes, garments and armor that I wasn't trained to wear. It always made the battle worse, harder somehow and it always leaves more casualties. I always found myself having to go back to You, wounded and beat up by the enemy.

"Father, this is now making so much sense! You are teaching me that David's training and armor and weapons were very specifically chosen and ordained by You, the Almighty God, for a specific purpose, a specific battle. I can see that the weapons chosen by You to defeat an enemy in battle will be exceptionally different than what my ideas might be.

"You had called David with a specific purpose and that was to kill Goliath who was tormenting Your children day after day. There was no way he could defeat this enemy wearing someone else's armor.

"Father, You have called all Your children to something significant, to fight strategic wars in strategic places, and we must never forget that we must not try to do it wearing someone else's armor.

"I understand that this doesn't mean that we can't accept help, advice, support, and learn from our brothers and sisters in Christ. It simply means that I shouldn't try to copy someone else's battle, training or calling. I need to especially make sure that I don't try to walk in their calling. I need to be walking in mine.

"Father, You have called me to accomplish great things in a very unique way, and I am to be obedient in that calling. David probably would have experienced great defeat and even possibly been killed himself if he would have tried to fight the enemy in the king's armor that wasn't made for him.

"I see, Father, that You are instructing me in several different issues here. First, to be aware of Satan offering me counterfeit garments. And second, I am to be the intercessor that You have called me to be. I am not to put on someone else's armor or to fight another's battle.

"I can't help but think about how different the battle would have been if David would have let his heart be filled with pride by making the decision to put on the 'king's armor.' I can see David walking out of the king's tent with the king's armor. Everyone in Saul's army would probably have bowed at David's feet, but when David went to fight Goliath, he would have not been able to defeat the giant. He would have become a laughing stock and Israel would have been slaughtered.

"Father, this is exactly what it would look like if I put on armor that I shouldn't be wearing. And this is exactly why so many people hate Christians. We put on the 'pride of a king' when we are called to be 'shepherds' that fight in humility under Your command!"

"Connie, you have learned much today! I am so proud of you! Take this lesson deep into the recesses of your heart, mind, will and emotions, and plant it in your spirit. You are always to make sure that you wear only that which I have given you.

"In doing this, in each and every battle you face, you will find that you are fully prepared and that your wardrobe fits you perfectly. This is how you will defeat your enemy. Your learning will always come through prayer, fasting, and intercession with Me."

"Father, I have also learned to stay close to You and be very watchful and awake! And I've learned that I will know immediately if I have on the wrong armor because it will become spiritually heavy and cause me to become tired, weak and weary. This is when I can give place to the enemy. The spirit of Pride, Complacency and especially Drowsiness are very real and they are just looking for an opportunity to take over. There is great danger in these three spirits.

"You have warned me that in these last days, there will be many of my brothers and sisters who have given into these spirits. They will be sleeping on the hour of Your return and will find themselves waking at the last hour, only to be ensnared and taken into the enemy's camp."

"Connie, the powers of darkness are very real and they are well trained. You will always need to remember that it doesn't matter which direction you choose to go; you will always encounter your enemy on every side. Their main purpose is to destroy My intercessors, My watchmen, My warriors and those I am reaching out to.

"I am the One who has built My Church on the life of My Son and I have clearly said in My Word, 'The gates of hell shall not prevail against it!'

"Now, I have one more lesson for you today My daughter. I want to caution your heart one more time regarding the garments and robes I have given you. Turn to one of your favorite books, Genesis, and read Chapter 37."

"Yes, Father I am very familiar with this chapter and cherish its story, even though it is heartbreaking."

"Connie, what was it that was stolen from Joseph?"

"Everything Lord! His freedom, his family and HIS ROBE! It says in Verse 23, *'So when Joseph came to his brothers, they stripped him of his robe, the richly ornamented robe he was wearing and they took him and threw him into the cistern.'*

"Oh Father, they stripped him of his Robe! The beautiful, ornamented robe that his father had made him because he loved him so much. You have given me many robes Father, are they going to be stolen too?"

"Connie, you need to know that there will be brothers and sisters in Christ who want to steal your robes, defiling them with false blood. The enemy would love nothing more than to steal the beautiful robes that I have placed upon you. You need to be fully aware of this, for your enemy will stop at nothing in hopes of disrobing you. Your robes are robes of authority and a sign of My love for you, and there will be those that hate you because you wear these robes.

"Now, daughter, I want you to jump to Chapter 29 of Genesis and tell me what happens."

"I see it already, Father. Potiphar's wife steals Joseph's robe too! She uses this against him and he sits in prison, innocent, but charged guilty. Wow, just unbelievable! I know you will have me putting together a whole study on this one.

"Father, as I sit here reading the rest of the story, I am so thankful that Joseph's robes were restored in Genesis Chapter 41. I know that there is a truth here, and I see it!"

As I start turning the pages of my Bible, my mind immediately goes to Elijah and Jezebel. She was trying to steal his robes too! Good thing in 1 Kings 19:19 it says that, *"Elijah threw his cloak around Elisha."* Elisha ended up with Elijah's robe! Whew! Close call! Then there's also the time in 1 Samuel 18, that Jonathan recognized the calling on David's life and the Bible says in verse 3, *"And Jonathan made a covenant with David because he loved him as himself. Jonathan took off the robe he was wearing and gave it to David and even his tunic, and even his sword, his bow and his belt."*

"Wow Lord, such love! But I do know that Saul tried to kill David for years after that, and I now understand that it was because You had placed a call upon his life.

"Father, this study is going to be going on for some time as my mind runs wild with the putting on and taking off of all the royal garments. We have the story of Esther and Haman's rage against Mordecai. Mordecai was honored with beautiful robes;

and then we have Joshua in the Book of Zechariah 3 and much more! Now I get it Father!"

"*Connie,* **whenever there is a calling of God placed on your life, you will have a robe placed on your shoulders and someone is going to try and steal it, so watch out!*"

"Well Father, I pray that as in the case of Joseph, Mordecai, Daniel and Joshua, the enemy will have to obey the King and may even be ordered by the King to put my royal robes right back where they belong! Thank you Father!

"I want to read Zechariah Chapter 3 one more time out loud before I leave this precious place."

"*Then he showed me Joshua the high priest standing before the angel of the Lord, and Satan standing at his right side to accuse him. The Lord said to Satan, 'The Lord rebuke you, Satan! The Lord, who has chosen Jerusalem, rebuke you! Is not this man a burning stick snatched from the fire?' Now Joshua was dressed in filthy clothes as he stood before the angel. The angel said to those who were standing before him, 'Take off his filthy clothes.'*

"*Then he said to Joshua, 'See, I have taken away your sin, and I will put fine garments on you.' Then I said, 'Put a clean turban on his head.' So they put a clean turban on his head and clothed him, while the angel of the Lord stood by. The angel of the Lord gave this charge to Joshua: 'This is what the Lord Almighty says: 'If you will walk in obedience to me and keep my requirements, then you will govern my house and have charge of my courts, and I will give you a place among these standing here.*

"'*Listen, High Priest Joshua, you and your associates seated before you, who are men symbolic of things to come: I am going to bring my servant, the Branch. See, the stone I have set in front of Joshua! There are seven eyes on that one stone, and I will engrave an inscription on it,' says the Lord Almighty, 'and I will remove the sin of this land in a single day. In that day each of you will invite your neighbor to sit under your vine and fig tree,' declares the Lord Almighty.'"*

31

Changing Your Robes Could Cost You Your Life

I **awaken each and every morning** excited to meet with my Father in my secret place of intimacy with Him. It never fails that He has something new to show me, or a new lesson to teach me. On this particular morning, the very moment I stepped inside my Tameion Chamber, I heard my Father speaking to me.

"Good morning Precious One! I have been waiting for you. My heart is blessed by your hunger for the wholeness of who I AM and what I have to offer you from the storehouses of My heavenly realm. There is a lesson I would like to impart into your life today, so I'm going to ask you Child, as the Author and Finisher of your faith, to pay very careful attention to what you are about to learn from Me today, for it is of great importance and I know it will be a blessing to you.

"I have spoken to you on many occasions about your uniqueness. I have also been teaching you for many years that you are never to be something I have not called you to be. I have designed you with a very specific purpose. You have a very unique calling, and it belongs only to you. There will not be a day that goes by that the enemy will not try to turn, twist and distort My call upon your life. He will offer you the great things of this world in order to turn your affections toward himself. And you will be tempted.

"The individual uniqueness of My children all along has been part of My plan because it is the one thing necessary in making up the whole of the Bride of My Son. It is only in the operation of My God-given gifts, talents and abilities that the purity of Her brightness and beauty can be seen in the darkness of the world.

"I long for My children to seek My heart regarding their importance to Me and how I have created them. The plans I have for them are far beyond what most of them could ever hope or

imagine. For many of My children, the enemy has distorted their view of who I have called them to be. I want you to encourage, equip and train up those whom I have placed in your path and in your care. They must learn of and about their uniqueness.

"So many of My children are not walking in what I have called them to be, and they have no idea of what My storehouse holds for them. They are walking around not seeing, not hearing and not perceiving their purpose.[23] The robes and garments they are wearing are not of Me or from Me, for their eyes are on the things of this world, and Satan, the angel of light, has turned their hearts to the doctrine of demons. He is having them mimic what they see in the world and what they are being taught in the worldly church. There is no distinction between those who call themselves My Bride and the World. They are watching men and are not learning from My Spirit. They have not entered the secret place of prayer, and they compromise truth by pulling out only what pleases them from My Word.

"I need them to understand that just as I took the dust of the earth and breathed the breath of life into Adam, My heart's desire is to create and breathe the breath of life into the Bride of My Son. She must be awakened from Her slumber, brought back to life, and then operate in such a manner and fashion that she is set apart for the sole purpose of My plan of Redemption, not only for Herself, but others.

"The timing of My Son's birth and the importance of His life upon the earth was not only appointed and ordained, but it was strategic! Before the creation of the world, I knew He would have to die. But I also knew that He would be the One sent to confront the sin and pride of a rebellious religion that had been birthed in Hell. This religion was and still is being carried out by the flesh of man in your time, not by the power of My Spirit.

"Daughter, I know you are familiar with My Word, but I want you to see and hear something you need to pay close attention to! Turn to Matthew Chapter 23 and read. What has My Spirit highlighted for you?"

I immediately do as my Father asks. I adjust my spiritual spectacles and start to read the chapter, looking, listening and

---

[23] See Mark 4:11-12

concentrating. I open the drawer that is in the table next to my chair and pull out my yellow highlighter.

I hear myself speaking to the Holy Spirit, "Show me what it is that I need to see." I finish the chapter and am determined to find out what it is I'm supposed to see, and there it is!

The Seven Woes And The Altered Robes. My

heart is pounding and my eyes fill with tears because I know it's not only a warning, but an expression of grief in the heart of my King, Jesus.

I have seen this before and I have read these scriptures so many times. But how could my spirit have been so blind of its warning? It is stated boldly for a reason! There is no mistaking by whom it was said! Not only is it written in red, but my King, Jesus says it seven times in this one chapter.

"Woe to you!"

"Father, I know that when Jesus was speaking to the men, women and children on the Sermon on the Mount in Matthew chapter 5, nine times He pronounced, *'Blessed Are.'* Now, here in Matthew 23, seven times He pronounced, *'Woe to You'* on those who were called to shepherd those same children.

"Father, You taught me long ago that if something is mentioned two times, I should pay close attention, and now this *'Woe to you'* seven times? I know this follows an established pattern that I have seen frequently throughout Your Word both in the Old and New Testament. It just dawned on me that in Isaiah 5:8-23, there are six *'Woe to you's,'* and in Habakkuk 2:6-20, there are five. And I'm aware of many more. Father, You know Your book. You wrote it and I don't have to tell You!"

"Daughter, these conversations you and I have, are partly how you learn. I love it when you talk to Me about My love letter to you."

"Father, my King, Jesus was talking to the religious leaders of His day and I notice something else that concerns me. They altered the priestly robes and garments that You had called them to wear."

"Yes, Daughter, the religious deception of Satan had overtaken the hearts of those I had called to shepherd My children in Israel, and it is still prevalent today. When My Son, Jesus walked

149

the earth as a man, these were the religious leaders, teachers of My law, and those whom I had called to be set apart for Holiness. The teachers of My law had disregarded My design and were purposely altering their priestly garments looking to impress men instead of obeying Me. They widened the phylacteries[24] and they lengthened the tassels[25] on their garments. They were full of pride and were indignant toward My Holiness. They mixed the unholy things with the Holy, and the ungodly things with that which belonged to Me. They took things that were set apart and replaced them with the ordinary, and this brought about defilement in their worship and offerings to Me. They were hardhearted and spiritually blind guides.[26] They replaced their Holy Garments with garments of deception. They allowed the enemy to come in and defile all that was set apart for Me.

"Connie, I always want you to remember these words that I am having you pen and what I am about to say to you. You must be watchful and humble for it is the prideful will of man that threatens My Holiness! As I have also shared with your husband, Greg, 'It is the ordinary that will always threaten My set apart ones!' The Bride that I am going to present to My Son must be pure. She must come to understand that every single part of her needs to be operating in the place of her own uniqueness and within the boundaries of the holiness I have called her too. I would not ask something of you that you could not attain. If I have called you to be set apart, then it is possible! If I have asked you to walk in righteousness and holiness, then it is possible.

"The time is now short and the return of My Son is sooner than most will expect. As it was in the days when My Son walked on the earth, so it is in your lifetime. As it was in the Days of Noah, so it is in your lifetime, Child. There is much defilement in the land and the American Church. They have mixed in the unholy things of this world and they do not Fear My Great Name. There are many pastors and teachers and those who claim to be My prophets who are nothing more than wolves in sheep's clothing.

---

[24] Phylacteries: a small leather box containing Hebrew texts on vellum, worn by Jewish men and Priests at morning prayer as a reminder to keep the law.
[25] Tassels; Hebrew "Tzitzit" are specially knotted ritual fringes, or tassels, worn in antiquity by Israelite are attached to the four corners of the _tallit_ (prayer shawl) and _tallit katan_ (everyday undergarment).
[26] Matthew 15: 12-14

Many have exchanged or altered their garments to please that of the men and women around them. They have become lovers of this world, lovers of money and even more so, they love the praise of men, which feeds their spirit of pride.

"My servant Paul, clearly warned Timothy, and I want you to be aware so that you do not fall into this snare yourself."

"Father, I don't ever want to deceive others by what I teach, so I ask that You keep my teachings true to Your Word. I also don't ever want to be deceived myself, so I ask that my heart would always be humble and that Your Holy Spirit would convict and assist me in keeping my motives pure."

As I speak this prayer out loud to my Father I want to make sure that all of heaven hears and will keep me accountable. I know that I am to read the familiar passage in 1 Timothy Chapter 4 and pay close attention. I know this passage well. It is short but full of warnings, revelation, instruction and teachings that are relevant for the days I am living in.

"The Spirit clearly says that in later times some will abandon the faith and follow deceiving spirits and things taught by demons. Such teachings come through hypocritical liars, whose consciences have been seared as with a hot iron. They forbid people to marry and order them to abstain from certain foods, which God created to be received with thanksgiving by those who believe and who know the truth. For everything God created is good, and nothing is to be rejected if it is received with thanksgiving, because it is consecrated by the word of God and prayer. If you point these things out to the brothers and sisters, you will be a good minister of Christ Jesus, nourished on the truths of the faith and of the good teaching that you have followed. Have nothing to do with godless myths and old wives' tales; rather, train yourself to be godly. For physical training is of some value, but godliness has value for all things, holding promise for both the present life and the life to come. This is a trustworthy saying that deserves full acceptance. That is why we labor and strive, because we have put our hope in the living God who is the Savior of all people, especially of those who believe. Command and teach these things. Don't let anyone look down on you because you are young, but set an example for the believers in speech, in conduct, in love, in faith and in purity. Until I

come, devote yourself to the public reading of Scripture, to preaching and to teaching. Do not neglect your gift, which was given you through prophecy when the body of elders laid their hands on you. Be diligent in these matters; give yourself wholly to them, so that everyone may see your progress. Watch your life and doctrine closely. Persevere in them, because if you do, you will save both yourself and your hearers" (1 Timothy 4).

"Father, I am so thankful for the teachings and truth of Your Word. It is powerful and effective and it has changed me at the deepest levels of my spirit. I am simply grateful and thankful for the hunger You have placed within me. My heart's desire is to never grieve Your Spirit, even though I completely understand that I am far from perfect. Please always convict me and continue to be patient with me as I grow. I can't stand the times that my heart becomes hard towards You, and I wish it would never happen again.

"Someday I will stand before You in the courts of heaven fully pure and without sin, but until that day I ask that You give me the strength to finish this race without grieving You. I am fully aware of the worldly sin that has overtaken Your Church, and I see but just a small portion of it. I know it must grieve You! I can't even begin to imagine and won't pretend too!"

Counterfeit Robes, Garments And Anointing.

"Daughter, My Spirit is not only trying to warn and bring conviction to the world, but it is being grieved at what I am seeing in those who call themselves apostles, prophets, evangelists, pastors and teachers. They claim righteousness for themselves when their hearts are far from Me!

"My Bride, especially the Ones whom I have called and appointed to shepherd My Church, must repent, humble themselves, take off their counterfeit garments and robes of pride, and pursue Holiness! Daughter, this is a must for you personally! There are no exceptions to this requirement of Mine. There have been times when your character has been the exact opposite of that which I required of the citizens of My Kingdom according to My Word in Matthew Chapter 18.

"My Church, starting with you, Precious One, must become healthy and whole so you will be without spot or blemish. Not all,

but many are wearing filthy garments just as you have in the past, and it is because the spirit of Pride still sits on the throne of their hearts. This will not allow the process of sanctification[27] to take place within them. They have pursued the doctrine of demons and exchanged the Truth of My Word for a lie. It is just as you have read in My Word. These teachings appear to have My approval, but they do not line up with the whole of My Word, teachings and requirements.

"At times, just as you have, the Church has come to Me asking that I forgive their sin, and yet they are not willing to remove their sin. They are looking for temporary relief from the one who torments them. They just shuffle their sin around throwing off an old garment or two here and there. They don't like the feeling of being naked and vulnerable before Me because it is so contrary to what they have learned from the father of lies! Before giving Me the opportunity to work, they rush back to their sin as if it were a comfortable pair of old sweats, and picking it up again, they place it over their head and no real inner change has taken place. They are excited about the idea of being great in My Kingdom but they are not willing to humble themselves so that I can work. They may at times even attempt to remove the blatant sin, but have only moved it into the basement of their lives. They attempt a cleaning of the surface but make no progress ending up in a condition seven times worse than they were to start with because they are afraid of the pain, the work and effort it will take to go deeper with Me."

"Yes, Father, there is that 7 number again! I am all too familiar with the condition of a man being 7 times worse according to Matthew 12 and Luke 11. I have walked down that road personally and I am so very sorry."

"Yes, Child, this is true! You have walked down that road too many times. I have watched you as you have changed back into your worldly garments. I knew that you were still very attached to them, for I would see you temporarily try on the ones I offered you, but because you still believed the lies about yourself thinking that they held the keys to who you were supposed to be,

---

[27] Sanctification is the act or process of acquiring sanctity, of being made or becoming holy. ... To sanctify is to literally "set apart for particular use in a special purpose or work and to make holy or sacred."

and because you were still in love with the old garments, My heart would break each time you would take off and lay aside the robes and garments I created for you. Each time you picked up the old ones, I knew you were out from underneath My protection and covering. Several times you ended up in a really bad way, this is true, and it could have cost you your life!"

It Could Cost You Your Life. "Cost me my life, really? Ok, Father, please explain. I'm not sure I understand."

"*Thank goodness Child, that your heart has now learned much and you don't ever wander too far from Me. You are quick to repent and tear off garments that are not part of My plan for you, but it wasn't always that way! You have had to learn some hard lessons in the past. Each time you come to Me and I see that your heart is serious about repentance, all of Heaven rejoices with Me because this is when I can destroy those old garments for you.*

"*When there are those such as yourself who truly desire inner change, then I can finally operate within the realm of freedom to do the spiritual housecleaning that is necessary and greatly needed in each individual. It's a very deep work that I do, as you well know, Precious One. I always rejoice when My children who have finally humbled themselves, have repented and are now willing to throw off their filthy dirty garments. There has not been a one of them who are not completely surprised to find that I have created a whole new wardrobe for them. They are in such awe of the gifts, talents, callings and treasures, not to mention the beautiful garments, robes, perfumes and armor that I have made just for them. They soon realize those old garments are no longer there, and I am able to cast them away as far as the east is from the west, never to be found again.*"

"Father, Psalm 103:11-14 has always been one of my favorite scriptures. '*For as high as the heavens are above the earth, so great is His loving kindness toward those who fear Him. As far as the east is from the west, so far has He removed our transgressions from us. Just as a father has compassion on his children, So the LORD has compassion on those who fear Him for He Himself knows our frame; He is mindful that we are but dust.*' I know You put it right there for all Your children such as me who have walked in the sin of heavy rebellion. Yet I love it when we

154

find ourselves broken before You with the ability to let it all go and repent, finding that You give us all a precious promise. You are not a man that You would lie.

"Daughter, You are the Ones who embrace the wholeness of My Word and know that a decision must be made with each and every new revelation I bring to you. So begins the work of My sanctification in your life and theirs.

"Precious One, My Son is worthy to be presented with a 'Perfect Bride,' a Bride who has made herself ready! I will settle for nothing less for My Son, for He is a King and His Name is Faithful, Worthy and True! Open My Word, Child, and go to 1 Corinthians 12. Read it to Me because I want you to be reminded of your uniqueness.

"Yes, Father!" I quickly turn the pages of my very loved and worn out Bible and find the beloved text.

"Just as a body, though one, has many parts, but all its many parts form one body, so it is with Christ...."

I finish the chapter and I know I have my part to play in the preparation of the Bride. I am excited as my mind and emotions are stirred by the wonder of it all!

The Robes Of Deception. "Father, I love Your Word

because it teaches ALL the details. There is nothing missed and everything Heaven has to offer is gained. But I am still curious about how the changing of my garments could cost me my life. I understand sin and I know I have been guilty in the past of picking up my old robes, but Your Words feels like a mystery to me right now. Please share Your Father's heart with me regarding this."

"Yes, Child, you have many questions and you also have a teachable spirit. I am thankful for this part of your character for I have grown to love it so deeply. I know that you have had to learn many lessons the hard way, but the truth is that you could have lost your life at any moment you stepped out from under My protection.

"It is especially dangerous to pretend to be something that you are not in My Kingdom realm. Walking in a counterfeit calling, seeking spiritual advice from ungodly spirits that are not

of Me, going into battles that I have not called you too... Yes, all of this could get you into real trouble and even cost you your life.

"Child, turn to 1 Samuel 28 and read it now. Tell me what you see."

"Father, I can clearly see in verse 8 that King Saul took off his royal robes, and Your Word says that, *'putting on other clothes,'* he went in to see the medium (witch) at Endor. Father, the next day King Saul was dead!"

"Child, now turn your attention to 1 Kings 22 and 2 Chronicles 18 and read and ponder these scriptures."

"Oh Father, here is Ahab, King of Israel, and he had decided to go into battle in disguise, and he took off his royal robes. Your Word says, *'The King of Israel said to Jehoshaphat, 'I will enter the battle in disguise, but you wear your royal robes.'*

"This is just terrible, Father, and it breaks my heart! He told someone else to wear their royal robes and that guy lived. But he himself, the King of Israel, took off his royal garments and went in disguise to the battle. Ahab did not enter the battle as who You called him to be!

"So You mean to tell me that someone just happened to randomly draw their bow, shoot it into the midst of the battle, and BAM, that day King Ahab was dead?"

"I think you are getting the picture My Dear One. My Word doesn't place these truths here for no reason, nor does My Word have silly fairy tales. These are golden treasures of wisdom, real truths and lessons that each of My children should be digging in My Word to find. These are the secrets that I love to share with those who are serious about their faith. They are not for the faint of heart, nor are they for those who like to compromise. These are Kingdom lessons that could save your life!

"My Precious Daughter, as I have watched your hunger for My Word grow over the years, and as I see you longing to know My ways, I can't help but hear the words of My Son, Jesus as He stated, 'Blessed are those who hunger and thirst for righteousness, for they will be filled.'[28] I believe that I am going to call you by a new name, but just for today! You are My 'Mela Ravah!'"

---

[28] Matthew 5:6

156

"Father that is so beautiful! Yes, I place upon myself my new name for today. I love it when you give me new names! I am Your 'Mela Ravah,' which means 'filled and saturated one!'"

I laugh at myself for just a moment as I completely understand why it is that this new name is just for today! I love it that He knows me deeply and all too well, for tomorrow I will be starving again and hungry for more of Him, His Word and anything else He will offer me.

"I'm glad I made you smile, Little One, for you truly are My Mela Ravah. Now turn with Me to 2 Chronicles and read Chapter 35."

The Tearing Of The Robes. As I finish the whole of Chapter 35, my tears are unstoppable. I feel like this is a truth that may get me stoned by the Bible scholars, pastors, teachers and prophets of today. I am shaking as I write everything down that is being poured into my spirit. My emotions are unsettled and raw because I had never put two and two together regarding King Josiah. Without a doubt I am seeing exactly what my Father wants me to see, for it is just as applicable today as it was over 2600 years ago, if not even more so. My heart is breaking as I know I have to go back to 2 Chronicles Chapter 34, and read it out loud.

"Josiah was eight years old when he became king, and he reigned in Jerusalem thirty-one years. He did what was right in the eyes of the LORD and followed the ways of his father David, not turning aside to the right or to the left. In the eighth year of his reign when he was still young he began to seek the God of his father David.

"In his twelfth year he began to purge Judah and Jerusalem of high places, Asherah poles and idols. Under his direction the altars of the Baals were torn down; he cut to pieces the incense altars that were above them, and smashed the Asherah poles and the idols. These he broke to pieces and scattered over the graves of those who had sacrificed to them. He burned the bones of the priests on their altars, and so he purged Judah and Jerusalem. In the towns of Manasseh, Ephraim and Simeon, as far as Naphtali, and in the ruins around them, he tore down the altars and the Asherah poles and crushed the idols to powder and cut to pieces

all the incense altars throughout Israel. Then he went back to Jerusalem.

"In the eighteenth year of Josiah's reign, to purify the land and the temple, he sent Shaphan son of Azaliah and Maaseiah the ruler of the city, with Joah son of Joahaz, the recorder, to repair the temple of the LORD his God. They went to Hilkiah the high priest and gave him the money that had been brought into the temple of God, which the Levites who were the gatekeepers had collected from the people of Manasseh, Ephraim and the entire remnant of Israel and from all the people of Judah and Benjamin and the inhabitants of Jerusalem.

"Then they entrusted it to the men appointed to supervise the work on the LORD's temple. These men paid the workers who repaired and restored the temple. They also gave money to the carpenters and builders to purchase dressed stone, and timber for joists and beams for the buildings that the kings of Judah had allowed to fall into ruin. The workers labored faithfully. Over them to direct them were Jahath and Obadiah, Levites descended from Merari, and Zechariah and Meshullam, descended from Kohath. The Levites—all who were skilled in playing musical instruments had charge of the laborers and supervised all the workers from job to job. Some of the Levites were secretaries, scribes and gatekeepers.

"While they were bringing out the money that had been taken into the temple of the LORD, Hilkiah the priest found the Book of the Law of the LORD that had been given through Moses. Hilkiah said to Shaphan the secretary, 'I have found the Book of the Law in the temple of the LORD.' He gave it to Shaphan. Then Shaphan took the book to the king and reported to him: 'Your officials are doing everything that has been committed to them. They have paid out the money that was in the temple of the LORD and have entrusted it to the supervisors and workers.' Then Shaphan the secretary informed the king, 'Hilkiah the priest has given me a book.' And Shaphan read from it in the presence of the king. **When the king heard the words of the Law, he tore his robes.** *He gave these orders to Hilkiah, Ahikam son of Shaphan, Abdon son of Micah, Shaphan the secretary and Asaiah the king's attendant: 'Go and inquire of the LORD for me and for the remnant in Israel and Judah about what is written in this book*

that has been found. **Great is the LORD's anger that is poured out on us because those who have gone before us have not kept the word of the LORD; they have not acted in accordance with all that is written in this book.'**

"Hilkiah and those the king had sent with him went to speak to the prophet Huldah, who was the wife of Shallum son of Tokhath, the son of Hasrah, **keeper of the wardrobe.** She lived in Jerusalem, in the New Quarter. She said to them, "This is what the LORD, the God of Israel, says: Tell the man who sent you to me, 'This is what the LORD says: I am going to bring disaster on this place and its people—all the curses written in the book that has been read in the presence of the king of Judah. Because they have forsaken me and burned incense to other gods and aroused my anger by all that their hands have made, my anger will be poured out on this place and will not be quenched.' Tell the king of Judah, who sent you to inquire of the LORD, 'This is what the LORD, the God of Israel, says concerning the words you heard: Because your heart was responsive and you humbled yourself before God when you heard what he spoke against this place and its people, and because you humbled yourself before me and tore your robes and wept in my presence, I have heard you, declares the LORD. Now I will gather you to your ancestors, and you will be buried in peace. Your eyes will not see all the disaster I am going to bring on this place and on those who live here.'

"So they took her answer back to the king. Then the king called together all the elders of Judah and Jerusalem. He went up to the temple of the LORD with the people of Judah, the inhabitants of Jerusalem, the priests and the Levites all the people from the least to the greatest. He read in their hearing all the words of the Book of the Covenant, which had been found in the temple of the LORD. **The king stood by his pillar and renewed the covenant in the presence of the LORD to follow the LORD and keep his commands, statutes and decrees with all his heart and all his soul, and to obey the words of the covenant written in this book.** Then he had everyone in Jerusalem and Benjamin pledge themselves to it; the people of Jerusalem did this in accordance with the covenant of God, the God of their ancestors. Josiah removed all the detestable idols from all the territory belonging to the Israelites, and he had all who were present in

*Israel serve the L*ORD *their God. As long as he lived, they did not fail to follow the L*ORD*, the God of their ancestors."*

I also turn to 2 Kings Chapter 22 and 23 and I read the whole of them. I let the lessons I am seeing burn deep into my spirit. When I am done reading, I stand up, walk over and sit at my Father's feet.

"Oh Father, this is the most incredible and yet the most important story ever! This is what myself, the president of our country, our congress, the religious leaders and the people in America need to do! I get the picture now and know that there is a time to tear your robes in repentance just as King Josiah did. I do believe this is a physical act that had a deeply spiritual meaning. He was tearing off his filthy robes in repentance before You, the One True God! His heart longed to know Your ways and You honored his heart of repentance as You revealed Your heart of Holiness to him.

"Father, Your Word, The Book of the Law, had been abandoned and discarded by the Children of Judah for approximately 75-80 years. The kings before Josiah ruled in wickedness encouraging Your children to become steeped in idolatry. They completely neglected Your temple as they ran and lusted after the gods of this world.

"Father, my heart breaks as I see our nation as a whole doing the same thing. Just as in the days of Josiah, You have always been in the temple. At that time, it was a man-made structure, but today we are the temple, I am the temple! I believe with all my heart that because there was a king searching for You that longed to know your ways, You revealed Yourself to him! I also believe that You will do the same for me even today! You reveal Yourself to anyone who is truly seeking to KNOW You! I don't believe after reading these chapters that King Josiah was the only one who was searching for You. There were others."

I have so many questions for my Father as I have noticed something new for me in His Word.

"Father, King Josiah's servant Hilkiah was the High Priest, and he was the one who found Your Word hidden in the temple, correct?"

160

"Yes, Child, He found My Word buried under the rubble in the Temple."

"He then gave it to Shaphan, the secretary and asked him to bring it to the King's attention. Correct?"

"Yes, Daughter, this is correct."

"Oh Father, I love that Hilkiah and Shaphan were obedient and took The Book of the Law into King Josiah and read it out loud to him."

All of a sudden I feel the urge to look up the meaning of the names of these two men. I start giggling to myself for just a moment as I learn that the name Shaphan means "rock badger."[29]

"Thank you Father, for in the midst of this burden that I'm feeling right now, You show me something that makes me laugh. Why would anyone give their child a name such at 'rock badger?'"

Again, my heart turns back to the seriousness of what I am being shown. I then look up the meaning of Hilkiah's name! It means, "Jehovah is my spirit and God is my portion."[30]

"This is just beautiful, and Father, these two men were after Your heart also!"

I have always had so many questions regarding these portions of scripture and have asked myself many times how My Father's precious "Book of the Law" could have been lost in the hearts of men and buried under rubble?

I clearly remember the day My Father helped me to understand through a commentary I was reading. I have never been able to forget what it said. "It would seem that the written law of God had passed from human knowledge, lost in the haze of heathenism, which for so long had enveloped the land... yet the narrative clearly indicates that the king and the people were strangers to its contents.... The natural meaning is that the written law had been lost, its substance meanwhile only existing in memory, or as a tradition. During these years the people had become steeped in idolatry, temple worship had been neglected, and most copies of the Law had been destroyed."[31]

---

[29] https://www.biblestudytools.com/dictionary/shaphan/
[30] Edersheim, Old Testament History, Bk 7, 560;
https://www.biblestudytools.com/dictionary/hilkiah/
[31] Preacher's Homiletic Commentary, Vol 8, 626-627.

"Father, it wasn't just lost under the rubble, it was lost in their hearts!"

I can't help but to contemplate the tragedy of my Father's law being lost, destroyed and replaced with idol worship back in Josiah's time. Unfortunately, it's not hard for me to comprehend that this same thing is going on today right here in America as at one time, it was far from my own heart also. But I do notice that there is one tragic difference between Josiah's time in history and the world I live in today.

"Little One, I can read your thoughts and sense the feelings of your spirit. Talk to Me about what you are feeling."

"Father, it's Your precious Word! It is so accessible today and it can be found everywhere in our nation! Our homes, including mine, are full of several translations and yet so few really read it, love it, and even less understand it! Even worse, those of us who read it have not heeded its warnings or applied its truths to our lives! We no longer teach our children from it and it has been removed from our schools.

"Precious Father, I believe this to be an even greater sin than that of those in King Josiah's day! I know it's true, at least for me, for I am guilty of these very things. Father, please forgive my foolishness in not cherishing Your Word as I should, and please forgive our nation for casting Your Word away from our hearts and turning to the ways of this world.

"Father, Your Word is not 'lost' in our society, it's just ignored! It is being preached through the lens of a distorted and twisted truth. It is buried under the rubble of the doctrine of demons, denominational differences and the American Dream of being filthy rich. It's mixed and blended with the approval of sin and the idols of this world. These are the things I have seen that have filled most of our churches here in America. The rubble of my day is the twisted gospel that is preached on Sunday mornings through the same technological idol that we have watched filthy dirty movies on the night before. There is no real conviction because we can stay in our sin, never leaving our homes. Or if we do go to church, we leave without being convicted by the preaching while patting ourselves on the back because we are satisfied with our new moral plane. Oh, Father, 'Woe unto us' as Your Son said 7 times in Matthew."

162

As I finish writing down all the personal convictions I just shared with my Father, my heart is grieved at the part I have played in all of this. I have also grieved His Spirit. If this were not so, there would be no proof, but the proof is all around me, and all too evident even in my own family. If this were not so, I would not see that the divorce rate in the church is at an all-time high. If this were not so I would not see the sexual sin in every shape, form and fashion tolerated by those who claim to be Christians, and in those who shepherd this people. If this were not so, I would not see the worst of all, the millions of babies that are killed through abortion in the name of convenience. None of this would be happening if we as a nation cherished His Word!

I hear my Father say, *"Daughter, all I need you to do is your part. You have been called away by Me, to live a life that is set apart. I have also asked your husband Greg to do the same as he is to preach the truth of My Word without compromise. Just keep your focus on Me, coming to your Tameion Chamber, repenting often and spending time with Me. This is the only way your life will be displayed in a way that others will desire to have what you have and know what you know! They will long for the same deep personal relationship you have with Me. This is where peace lives. I have no doubt in whom I have created you to be, so be encouraged Little One, you and your husband will make a difference.*

"I have many set aside such as yourself and your husband, Greg, who seek no glory for themselves. Child, don't be discouraged. It's just that they are also hidden away, just as the two of you are!"

"Yes, Father, I know there are others and I thank You for that! I will be faithful to do what you have asked of me! But honestly, I am struggling with the implications of this truth regarding Your church. Is it really this bad? And if so, will anyone listen as Greg and I speak what You have shown us?"

"Yes Daughter, there will be those that I will send to listen to what you both have to say, but only if you continue to present the truth of My Word through humility, love and with a servant's heart."

"Ok, Father, I trust You completely in this! I will stand firm on what I have learned."

The Keepers Of The Wardrobe. "Father, I want to go back to the lesson of Josiah and his torn robes. He would have needed new ones, right?"

"Yes, Precious One. King Josiah would have needed new robes because I was doing a new work in him. But not only in him, but in a whole nation. I had someone in mind who knew exactly what kind of robes this changed king would need to be wearing."

"Father, I do understand that the tearing of his robes was an expression of horror and astonishment of the sin of the kings before him, even his own Father, King Amon. I believe that in the strongest sense possible, Josiah was showing his repentance and grief! This was not only on his own account, but also on the account of the nation he was called to rule. This was an expression of deep conviction of sin, which was a good thing, right?"

"Yes, Connie, revival and spiritual awakening are marked by such expressions as Josiah displayed on that day. It wasn't that King Josiah knew much about Me or about My ways, or even knew how to seek My face. This is clear through his reaction after hearing that My anger burned against his fathers who did not obey My law. But make no mistake Child, My hand was upon him! I may have been furious, but I loved him as well as every man, woman and child who lived in that time of history. And it was because of My love that I had kept this very worthy man for Myself. I was honored to call him the King of Judah! I not only kept him, but his life was a prophecy that had been established long before he was actually born.[32] I created him for a very specific time and unique purpose, and that was to set My house in order!

"Child, it is very important that you take note that King Josiah did not start with the cleansing of the temple. He started with the purging of the land, then he cleansed himself and then he cleansed the people. It's only then that He then turned his attentions to repairing the Temple of the Lord.

---

[32] See 1 Kings 13:2

"While having My place of worship restored, He discovered My Word! There are mighty and wonderful lessons to be learned here. Before My Word was discovered, he was simply led by My Spirit, and upon the hearing of My Word, he tore his robes because the sin in his nation was so great that My anger was burning against his fathers and the people. Under the conviction of the Holy Spirit and with great humility and haste, he put his face to the dust and cried out to Me, the God of Israel."

"Yes Father, I am seeing something here but I am not sure how to put all the pieces together. I know that You will be faithful to show me. I can't help but feel that it has everything to do with everything!

"I did notice that King Josiah sent his servants to inquire of You on the blueprint for the restoration process that would be necessary for the land and the people. I know they were sent to the prophetess Huldah, who was the wife of Shallum son of Tokhath, the son of Hasrah! I also see that her husband was the.....oh my goodness! He was **'keeper of the wardrobe!'**

"Wow! Your Word says right here that...*"When the king heard the words of the Book of the Law, **he tore his robes.** He gave these orders to Hilkiah the priest, Ahikam son of Shaphan, Akbor son of Micaiah, Shaphan the secretary and Asaiah the king's attendant: 'Go and inquire of the LORD for me and for the people and for all Judah about what is written in this book that has been found. Great is the LORD's anger that burns against us because those who have gone before us have not obeyed the words of this book; they have not acted in accordance with all that is written there concerning us.' Hilkiah the priest, Ahikam, Akbor, Shaphan and Asaiah went to speak to the prophet Huldah, who was the wife of Shallum son of Tikvah, the son of Harhas, **keeper of the wardrobe.** She lived in Jerusalem, in the New Quarter'* (2 Kings 22:11-14).

"Oh Father, King Josiah had torn his royal robes in repentance and now he was asking the priests to inquire of the Lord on his behalf! He was NOT going to take another step until he heard from You. The priests sought out the Prophetess Huldah!"

As I ponder this amazing woman and her husband, I can't help but stand astonished at my Father's strategic timing. They were born for a very unique and important purpose! I study a little more and find that Huldah was one of seven prophetesses mentioned in the Bible along with Sarah, Miriam, Deborah, Hannah and Abigail. These prophetesses lived in different times according to My Father's need for the very specific and unique gifts He had placed upon each of their lives. They are tucked away in special places in the Bible, barely to be noticed, but they always seem to jump out of my Bible, come to life and teach me when I least expect it!

But for this amazing Prophetess named Huldah, it was during the reign of King Josiah that the spirit of prophecy came upon her with great boldness and purity. She was known not only as a prophetess within Jerusalem, but according to the Midrash,[33] it states of her "....that Jeremiah prophesied in the streets of Jerusalem; Zephaniah delivered his prophecies in the synagogues; **and Huldah had a school for women in Jerusalem, whom she taught the word of God as it pertained to the Jewish women, mothers and daughters of that time.**" Here I sit all these years later and she is still teaching me.

I also know that in the Talmud[34] it is stated that Huldah was a relative of the prophet Jeremiah. I can truly say in her case, "The apple doesn't fall far from the Prophet's tree!"

She would have held a place and position of prominence in the life of not only her husband, Shallum, *who was the keeper of the wardrobe,* but King Josiah and the rest of the people of in Judah and Jerusalem! Huldah would have sat at a gate in Jerusalem and held court. The ancient "Huldah's Gate,"[35] along with her tomb is still there in Israel to this day.

"Father, Huldah's husband, Shallum, also held a position of prominence in the life of King Josiah and would have known him intimately. As keeper of King Josiah's wardrobe,[36] Shallum would have taken care of all those royal garments and robes knowing what was necessary for every single occasion. He was

---

[33] Midrash: an ancient commentary on part of the Hebrew scriptures, attached to the biblical text. The earliest Midrashim come from the 2nd century AD, although much of their content is older. Pesikta Rabbati, ch. 26.
[34] https://www.gotquestions.org/Talmud.html
[35] https://en.wikipedia.org/wiki/Huldah_Gates
[36] https://en.wikipedia.org/wiki/Shallum

also one of King Josiah's instructors! King Josiah began his reign as a child and needed instruction. I can't imagine what was in his memory regarding his father, Amon, who had turned to idolatry at the deepest levels imaginable. It is sad to think that King Amon was murdered in a plot by his own palace servants. I just pray that Josiah didn't have to see it and understood it all somehow. Father, we think we have drama and pain today???"

As I ask the Lord to bring all that's in my mind and my heart to clarity, I reach again for my journal and pen, and continue to sit at my Father's feet writing away. I still stand in awe of His ways! My mind goes wild as I can see how My Father had protected little King Josiah as no one else could. I read that the meaning of King Josiah's name is "Healed by (Yah) the God of Israel" and "Supported by (Yah) the God of Israel."[37] I see clearly that my Father had such a plan for this young man's life! His ways were nothing short of a miracle. The timing was nothing short of strategic! The placement of men and women around him who feared Yahweh's Great Name was nothing short of astonishing!

I know through my studies that there were many who had Yahweh's heart placed around this king. There was Hilkiah, the High Priest, who was the great-grandfather of Ezra the Scribe. The prophet Jeremiah was in his life, as was Shafan the scribe, and his son, Ahikam! But it was Shallum and his wife, Huldah the prophetess who took special notice of King Josiah in his early childhood. Under their teaching and influence, King Josiah developed a hunger for my Father's ways and he stayed far away from following in the footsteps of his own wicked father, Amon.

His grandfather was no gem either! I quickly look up the scripture I have underlined about Manasseh in my Bible and I shudder at the thought of what it says, *"Moreover, Manasseh also shed so much innocent blood that he filled Jerusalem from end to end besides the sin that he had caused Judah to commit so that they did evil in the eyes of the Lord"* (2 Kings 21:16). Josiah's grandfather was not a nice guy! No wonder Judah turned to worshipping idols and then reveled in their idolatry. With leaders like that, the gates of hell were wide open!

---

[37] https://en.wikipedia.org/wiki/Josiah; http://biblehub.com/hebrew/3050.htm

As I sit very still, I can't help but ponder something my husband Greg has always told me. He says that if there is sin and complacency coming from the man who stands in the pulpit or is in church leadership, you will see sin and complacency flowing throughout the congregation. It's no different in our nation. As we have seen the unrighteous rule, the floodgates of hell have opened wide. What comes from the top flows down over the people of our cities and nation.

This statement can truly be seen in the application of this story. I'm just so thankful that King Josiah had a great-grandfather whose name was Hezekiah, and that he did what was right the eyes of the Lord.[38] Josiah was following full-fledged in the footsteps of his great-grandfather who had also removed the high places, smashed the sacred stones, and cut down the Asherah poles. And that was just to start! I wish King Hezekiah had been able to see that he had passed on a godly bloodline, one that my Father was able to raise up again, a legacy that changed the course of history.

"Father, looking at Your Word as a whole is just fascinating to me! I would have assumed that because there were other great prophets in Judah, that Hilkiah the priests Ahikam, Akbor, Shaphan and Asaiah would have gone to them! We have proof that Josiah also knew of them and that they knew of him! Why did they go to Huldah?

"Father, there was Jeremiah the Prophet![39] He was available, but neither Josiah nor the priests ever mentioned him by name. Why not? And then there was Zephaniah! He was also operating in the office of a prophet during Josiah's reign.[40] Why not him?"

"Well Daughter, what do you think? What's on your mind Child? Feel free to speak up."

"I believe there is a reason they chose to hear from the Lord through Huldah. She was the one who knew the intimate inner workings of the king's private chambers! She would have understood the importance of the garments, robes and probably even the armor that King Josiah wore on a daily basis, not to

---

[38] See 2 Kings Chapter 18
[39] See Jeremiah 22: 15-16
[40] See Zephaniah 1:1

mention all the priests and attendants and even the servants! She would have watched King Josiah grow into a man and she would have more than likely had the calling and heart of an intercessor, praying continuously and fervently, interceding for King Josiah. Your true prophets usually walk in the calling of an intercessor.

"Your Word tells me that Huldah's husband was Shallum, keeper of the robes and most scholars agree that he was the organizer of the king's royal wardrobe. I know that it might not make a lot of sense to most as to why his job would have been so important. People might have even seen her husband as nothing more than a tailor. But I believe there is a deeper meaning to this 'tailor' and his wife who would have had daily access to the king, and who would have met with him often in relative privacy, in an intimate setting.

"Father, Shallum was placed right there by You, and there may have been no one better to talk with King Josiah. He was so young, just a mere boy when he first became king. The young king would have needed advice, training and counsel. And of course he would need someone he could trust who could create the garments as King Josiah grew.

"Father, the most powerful men and women of God throughout history have worked quietly behind the scenes. I believe it was no different for Huldah and her husband, Shallum. Huldah's gift was known, but even more extraordinary to me, is that she correctly and precisely interpreted Your Word and it's meaning, and her interpretation was taken seriously!"

I sit back to ponder all I have learned about this woman, but I have to know one more thing. Sitting at My Father's feet, I quickly study the meaning of her name. Again, I start to giggle as I see the name "Huldah" means "a burrowing animal."

It makes perfect sense to me because that is what most of my favorite scholars do. They burrow down deep and seek out the mysteries of God's Word. They examine the precious pieces of knowledge and wisdom that this beloved book has to offer. They know that it will not only nourish their mind, their will and their emotions, but most importantly, it will feed the spirit and the heart of every man or woman who takes His Word seriously. Huldah was just such a woman!

"Father, without her love for You and knowledge of Your heart, there may not have been revival and restoration in the land of Judah and elsewhere. Your written Word had gone missing! Was she the intercessor of that time that prayed for Your Word to be brought back out into the light? Was she the one who fasted and cried tears of repentance for the people and the sin that was being committed in the land? Was she the one who prayed protection over this little boy king as he grew to be one of the Bible's most cherished and honored kings?"

I consider this precious lesson and my mind stays focused on what a righteous ruler King Josiah really was and how God had placed a woman prophet in his life that was willing to speak the truth without compromise.

"Father, we need evangelists, prophets, pastors and teachers with the heart of King Josiah! We need the rulers of our government to have a heart like his. We need a president just like this!"

My tears continue to flow as I consider the heart condition of my nation. I know there is change coming, but what is our exile going to look like?

"Daughter, I can see by the look on your face that you still have many questions for me."

"Yes Father, You allowed King Josiah to be killed at the young age of 39! I am still bothered by the way he died and have way too many questions. He was such a good man!

"Father, King Josiah died fighting a battle he was not supposed to be fighting! Why would he do that? Did King Josiah have to be taken out of the way because Judah had fallen back into sin and disaster was coming?

"The prophecy did say, *'Because your heart was responsive and you humbled yourself before the* LORD *when you heard what I have spoken against this place and its people—that they would become a curse and be laid waste and because you tore your robes and wept in my presence, I also have heard you, declares the* LORD. *Therefore, I will gather you to your ancestors, and you will be buried in peace. Your eyes will not see all the disaster I am going to bring on this place'"* (2 Kings 22:19-20).

I can't help but choke up as I remember that after the greatest cleansing of a land, after everything detestable that could be imagined had been destroyed from God's sight, King Josiah made one last and fatal mistake.

I read the passage again trying to comprehend it all. *"After all this, when Josiah had set the temple in order, Necho king of Egypt went up to fight at Carchemish on the Euphrates, and Josiah marched out to meet him in battle. But Necho sent messengers to him, saying, 'What quarrel is there, king of Judah, between you and me? It is not you I am attacking at this time, but the house with which I am at war. God has told me to hurry; so stop opposing God, who is with me, or he will destroy you.' Josiah, however, would not turn away from him, but disguised himself to engage him in battle. He would not listen to what Necho had said at God's command but went to fight him on the plain of Megiddo. Archers shot King Josiah, and he told his officers, 'Take me away; I am badly wounded.' So they took him out of his chariot, put him in his other chariot and brought him to Jerusalem, where he died. He was buried in the tombs of his ancestors, and all Judah and Jerusalem mourned for him"* (2 Chronicles 35:24).

"I know this is only speculation on my part, but Father, if Huldah's husband was the 'Keeper of the Kings Garments' then King Josiah would have had on brand new beautiful robes, right?"

"Yes, Child, this is correct. He would have been wearing his royal robes."

"Why in the world would he have taken them off and disguised himself to go and fight in a war that he was not called to fight? Father, could You not have let him rule in righteousness just a little longer? Did he make a critical final mistake in that he took off his royal robes?"

"I do cherish every question and even all your hearts concern, Child and yes, there is many a lesson to be learned here! Connie, you are right in that King Josiah should not have disguised himself. I called him to be a King. You should never pretend to be something I have not called you to be. My ways regarding King Josiah and his death will continue to be a mystery to you, but please know that there is always a reason. You must just simply trust Me.

"The lesson that I want you to learn and to teach others is that if I have called you to be a king, stay in your kingly garments.

171

If I have called you to be a priest, stay in your priestly garments. If I have called you to be a pastor, stay in your pulpit. If I have called you to be a plumber stay under your sink and pray. If I have called you to be a mom, raise your children up to have burning hearts for Me[41] teaching them in My ways! You get the point, Precious One. Operating in a calling that is not yours could cost you your life! Child, remember Huldah! She is a good example for you to follow."

"Yes Father, and thank you!" I wipe my tears into the beautiful robes I am wearing and I remember that I am right here in my Tameion Chamber with the One my heart loves.

As I read the portions of scripture quietly to myself one more time, my heart stands in awe of the fact that a simple **woman**, possessed and protected the true Word of God deep within her spirit for a king! I can also see that My Father had such a plan for this young man's life. He had a tender heart towards the things of God and I can't help to think that she had something to do with it! I quickly realize that this King Josiah may have carried a heart that was even greater than the Judean royalty lineage that he was born into which was that of King David, King Solomon, and King Rehoboam.[42]

I quickly turn to the passage in 2 King 23 and underline with my yellow highlighter verse 25. *"Neither before nor after Josiah was there a king like him who turned to the LORD as he did—with all his heart and with all his soul and with all his strength, in accordance with all the Law of Moses."*

Because of this scripture I believe that Huldah the very humble Prophetess may have had more knowledge of the situation at hand than even the best prophets of that day regarding this precious King Josiah.

The Stirring. Immediately I'm aware of a stirring in my heart! I recognize it as grief, grief over my own sin. Grief at the thought of anyone who would boast of their great calling as a prophet. Not that I have ever said that about myself, nor would

---

[41] Recommended reading: Bootsma, Patricia "Raising Burning Hearts-Parenting and Mentoring Next Generation Lovers of God" Forerunner Publishing; ISBN 978-1-938060-18-2

[42] See Matthew 1:6-11.

172

I. And I'm also not referring to Jeremiah and Zephaniah in Josiah's time. They were the real deal!

I am concerned with that which is so common around me today. There are many who claim to walk in the office of a prophet, but who in truth are peddlers of false promises, false words of wisdom and have revelations that have been birthed from a different gospel than that which I see in my Father's Word. I'm talking about those I see running from church to church, conference to conference, place to place, prophesying in His Great Name with no Fear of the Lord regarding the things that they have spoken over the wandering flocks.

If our time period was found to be back in the days when the true prophets of God walked in the Fear of the Lord, many of today's prophets would be stoned!

As I ponder my own foolish heart, I know that there will come a time, and I believe that time is now, when people will not put up with sound doctrine. Instead, to suit their own desires, they will gather around them a great number of teachers to say what their itching ears want to hear. They will turn their ears away from the truth and turn aside to myths.[43]

I stand in awe knowing that My Father is not only showing me the heavenly truths that secure my future with Him, but He has encouraged me through a precious woman who is called by name in His Word. There is only one Prophetess by the name of Huldah in the Bible, and she is unique! It's hard to believe that I am holding proof that she existed in my hand. To me, she is now part of more than just an amazing story! She has touched my life in a very powerful way! I only hope that I can be as bold as she was. Huldah could have lost her life by speaking to the King in this manner. But she feared my Father more than what a mere man could do to her. Her "Words of the Lord" to King Josiah were the truth of the condition of the heart of a people He had called to be set apart. And for this tenderhearted young king, the Word of the Lord was harsh, yet loving. It brought conviction, but it also came with a promise!

"She said to them, "Thus says the LORD God of Israel, 'Tell the man who sent you to me, thus says the LORD, "Behold, I bring evil on this place and on its inhabitants, even all the words of the

---

[43] 2 Timothy 4: 3-4

book which the king of Judah has read. *"Because they have forsaken Me and have burned incense to other gods that they might provoke Me to anger with all the work of their hands, therefore My wrath burns against this place, and it shall not be quenched."' "But to the king of Judah who sent you to inquire of the LORD thus shall you say to him, 'Thus says the LORD God of Israel,* **"Regarding the words which you have heard, because your heart was tender and you humbled yourself before the LORD when you heard what I spoke against this place and against its inhabitants that they should become a desolation and a curse, and you have torn your clothes and wept before Me, I truly have heard you," declares the LORD. "Therefore, behold, I will gather you to your fathers, and you will be gathered to your grave in peace, and your eyes will not see all the evil which I will bring on this place.** *So they brought back word to the king"* (2 Kings 22:15-20).

I know the story well, that after the "Word of God" was spoken through Huldah to King Josiah, he immediately moved forward and embarked on a bloody battle against the priests of Baal and Asherah, even burning their bones! (2 Kings 23:16). He started the process of cleansing the land. It was just a few years after his death that King Nebuchadnezzar fulfilled Huldah's prophecy against the people of Judah because they had fallen right back into their sin. King Nebuchadnezzar carried them off to Babylon as slaves and they were put into exile, just as His Word had said. (2 Kings Chapters 24 and 25)

"Father, it was only then that Your children began to take You seriously at Your Word! What is it going to take for America to become serious about Your Word? It was only after they went into exile that Your Word began to take shape, and to this day it is still in the shape of a Sword. I do thank You for the hope that I can see as many years later, Ezra and Nehemiah led the return of the children back to Judah to build Your Alter, Temple, Gates and Walls.[44] My faith and Christianity would never have

---

[44] Ezra–Nehemiah is made up of three stories: (1) the account of the initial return and rebuilding of the Temple (Ezra 1–6); (2) the story of Ezra's mission (Ezra 7–10 and Nehemiah 8); (3) and the story of Nehemiah, interrupted by a collection of miscellaneous lists and part of the story of Ezra.

come about without all of these terrible things coming to pass, and yet there is always a promise of restoration.

"Father, You used this precious prophetess whom You called by the name of Huldah, in a mighty way! She was created by You to be a scholar and a seer! Her character as a woman who feared the Lord was known among the people of Jerusalem. I am so grateful for her example, and yet...."

Recognizing The Anointing. ...My Father's voice

interrupted my unsettled thoughts. *"Precious One, I want you to read a story that will give your heart the peace it seeks. There are occasions when you are to either accept or give away your garments. We have briefly talked of this before, and I want you to write down what I say to you."*

"Yes, Father, I do remember!"

"Daughter, there may be very few occasions that I ask you to take off your garments, robes, armor or anointing. And there may come a day when I will ask you to pass your mantle on to someone else, but this will only happen when I have brought a replacement garment for you to wear. You may even receive a cloak or garment from someone of My choosing. Either way it will be someone who will add beauty to the tapestry that I have been weaving of your life.

"When this happens, if you have continued with a prayerful and humble life that has sought Me with all of your heart, you will never question that I am in the season of change set before you. A perfect example of this is Jonathan and David. You know the story well."

"Oh Father, I have always loved the fact that Jonathan noticed and was attentive to the call You had placed on David's life. King Saul had great sin in his life and couldn't see Your anointing on David, but I believe Jonathan saw it clearly. When David spoke with Saul at length, I do believe Jonathan was listening with spiritual ears. David may have explained his actions and expressed his faith and love for You, the Lord His God! I just have a feeling that this was what attracted the love and loyalty of Jonathan's heart. Their friendship continued even when it became clear that David was to replace himself as successor to his father's throne.

175

"Father, Jonathan was the one that made a covenant with David, the initiative came from Jonathan and it was heartfelt and pure. He pledged his loyalty to David and accepted David as his equal. Jonathan confirmed their covenant in an act that symbolized the giving of himself to David. He recognized David as his King and placed upon his shoulders his own royal robes. Father, this is an example of the garment changing process.

"I never tire of this portion of Your Word! '*Then Jonathan made a covenant with David because he loved him as himself. Jonathan stripped himself of the robe that was on him and gave it to David, with his armor, including his sword and his bow and belt*' (1 Samuel 18:4).

The Double Portion. "*Daughter, you are also aware of many other examples in My Word where there is, as you would say, 'A changing of the guard!' Please remember that these things are written down for your instruction.*

"*Please take each lesson you learn from Me seriously because I have placed the gift of teaching upon your life. Always be watching for the life that you are to plant that lesson in. There will always be someone I want you to train and raise up.*

"*I want your life to look like the life of Elisha who lived over nine centuries before My Son, Jesus. Elisha followed Elijah around not ever wanting to leave him. He watched as his mentor, Elijah, boldly stood in the face of the evil kings of his day. One of those kings was Ahab, the husband of Jezebel, and the other was Ahazia, their son.*[45]

"*Elisha was Elijah's servant, and as Elijah's time on earth was coming to an end, Elisha did not want to leave him. You know the story well Child.*"

"Father, Elisha asked for a double portion Elijah's spirit. He was not asking for a worldly advantage, but for a God-given spiritual power. You have clearly lined out the qualifications of a 'double portion' in Your Word. The double portion was always the portion that was given to the firstborn, the right of the oldest son according to Deuteronomy 21:17. Since Elijah had no children, Elisha was simply claiming to be acknowledged as

---

[45] https://en.wikipedia.org/wiki/Ahaziah_of_Israel

176

Elijah's firstborn spiritual son, his spiritual heir. He would have needed this double portion to finish the work that his spiritual father had started.

"The honor for which Elisha was asking came with a heart of great humility. He had carried a servant's heart for Elijah that was very real. We all need to start out with the heart of a servant. I have gladly cleaned my share of toilets in the churches I have attended."

"Yes, My Precious One! I have seen the many times you and your husband Greg have cleaned the toilets in the churches you attended. Your hearts were pure in all that you have done."

"Father, all we wanted to do was serve You with all of our hearts, and nothing has changed even today. I would gladly clean any toilet anywhere You ask!"

"I know sweet Child, I know!"

I turn to 2 Kings in my Bible and read the whole of Chapter 2. *"When the LORD was about to take Elijah up to heaven in a whirlwind, Elijah and Elisha were on their way from Gilgal. Elijah said to Elisha, 'Stay here; the LORD has sent me to Bethel.' But Elisha said, 'As surely as the LORD lives and as you live, I will not leave you.' So they went down to Bethel. The company of the prophets at Bethel came out to Elisha and asked, 'Do you know that the LORD is going to take your master from you today?' 'Yes, I know.' Elisha replied, 'so be quiet.'*

"Then Elijah said to him, 'Stay here, Elisha; the LORD has sent me to Jericho.' And he replied, 'As surely as the LORD lives and as you live, I will not leave you.' So they went to Jericho. The company of the prophets at Jericho went up to Elisha and asked him, 'Do you know that the LORD is going to take your master from you today?' 'Yes, I know,' he replied, 'so be quiet.'

"Then Elijah said to him, 'Stay here; the LORD has sent me to the Jordan.' And he replied, 'As surely as the LORD lives and as you live, I will not leave you.' So the two of them walked on. Fifty men from the company of the prophets went and stood at a distance, facing the place where Elijah and Elisha had stopped at the Jordan. Elijah took his cloak, rolled it up and struck the water with it. The water divided to the right and to the left, and the two of them crossed over on dry ground. When they had crossed, Elijah said to Elisha, 'Tell me, what can I do for you before I am

taken from you?' 'Let me inherit a double portion of your spirit,' Elisha replied. 'You have asked a difficult thing,' Elijah said, 'yet if you see me when I am taken from you, it will be yours— otherwise, it will not.'

"As they were walking along and talking together, suddenly a chariot of fire and horses of fire appeared and separated the two of them, and Elijah went up to heaven in a whirlwind. Elisha saw this and cried out, 'My father! My father! The chariots and horsemen of Israel!' And Elisha saw him no more. Then he took hold of his garment and tore it in two. Elisha then picked up Elijah's cloak that had fallen from him and went back and stood on the bank of the Jordan. He took the cloak that had fallen from Elijah and struck the water with it. 'Where now is the LORD, the God of Elijah?' he asked. When he struck the water, it divided to the right and to the left, and he crossed over.

"The company of the prophets from Jericho, who were watching, said, 'The spirit of Elijah is resting on Elisha.' And they went to meet him and bowed to the ground before him. 'Look,' they said, 'we your servants have fifty able men. Let them go and look for your master. Perhaps the Spirit of the LORD has picked him up and set him down on some mountain or in some valley.' 'No,' Elisha replied, 'do not send them.' But they persisted until he was too embarrassed to refuse. So he said, 'Send them.' And they sent fifty men, who searched for three days but did not find him.

"When they returned to Elisha, who was staying in Jericho, he said to them, 'Didn't I tell you not to go?' The people of the city said to Elisha, 'Look, our lord, this town is well situated, as you can see, but the water is bad and the land is unproductive.' 'Bring me a new bowl,' he said, 'and put salt in it.' So they brought it to him. Then he went out to the spring and threw the salt into it, saying, 'This is what the LORD says: 'I have healed this water. Never again will it cause death or make the land unproductive.''' And the water has remained pure to this day, according to the word Elisha had spoken.

"From there Elisha went up to Bethel. As he was walking along the road, some boys came out of the town and jeered at him. 'Get out of here, baldy!' they said. 'Get out of here, baldy!' He turned around, looked at them and called down a curse on them in the name of the LORD. Then two bears came out of the woods and

178

mauled forty-two of the boys. And he went on to Mount Carmel and from there returned to Samaria."

"Father, there is so much to learn here! I don't even know where to start. But what catches my eye is that Elisha **tore his own garments in two** and picked up Elijah's cloak that had fallen from him and then he asks, *'Where now is the Lord, the God of Elijah?'*

"Father, I believe that Elisha was asking You to appear before him immediately, showing and displaying Your powerful hand. Elisha knew that the mantle would mean nothing without Your anointing and power upon it. This is why he asked, *'Where now is the Lord, the God of Elijah?'* You answered him and You showed up in a mighty way! You then confirmed his position as the prophet who would replace and carry a double portion of the mantle and anointing of Elijah, for the company of prophets who saw yelled out, *'The spirit of Elijah is resting on Elisha.'*"

As I read this passage again, I believe that Elijah had been a good teacher to Elisha. He was a good example of what a "God Fearing Man" should look like. I also believe that Elisha welcomed his wisdom with inspiration and humility. Oh how I would have loved to be a bowl on the table as they discussed the ways of the One True God.

"Father, my questions from this lesson are many. Who are the Elijah's in my life? Who are the godly men and women who have shown me the way of righteousness and have taught me the truth of Your Word? Who have You set before me as an example of how I am to live? Who are those whom You have used to encourage me on my journey with You? Whose *mantle* am I to receive, and who will be receiving my *mantle*?

I take a moment and do a quick word study on what a *mantle* is according the Word of God. I find that the main idea is that of a covering such as a cloak or other article of clothing. The New American Standard Bible uses the word "*mantle*" in Joshua 7:21 and Hebrews 1:12. In the former passage, the ESV translates the word as "cloak" and in the latter, "robe." In biblical times, a mantle was typically a large, loosely fitting garment made of animal skin, probably sheepskin. Several people are mentioned as wearing a mantle, including Job (Job 1:20) and Ezra (Ezra 9:5).

179

Prophets were known for wearing mantles as a sign of their calling from God (1 Kings 19:13). The prophet Samuel wore a mantle (1 Samuel 15:27). The prophet Elijah "threw his cloak around [Elisha]" as a symbol of Elijah's ministry being passed on to Elisha. The prophet's mantle was an indication of his authority and responsibility as God's chosen spokesman (2 Kings 2:8). Elisha was not confused as to what Elijah was doing; the putting on of his mantle made his election clear.

Some theologians see the mantle as a symbol of the Holy Spirit. For example, in 2 Kings 2:14, Elisha takes the mantle that had "fallen" from Elijah; similar to how Jesus received the Spirit "descending" on Him at His baptism (Matthew 3:16). The audible voice of God in Matthew 3:17 confirms Jesus as God's chosen servant (cf. Isaiah 42:1). We see a similar "falling" of the Spirit in Acts 8:15–16 and Acts 10:44. It's only after Elisha takes the fallen mantle that he performs miraculous works (2 Kings 2:14, 21, 24). The Holy Spirit is the Person who empowers God's people to do God's work (Micah 3:8; Matthew 12:28; Ephesians 3:16).

The mantle served the practical purpose of keeping people warm and protecting them from the elements. It also served a symbolic purpose, and in the case of the prophets, it showed that they were wrapped in God's authority. Like all imagery in the Old Testament, the mantle presents a visible representation of a New Testament principle. The mantle can be seen as a symbol of the anointing of the Holy Spirit whom God so graciously gives to all Christians, the people of His choosing (1 Thessalonians 1:5–6; 1 Peter 2:9).[46]

"Father, there is no shortage of things I could study in Your Word. I can see myself going down a hundred rabbit holes and getting lost. What a wonderful journey that would be with You!"

I see my Father smiling at me as He says, *"Connie, you are now ready for your day! See you in the morning!"*

---

[46] https://www.gotquestions.org/mantle-Bible.html

180

32
*L*eaving *T*he *T*ameion *C*hamber

*I*t **is time to leave my chamber,** this very wonderful secret place, and to go about my day. I am assured that, *"If the Lord delights in my way, He will make my steps firm; though I stumble, I will not fall, for the Lord upholds me with His hand"* (Psalm 37:23).

Once again, as I take up God's Word it transforms into a Sword, which I tuck into my Belt of Truth. I pick up my Spear, Shield of Faith and Rod of Authority, and as I walk toward the door, I notice on the right, a set of keys hanging on the wall.

Yes, I know these keys well and recognize them as the **Keys of the Kingdom.** I grab them and place them in the holder inside my Belt of Truth that has been made just for them (Matthew 16:19).

I look forward to coming back into my chamber each and every day, early in the morning, for this is the time that I love being with my Father. He has promised me that *"....those who seek Him early shall find Him"* (Proverb 8:17, KJV).

There are robes yet to be worn in my closet, treasures I have yet to find, and armor and battle plans I have yet to be given. I will stay in my Father's Word and daily renew my mind, keeping His promises close to my heart. I can't wait for the gifts He gives. I have such a glorious hope, in knowing my Savior - He lives!

"For we know that if the earthly tent we live in is destroyed, we have a building from God, an eternal house in heaven, not built by human hands. Meanwhile we groan, longing to be clothed instead with our heavenly dwelling, because when we are clothed, we will not be found naked. For while we are in this tent, we groan and are burdened, because we do not wish to be unclothed but to be clothed instead with our heavenly dwelling, so that what is mortal may be swallowed up by life. Now the one who has fashioned us for this very purpose is God, who has given us the Spirit as a deposit, guaranteeing what is to come. Therefore, we are always confident and know that as long as we are at home

in the body we are away from the Lord. For we live by faith, not by sight. We are confident, I say, and would prefer to be away from the body and at home with the Lord. So we make it our goal to please him, whether we are at home in the body or away from it. For we must all appear before the judgment seat of Christ, so that each of us may receive what is due us for the things done while in the body, whether good or bad" (2 Corinthians 5:1-10).

33
*W*edding *P*reparations

I would like to change gears now and talk about some of the things that are pertinent in the wedding preparation process.

Weddings are a lot of work and if you have ever planned one you know what I am talking about. Unfortunately, the Bride-to-be is usually the most difficult one to deal with when it comes to all the planning. We have TV shows like "Say Yes to The Dress" and "Bridezillas," and we stand with jaws dropped at the attitude and actions of some of these beauties.

There are many aspects to a wedding, and in America most brides tend to be focused on the dress, the ring, the setting, the flowers, the cake, the bridal court, the dinner and about a thousand other tiny details.

Unfortunately, today we stay connected to our fiancés and spouses only as long as they are meeting our particular needs at an acceptable cost to us. When we cease to make a profit—that is, when the relationship appears to require more love and affirmation from us than we are getting back—then we "cut our losses" and drop the relationship. This has also been called "commodification," a process by which social relationships are reduced to economic exchange relationships, and so the very idea of "covenant" is disappearing in our culture.

"Covenant" is therefore a concept that is increasingly foreign to us, and yet the Bible says it is the essence of marriage, so we must take some time to understand covenants.

*T*he *V*ertical and the *H*orizontal. A serious reader of the Bible will see covenants literally everywhere throughout the entire book. *"Horizontal covenants"* were made between human beings. They were established between close friends (1 Samuel 18:3; 20:16) as well as between nations. But the most prominent covenants in the Bible are *"vertical covenants"* made by God with individuals (Genesis 17:2), families and peoples (Exodus 19:5).

The marriage relationship is unique in several ways, and is the deepest covenantal relationship possible between two human beings. In Ephesians 5:31, Paul evokes the idea of the covenant when he fully quotes Genesis 2:24, which is perhaps the most well known text in the Old Testament regarding marriage. *"For this reason a man will leave his father and mother and cleave to his wife, and the two shall become one flesh."*

In Genesis 2:22–25 we see the first marriage ceremony. The Genesis text calls what happens, "cleaving." This archaic English term (which you can find in the King James Version) conveys the strength of the Hebrew verb, which modern translations render "united to." It is a Hebrew word that literally means to be glued to something. Elsewhere in the Bible, the word "cleave" means to unite to someone through a covenant, a binding promise, or oath.

Why do we say that marriage is the most deeply covenantal relationship? It is because marriage has both strong horizontal and vertical aspects to it. In Malachi 2:14, a man is told that his spouse *"is your partner, the wife of your marriage covenant."* (See also Ezekiel 16:8)

Proverbs 2:17 describes a wayward wife who has *"left the partner of her youth, and ignored the covenant she made before God."* The covenant made between a husband and a wife is done *"before God"* and therefore with God as well as the spouse. To break faith with your spouse is to break faith with God at the same time.[47]

Before we are ready to get dressed in our wedding garments, we need to fully understand the **vows and covenants** we are preparing to not only take, but to make.

The reason why this is so important is because the majority of Christians today do not understand the language of covenant. God's Word itself is a language of covenant and all that is contained within its pages should be seen as such and understood as such. If we can't understand the meaning of a

---

[47] Adapted from the book by Keller, Timothy, *"The Meaning of Marriage"*. Penguin Random House Publishing. www.global.penguinrandomhouse.com

covenant, how can we take our vows as the Bride of Christ seriously?

So many have stood half-hearted before friends and family, speaking their vows and signing the marriage certificate without the knowledge of, and/or being prepared for the cost involved, the price to be paid.

If you were to walk up to someone on the street and ask them to explain a covenant, they may not know what that means. If asked about broken vows, most would agree that we are a nation that makes and breaks vows all the time according to what would suit us at that moment.

Most Christians are no different from the world in this area. According to The Barna Group,[48] statistically, the church in America has just as high of a divorce rate as that of the world, which shows how lightly we, as the Church, view the importance of vows and covenants. But God takes the making and breaking of vows and covenants very seriously.

There is a difference between a "vow" and a "covenant." **Vows** *are about the words we speak out of our mouths.* **Covenants** *are made more out of the true intentions of our hearts.* A "vow" *is a promise or a binding agreement that is "spoken" between two parties.* There are several Hebrew words for the meaning of "vow" but we will briefly look at just one, Neder,[49] which means *a promise to God "spoken" concretely that can't be moved.* It's a promise spoken with the intent to keep that promise, pledge, or personal commitment between you and God or you and another person. It is very serious. We can also vow things in our hearts like, "I'll never let that happen again." Or "Oh God, I'm not going to trust You with that." We must be very careful with what we believe in our hearts or say with our words, for those are vows.

"Blood covenants" are a whole different thing, and are the most powerful and binding of covenants because God states in His Word that life is in the blood (Leviticus 17:11). The **Hebrew Word for covenant** in the Bible is "bereth,"[50] and *it carries a connotation of the shedding of blood. This word implies pact,*

---

[48] https://www.barna.com/research/new-marriage-and-divorce-statistics-released/
[49] https://www.blueletterbible.org/lang/lexicon/lexicon.cfm?t=kjv&strongs=h5088
[50] https://www.blueletterbible.org/lang/lexicon/lexicon.cfm?t=kjv&strongs=h1285

contract, and treaty or agreement between two parties, and it is likely derived from the Hebrew verb "barah,"[51] which means to cut.

I was once asked, "Why do I need to be covered by blood? Blood is disgusting! Why a blood covering for sin? Why not something else, like water?"

This is actually a good question. Blood covering can be a little hard to explain, especially when most of the world today does not understand or grasp the importance and significance of human life. It is important that we understand the reason for and the great love behind the application of the Blood of Jesus on a life.

For many years, I really didn't understand covenants or vows or the width, depth, height and length of this very real love language in its fullest sense, and in no way can we cover it in just this book alone. I do have a deeper study online and I would encourage you to check it out.[52] For now, I'll briefly explain this mystery of being covered in the blood that will help us to establish an answer to the question above.

Satan was a "covering cherub" before he sinned, and was a very important part of the divine council that God established in heaven as stated in Psalm 82:1. The understanding of our enemy's position in the past is vital to our understanding of the part he now plays in our current lives and our future.

Dr. Michael Heiser explains the divine council. "The term *divine council* is used by Hebrew and Semitic scholars to refer to the heavenly host, the pantheon of divine beings who administer the affairs of the cosmos. All ancient Mediterranean cultures had some conception of a divine council. The divine council of Israelite religion, known primarily through the psalms, was distinct in important ways.[53] (Psalms 82:1; Ezekiel 28:14-16).

Knowing that Satan was a part of the inner-workings of God's divine council helps us understand that he fully understood that anything sinful and uncovered could not be in the presence of a holy God because it carried a consequence of

---

[51] https://www.blueletterbible.org/lang/lexicon/lexicon.cfm?strongs=H1262&t=KJV
[52] https://www.igniterevivalministries.com/written-bible-studies
[53] http://www.thedivinecouncil.com/DivineCouncilLBD.pdf

death and to this very day, he and his cohorts will do anything and everything to try and keep mankind uncovered.

Before the fall, God clothed Adam and Eve in His pure and sinless "glory covering," which allowed them access to His presence at any time. Wearing these "glory garments" also gave them the ability to live forever with God. The serpent knew that in order for him to gain authority, he had to deceive them into taking off their glory garments. God had established the boundaries of His covenant clearly to Adam and Eve, that they were not to eat from the tree of the knowledge of good and evil (Genesis 2:17-17). Yet, because they had freedom of choice, they chose to disobey, to break covenant with God and to disrobe.

It is no coincidence that they immediately realized they were uncovered (naked) and saw their need to be covered quickly by something, anything. They grabbed what they could, fig leaves! They now understood that they were vulnerable and exposed, no longer able to be in God's presence. In Genesis 3 the Bible says, *"they hid from the Lord God in the trees of the Garden."* Not only had sin entered their hearts, but the Spirit of Fear showed up for the first time. It was not simply their nudity that made cover necessary, it was their nudity coupled with the knowledge of evil that left them exposed and in grave danger.

The word "naked" in Hebrew is *"eryom"*(H5903)[54] but it comes from the root word "aram" (H6191).[55] I find it no coincidence that the word "aram" means to be cunning (usually in a bad sense) and to take crafty counsel. In other words, Adam and Eve both listened to bad counsel and a seed was planted, the "seed of doubt" regarding God's covenant spoken Word. It was planted in their minds, and the "seed of Fear" about His character was planted in their hearts. Eve listened to the serpent and Adam listened to Eve, and they both broke covenant with the God who loved them.

The Bible is very clear that God's Word is seed, seed that brings life (Luke 8:11; 1 Peter 1:23). In these verses, the Greek word for seed is "sporos" (G4703)[56] and it is a seed that grows. It is no different with our words as they can also bring life or

---

[54] https://www.blueletterbible.org/lang/lexicon/lexicon.cfm?Strongs=H5903&t=KJV
[55] https://www.blueletterbible.org/lang/lexicon/lexicon.cfm?strongs=H6191&t=KJV
[56] http://biblehub.com/greek/4703.htm

death (Proverb 18:21; 21;23; 25:15). Because Adam and Eve partook and believed the twisted words of the serpent to be truth, the seeds of sin, doubt, fear, and the knowledge of good and evil was planted within them that day. They were now disrobed from their glory covering (Genesis 3:16) and naked. Once this seed of sin and evil had been set loose in the hearts and minds of Adam and Eve, they were in big trouble. From that moment man's physical blood became tainted, and to this day our human bodies are now subject to corruption, decay and ultimately death.

This was a hard concept for me to grasp and I love the simplicity with which Dr. Michael Heiser explains this biblical mystery. "Adam's sin placed humanity outside the conditions that Adam and Eve enjoyed in the garden...God's superintending influence and presence in Eden was the primary agent or force that kept Adam and Eve sinless. Once humans were removed from that, they had no hope of *not* sinning (and notice in Genesis 3 that Eve is not in the presence of God when she is deceived, and Adam is also not with God when he sins; the writer is making a point)."[57]

God's glory covering has always been our protection. As women of God we must remember the importance of staying in covenant with our God and under the glory covering of His presence. This can only come through a relationship with Him and the blood of His Son, Jesus. We must never forget that we can still be deceived by the serpent, and as women, our influence over man can be amazingly good or terribly bad.

Adam and Eve lived in the garden with the eternal lifeblood and Spirit of God in them and covering them until the eternal lifeblood and Spirit of God left them through their choice to listen to the serpent. That was their death sentence!

God had to immediately shed the blood of an animal and the Bible says, *"The Lord God made garments of skin for Adam and his wife and clothed them"* (Genesis 3:21). This shedding of blood that God provided had an implication of death and of sacrifice and of a new and different covenant. But why? Why did there have to be the death of a living thing, and why did God have to use blood to cover sin?

---

[57] http://drmsh.com/romans-512-part-4/

In God's great wisdom and within His purest love He knew exactly what needed to be done for fallen man, and we need to trust Him in that. It was a foreshadow of what was to come at just the right moment in history. God knew that the only answer to this problem of eternal death could be that of divine love and divine intervention thousands of years later through a man called Jesus, the Son of this Living God who used to walk in the garden and fellowship face to face with Adam and Eve.

Let's back up and grab a little female history before we jump back to the importance of covenants. Let's briefly review a bright spot in the Biblical perspective of our creation as women, the how's and why's of us! It's actually quite a beautiful story.

Adam was created from the dust of the earth and it wasn't until God breathed His breath (neshâmâh, H5397)[58] into that dust that he, Adam, became a living, breathing, thinking, blood filled, perfectly created man made in the image of God Himself. He was created to live forever and his DNA was perfect. In this perfect paradise however, there was something missing, and this "something" was so important that God mentions it twice in Genesis Chapter 2.

"The Lord God said, 'It is not good for man to be alone. I will make a helper suitable for him.'" And, *"But for Adam no suitable helper was found. So the Lord caused the man to fall into a deep sleep; and while he was sleeping he took one of the man's ribs and closed up the place with flesh. Then the Lord God made a woman from the rib he had taken out of the man and he brought her to the man."* (Genesis 2:18; 20b-22)

I want to take a quick look at the Hebrew word "MADE" because I find it quite fascinating. The word is bânâh 'to build' (H#1129). *"And the rib, which the LORD God had taken from the man, 'MADE' (bânâh) He a woman"* (Genesis 2:22, JPS).

The first three uses of bânâh, "to build" (H1129), reveal its range of application. Genesis 2:22 describes God's "building" of a woman out of Adam's "rib" or "side tsêlâ'. Interestingly, in the study of words, bânâh begins with the Hebrew letter bêth and the pictogram of a house, for which the Hebrew word is bayith (H1004). This just serves to affirm the foundational idea

---

of construction, combining, building out of materials, at the heart of bânâh.

So we can see from this word "MADE," that Eve was built, not created as Adam was, and that she was built intelligently. Now the Bible says that God had taken from the man a "rib." The word "rib" in Hebrew is tsêlâ' (H6760);[59] a rib (as curved), literally (of the body) or figuratively (of a door); hence a side, literally (of a person) or figuratively (of an object or the sky, that is, quarter); architecturally a timber (especially floor or ceiling) or plank (single or collectively, that is, a flooring): beam, board, chamber, corner, plank, rib, side (chamber).[60]

A lot of these words are pretty hefty and have some serious meaning to them but I love the fact that we came out of the "side chamber of man." If we were to put the scientific application to the woman who was "MADE" for Adam, we could easily say that Eve was literally constructed from the DNA curved rib-bone of Adam. I do not think it any coincidence that scientists have given our DNA the name Helix Curve. Because of God's great mysteries, which "woman" most certainly is a mystery, we are so far beyond comprehension that it's been easier for our pastors, parents, Sunday School teachers, etc. to teach us that God just put Adam to sleep and then pulled out a tiny little rib, sewed up his side, and WALLA! There she was, WOMAN! The truth is, we are so much more than that and our origins are precise and beyond amazing. As I wrote this book about a "chamber," I was pleased to learn that as a woman, "chambers" are part of my DNA!

We know through scripture that God had made Adam from the dust of the earth and also brought forth all male and female animals from the ground, (Genesis 2:19) but there was still something missing. Most would assume that God would have made woman out of the dust of the ground, but He didn't. Why not? So now God decides to use a rib, instead of a finger or a toe, or an ear? Why? Do you ever ask yourself these questions?

I personally believe that something far more meaningful is being expressed through God's precious Word in this biblical

---

[59] https://www.blueletterbible.org/lang/lexicon/lexicon.cfm?t=kjv&strongs=h6763
[60] https://www.studylight.org/language-studies/hebrew-thoughts.html?article=877

account of the creation of woman. If we look closely at the Hebrew word for rib, we will learn something new and unexpected. Let's jump outside the box of Sunday School theology for just a moment and get our hands a little dirty by digging into the original Hebrew.

We can see right away that what God took from Adam was a lot more than a small rib bone. It was a lot sturdier than just a 2 X 4, and much more durable than double dust refined. I do believe that we should consider the implications that God literally divided Adam in half to create a woman for him.

Eve was every bit the image of God that Adam was, and it is confirmed in the scriptures. We can see in Genesis 1:27 that God says, "*In the image of God He created him, male and female He created them,*" suggesting that they were equal in God's sight. My purpose in implementing this information is that I want every woman who reads this book to know that she has not been created less than, but equal to.

I have a quote by Matthew Henry written down in the margin of my Bible next to Genesis 2:23. It says, "The woman was made of a rib out of the side of Adam; not made out of his head to rule over him, nor out of his feet to be trampled upon by him, but out of his side to be equal with him, under his arm to be protected, and near his heart to be beloved."

Eve did begin her life literally as half of Adam. We were a much needed desire of God's heart for the man that He created out of the dust of the earth, but for us as women we can literally say we were "MADE" out of a living, breathing image of God. The words "bone of my bone" and "flesh of my flesh" take on a whole new meaning when viewed through this lens.

It would take the writing of another book to explain all the wonderful mysteries of us as women in our fullness, but let's just think about a couple of points for just a moment.

Not only as a woman did we come out of the "rib" or "curved chamber" of man, but unlike Adam we are not made out of dust. Let's take a quick look at this amazing, beautiful Hebrew word, rib ("tsêlâ'). When we tear it apart, we find that we are made with very specific callings and gifting's as "women" who were taken out of the chamber of a living, breathing man.

The word tsêlâ' is made up of three Hebrew letters; Tsadhe, Lamedh and Ayin; **צלע**. These Hebrew letters when put together make for a powerful force to be reckoned with. I won't go into great depth in their meaning but I will at least give you a picture of how beautiful the Hebrew language is.

The first letter in Hebrew is **צ** "*Tsadhe*" and means "side," but is also related to the idea of a stronghold, which is often built on the side of a mountain. The Hebrew pictograph of the letter "*Tsadhe*" is a picture of a trail **ᴧ** as leading up to a destination or stronghold. It also has the meaning of a trail leading to a destination such as a watering hole. This is a really beautiful picture if we think about it. As women, we are able to lead others to safety and also can lead anyone who is thirsty to the Lord so that they can drink (John 7:37).

The second letter in Hebrew is "*Lamedh*" **ל**, which means a shepherd's staff. The shepherd staff was used to direct sheep by pushing or pulling them. It was also used as a weapon against predators to defend and protect the sheep. The Hebrew pictograph of the letter "*Lamedh*" is of a staff **⌐** . It carries many powerful meanings such as "authority" because it is a sign of the shepherd, the leader of the flock. The Hebrew shepherd always carried a staff, which could be used as a weapon to protect the flock from predators as well as to discipline the sheep. The staff also had a bent end that could be used to pull a lamb. This picture of "pulling a lamb" reminds me of many beautiful midwives pulling those babies out. Having raised boys, I can picture myself chasing my little ones, hooking them with my staff and getting them under control, and I can also see myself protecting my children from the enemy. We have been given spiritual attributes that will spiritually guard and protect our husband and children, especially through prayer and intercession.

The third Hebrew letter is "*Ayin*" and it means eye. The ancient Hebrew pictograph for the letter "*Ayin*" is **⊙**. This letter represents the ideas of seeing and watching as well as knowledge, for the eye is the window of knowledge. As women of God, He has given us the ability to keep an eye on things, to search out and seek the wisdom of God and learn the knowledge of His ways and dig for the treasures of Heaven if only we will seek them with all our hearts (Matthew 6:19-21).

Words of Warning! Ladies, because of the great power and influence that can be manifested through us as women of God by the Spirit of God, we have a big enemy! I want to warn you and ask that you become familiar with and prepared for war against this spirit that is out to destroy and overtake us as women of God! This spirit's goal is to destroy our husbands, families, churches, cities and nation. It would love nothing more than to operate through us as women. This spirit can operate through men also, but it's prominent in women. This spirit's name is Jezebel.

We must be careful that we don't allow this spirit to overstep or overrule our husbands, children, pastors or those in leadership over us. The spirit of Jezebel is a very real spirit that is fully operational in the American Church and our nation. It is very powerful and operates through manipulation, deceit, seduction, bondage and a plethora of other things. It has taken down the best of marriages and ministries. The Bible is very clear regarding this spirit of Jezebel with Jesus' warning to us in Revelation Chapter 2, that we are not to tolerate her period! Jesus' warning alone should put the Fear of the Lord in every person who claims to be a Christian, but it hasn't. Because Jezebel has been tolerated for so long, we continue to see her undermine the authority of God in our homes and nation.

There are many books written on the Spirit of Jezebel, but there are very few whose teachings are biblically correct. However, I would like to highly recommend Jennifer LeClaire's book, *"The Spiritual Warriors Guide to Defeating Jezebel."* In her book she asks the question, "Are You Armed for Battle?" She writes, "Right now, we are witnessing Jezebel both perverting and making puppets out of prophets at the same time. I believe a showdown lies ahead. Jehovah wants you to serve Him with all your heart, all your soul and all your strength. Jezebel wants your devotion, too. The difference is, Jesus will not manipulate you into serving Him. The Holy Spirit will never try to control you. Jezebel will. All of us come to a time in our lives when we reach the Valley of Shechem. The Lord is saying to you, 'Choose

193

this day whom you will serve' (see Joshua 24:15). Sadly, much of the church is completely ignorant of this war in the heavens and much of the Church is fighting the spirit of control thinking it is Jezebel. This deception must not continue. We must stop being distracted by the red herrings that divert us from the truth. Jesus promises authority over nations to those who conquer Jezebel and judgment to those who follow Jezebel's false doctrine.

"Since many Christian leaders do not understand the deeper danger of the Jezebel spirit, few are working to equip the saints with truth to combat its wicked strategy. Let's face it: Jezebel is a topic that draws a crowd and sells books. But, again, Satan is probably sitting back laughing as we continue to produce incomplete teaching on the subject of Jezebel that keeps the Lady of the Kingdoms hidden from our view.

"Yes, Babylon and the spirit of Jezebel will one day fall in judgment. But so will all those unrepentant people Jezebel has seduced into idolatry and immorality. We should be warring against this! Armed with a fuller understanding of what Jezebel really is, we can avoid falling into its trap through misguided teaching on grace or plain ignorance of this principality's devices. Armed with truth, you can walk free from the sinful influences of Jezebel. But you need the whole truth..." [61]

As women of God, we need to make sure that we walk in our giftings humbly and with a teachable spirit. There is an order to the way the Kingdom of God operates and the way the Lord has set up our roles as women. The spirit of Jezebel wants nothing more than to operate through us regardless of where we are spiritually. We must be accountable to God for our own actions, so I must warn you regarding the spirit of Jezebel. Make sure you are ready for war. It must not be tolerated in you!

Now *Back* *To* *Covenants!* We can see the importance of covenant throughout scripture and it makes for a wonderful and fascinating study. Our God is full of surprises and His Word is full of mysteries and wonder! It immediately brings

---

[61] Jennifer LeClaire, "The Spiritual Warrior's Guide to Defeating Jezebel. How to overcome the Spirit of Control, Idolatry and Immorality" Chosen Press, Bloomington, MN. 2013. Pages 24-25

to my mind some of the most fascinating situations and examples found in the Bible.

The first one is in Genesis Chapter 15. *"When the sun had set and darkness had fallen, a smoking firepot with a blazing torch appeared and passed between the pieces. On that day the Lord made a covenant with Abram and said, 'To your descendants I give this land, from the Wadie of Egypt to the great river, the Euphrates...'"* (Genesis 15:17-20, see also Jeremiah 34:18).

Abram followed God's commands to cut the three animals in two and placed them in such a way that the blood actually formed a pathway that only God could walk through to validate this covenant. Why? For this particular covenant, only God was able to establish it, which meant that He personally would have to bare and carry the responsibility of it. It would fall solely on Him to keep this particular covenant, and He has done so to this day.

God showed up and manifested in the form of a smoking, burning Fire Pot with a blazing torch! Fascinating! It represents His Burning Presence, similar to how He manifested as a pillar of fire in the desert at night and a cloud by day. He entered into this covenant wholeheartedly and walked right through the blood to confirm the covenant between Himself and Abram.

Another amazing example would be when God had the Children of Israel put the blood of a lamb on the doorposts of their homes. His covenant with them would be honored in their obedience of doing what He asked. If the destroyer saw the blood upon the doorpost, the destroyer would not be able to come into their home. *"You shall take a bunch of hyssop and dip it in the blood which is in the basin, and apply some of the blood that is in the basin to the lintel and the two doorposts; and none of you shall go outside the door of his house until morning. For the LORD will pass through to smite the Egyptians; and when He sees the blood on the lintel and on the two doorposts, the LORD will pass over the door and will not allow the destroyer to come in to your houses to smite you"* (Exodus 12:22-23).

Before Christ, God continually had the Children of Israel use animal sacrifices to seal covenants. The shedding of Jesus' blood at His death was the final and ultimate blood sacrifice covenant that God would make, and we would no longer have to use the blood of animals.

There is still a precious covenant that involves the shedding of blood today, and I wish our world would take this covenant a little more serious. It's found in marriage the way God intended it to be. If a young woman saves herself for her husband and is a virgin when she marries, the hymen is broken during sex. I completely understand God's forgiveness and grace, but I wouldn't be honest if I didn't express some regret in the fact that I did not save myself for my wonderful husband, Greg. So now, I make sure to encourage other young women to make the effort to stay pure for their earthly husband.

Vows and covenants are taken so seriously by God that there are only three cases I've found in the Bible where He will release someone from a vow or covenant. The first is in marital unfaithfulness or adultery, and the second is death. The third is when the authority of either a father or husband opposes the vow that his daughter or wife has made. Numbers 30:1-16 explains that if a father opposes a vow that his daughter has made, then she will not be held to that vow and the Lord will forgive her because her father opposed her; and if a wife makes a vow, when her husband hears of it, if he makes it void, then she is released from that vow.

Marriage Vows To Christ.

Do you consider yourself a Christian? If so, as the soon-to-be Bride of Christ, I want you to look at, ponder, and contemplate the vows and the covenant you made when you gave your life to Christ. The price He paid was extremely high and it was brutal and bloody! I'm talking about the commitment level your heart has truly made to your God regarding the death of His Son, your purchase price.

Has your commitment to Him intensified or grown cold? Do you really understand what you have committed to? The Bible is very clear that when we give ourselves to Him we are talking about a lifetime of committing ourselves, setting ourselves apart to God alone in the good times and in the bad, and keeping ourselves pure to the best of our abilities as we grow and mature in our faith. During this time of commitment, we should also be in a continuing state of preparation for our wedding day. This marriage to His Son is the real deal and this life is our boot camp. He has gone away for a time to prepare a place for you, and you should be faithfully reading the love letter He has left behind until He returns. We should be daily pledging forever our commitment to love and to cherish Him.

My heart is to challenge you briefly in the area of the vows and the covenants you have made to God regarding your faith in Him and your future marriage to His Son, Jesus. He will be returning soon to get His Bride.

Are you His Bride?

I challenge you in this area because we have a Church body in America that doesn't look much different than those who have committed themselves to the world. A lot of people don't hesitate to say with their mouth that they are committed to Christ, even saying that they would die for Him, but if we look to scripture we should be able to see a clear difference between those committed to Christ and those committed to the world. If we see no fruit or rotten fruit out of any person who claims to be part of the body of Christ, we have a problem. We should be able to see clearly the good fruit and the preparation process taking place in the life of one who claims to be a Bride, readying herself, spotless and without blemish. This is the Bride He is coming back for! (Ephesians 5:26-27). This does not mean we are perfect, but it does mean we are quick to repent and that the characteristics of love and humility are very evident in our lives.

I'm hopeful that as you contemplate the seriousness of the vows and covenants you have made, it will realign your commitment to the Father and His Son, Jesus. You will either make the decision to fully commit, recommit, or you will want to make sure that your house is in order. There should be a daily preparation taking place, for the return of the King of Kings and Lord of Lords is no small thing. A lot of us have made vows in the past and have broken them, but there is still time to fully commit. Don't put it off any longer.

WARNING! Earlier this year the Father spoke very clearly to me in my Tameion Chamber. ***"Connie, it is no small thing to enter the service of a King."*** This is why we must truly consider what we are committing and who we are committing to.

197

Broken Vows and Unholy Covenants. I did not come to know Christ as my Lord until I was 23 years old, and up until that time I had lived a pretty rough life. By that age, I had three children by three different men. I lost one of my boys when he was a year and a half old because of my lifestyle, and have missed out on a relationship with him because of my sin. I had lived a life that would terrify most, and was truly running down a path of destruction. Since we are on the subject of being a bride and making vows, the two divorces I had under my belt were the least of this drug addict's problems. I had not only a lot of broken vows, but had made unholy covenants with Satan himself. I had even cursed heaven and the Lord of Glory more times that I could ever count. So when I came to Christ, I was, as I call it, "road hard, put away wet, and filthy dirty." I was not a pretty sight nor could I imagine how God could ever love anything like me, let alone want me to be the Bride of His Amazing Son, Jesus.

For the first three years of my new life in Christ, I was blessed to have some pretty amazing spiritual moms raising this hardhearted, rebellious new believer. I have no doubt that I was a handful at every level as they had to confront all my demons, literally. My spirit was now saved, but my flesh was going to need lot of heavy deliverance.

After about a year of being saved, they would tell me that I should think about marriage again. I would laugh on the outside, but on the inside my heart was questioning, "I am a single mom, twice divorced, and I'm seriously even listening to these ladies? Am I really thinking I could ever marry again? Who would want me if they really knew my story?"

However, these women encouraged me not only to pray for a husband, but to pray for him personally every single day even though I didn't know him. So I set my heart to do just that! My boys and I prayed every evening for a man we had never even met. They needed an earthly father and I needed an earthly husband. I walked with the Lord for 2 more years after I had started praying, and it was not without my fair share of trip-ups, trials, temptations and failures.

About 2 years after praying, I met a man named Greg, who was at that time, a pastor at the Assembly of God church next to the business I was working for. He had also been testing for the CHP Academy and had applied to be a California Highway Patrol Officer. At first, I thought that there was no way this relationship could work because it felt kind of like the book of Hosea. He was Hosea, the godly man, and I was Gomer, the prostitute. Not to mention that I had not had good encounters with that side of the law for the most of my life. If you could only see inside my brain and heart as I asked God about this man who was so different in every way from my past experiences.

To make a short story shorter, we only dated eight weeks because God was in it, and we've been married now going on 29 years. I'm very grateful that my God is a God of redeeming love. When I thought that nobody would ever have me again, God gave me the most incredible, amazing and wonderful husband and father for my boys. We've kept our vows and the covenant we made not only to ourselves, but to God, faithfully. That doesn't mean that it's not been hard work or that it's always perfect. He inherited a lot of work when he married me.

Now back to the purpose for this book. I truly believe that the time is drawing close for Christ's return and that He is coming soon for His Beloved Bride, but she must ready herself. The Bible is very clear in Matthew 25 that "all" the virgins were asleep and they "all" woke up but only half were ready! The vows and covenants that we make are serious business before a Holy God and He does not take them lightly. Only half of the virgins had made a serious vow and covenant commitment. Yes, He is a good, good, Father, but He is also a Holy, Righteous God, and He paid a high price for a Bride for His Beloved Son.

We must get back to the basics of the Bible and see the truth of God's Word. We can no longer put God in a neat little religious box, believe the lies we have been told and take Him out of that box only when we feel its necessary.

When was the last time you really asked the God of all creation to get into your space and rearrange your world to fit His purposes? Have you ever asked God to prepare you for your wedding day to His Son? We are not taught to ask these questions in most of our churches.

One of my favorite men of God is John Paul Jackson who is now home with the Lord. He wrote, "In order to implement the fullness of God into our daily lives, our view of eternity and spiritual life must be so much larger than our temporal existence here. We are not human beings having a temporary spiritual experience; we are spiritual beings having a temporary human experience. We could never describe the whole of eternity, its beginning or ending, for God has no beginning. He has no ending. All was created by the sound of His voice or with His own hands. He has always simply been, stretching on and on before us and on and on after us. He will always be."[62]

God is so much bigger than we can even begin to imagine, and we need to get back to a spiritual perspective of our life with Him in it. My husband Greg preached a sermon this last year titled, "The Judgment Seat of Christ"[63] and we were both surprised at the amount of believers that did not realize that they would be judged for their time spent here on earth. As I stated above, He is a good, very good Father, but someday we will all have to stand before this Righteous Judge and give an account for everything we did and did not accomplish on this earth including, what we did and did not do to ready ourselves for the wedding day.

2 Corinthians 5:10 says, *"For we must all appear before the judgment seat of Christ, so that each of us may receive what is due us for the things done while in the body, whether good or bad."*

So, remembering who He is as Holy and Righteous, let's take a brief look at some scriptures that talk about God's view of vows and covenants. I'm only giving you a couple of scriptures and I would encourage you to study it out someday. Remember that we are looking at how God feels about vows and covenants.

"If a man makes a vow to the Lord, or swears an oath to bind himself by some agreement, he shall not break his word; he shall do according to all that proceeds out of his mouth" (Numbers 30:2).

---

[62] John Paul Jackson, 7 Days Behind The Veil: Throne Room Meditations. Streams Publishing House. Pages 8-9
[63] Pastor Greg A. Stoffel, "The Judgment Seat of Christ" www.igniterevival.org 7-16-17. https://youtu.be/7PdFweW8Iso

"It is a snare for a man to devote rashly something as holy, and afterward to reconsider his vows" (Proverbs 20:25).

"Again you have heard that it was said to those of old, 'You shall not swear falsely, but shall perform your oaths to the Lord.' But I say to you, do not swear at all: neither by heaven, for it is God's throne; nor by the earth, for it is His footstool; nor by Jerusalem, for it is the city of the great King. Nor shall you swear by your head, because you cannot make one hair white or black. But let your 'Yes' be 'Yes,' and your 'No,' 'No.' For whatever is more than these is from the evil one" (Matthew 5:33-37).

Wow! Think about it... Let your yes be yes or your no be no...anything more comes from the evil one! God would rather not have us make a vow than to make one and not keep it, because if we make a vow and don't keep it, we are guilty of sin. *"If you make a vow to the LORD your God, do not be slow to pay it, for the LORD your God will certainly demand it of you and you will be guilty of sin"* (Deuteronomy 23:21).

I propose that we need to revisit the importance of the vows and covenants we have made to God with a serious heart. We need to choose whether or not we want to become the Bride of Christ. This may be the first time you are considering making a covenant, or if it is a renewal of your vows, it is something that you should think long and hard about.

Count The Cost. In making this choice, we need to count the cost. Many jump right into relationship with Christ and have no idea who or what they are truly committing to. They don't understand the cost involved, and you can literally see the dust flying as they end up leaving Jesus at the altar. Because of this, when I share the Lord with somebody, usually having discipled them for some time and they feel they are ready to accept Christ as their Savior, I usually tell them to wait. I try to talk them out of salvation. What??? Yes, I do this because I truly believe they need to know what they are signing up for. So I'm going to talk to you about what it looks like to make vows and covenants before the Lord.

Marriage is work and it's no different in our relationship with Christ. Some of you who have entered into these vows and covenants with Christ didn't really count the cost when you made the commitment. You may have even said, "This isn't what I signed up for!"

How many of you gave your life to the Lord and then all hell broke loose? If this has happened to you, let me validate you right now! You're not crazy! It's true, all of hell is really nipping at your heels like a pack of vicious wolves. If you happen to be a much stronger Christian, you know exactly what I'm talking about.

How many people do you know that have given their life to the Lord but are not living for Him? They have separated themselves from Christ and are denying Him. Jesus says, "*If you deny Me before men, then I will deny you before My Father*" (Matthew 10:33).

We see broken vows, covenants and commitments to Christ all the time. This is why I want to make sure that anyone I lead to Christ will stick with Him through it all.

My heart is for you to choose Jesus and to commit to Him, your soon coming King. A lot of what I have said throughout this book might be uncomfortable and it might even offend you. But we must understand the weightiness that our commitments, vows (words spoken) and covenants carry. We must be willing to continually evaluate and count the cost of what our commitment level is as the Bride of Christ. What does it really mean to "put on" the wedding dress? Most of the Christians I encounter have no idea what this is supposed to look like. My heart is broken over this because I see it and deal with it everyday as a pastor's wife. I don't know what else to do except to pray, intercede and share the experience of what I seem to be encountering in this culture. So please take seriously your willingness to commit to the King of Kings and Lord of Glory.

"For it is no small thing to enter the service of a King."

34
*T*he *B*ridal *P*ath

"But when you pray, go into your room, close the door and pray to your Father, who is unseen. Then your Father who sees what is done in secret will reward you. And when you pray, do not keep on babbling like pagans, for they think they will be heard because of their many words. Do not be like them for your Father knows what you need before you ask him."
Matthew 6:6-8

"No one can come to me (Jesus) unless the Father who sent me draws them, and I will raise them up at the last day. It is written in the Prophets: 'They will all be taught by God.' Everyone who has heard the Father and learned from Him comes to me. No one has seen the Father except the one who is from God; only he has seen the Father. Very truly I tell you, the one who believes has eternal life. I am the bread of life."
John 6:44-48

"He (Jesus) went on to say, "This is why I told you that no one can come to me unless the Father has enabled them."
John 6:65

*I*t is very clear throughout scripture that we are to learn from God the Father. Jesus Christ His Son is a perfect example of this in that He would only do what His Father commanded Him to do. And when Jesus was resurrected, He clearly taught us that the Holy Spirit would be left in His place here on earth to teach, guide, counsel and instruct us. There is a part they all play in the bridal preparation process.

The Biblical principles in the above scriptures apply to us and are an extremely important part of the bridal path we are to walk. I would like to turn your attention to Ephesians 5:22-32 for just a moment. Paul gives us a clear picture of the part that Christ plays as well as His expectations of the wife He will be accepting and presenting to Himself.

Paul is very clear that she will be a Bride that is not only submitted, but also holy, and explains how this process of

203

becoming holy takes place. In our submission we are to allow Christ to cleanse and wash us with the water of the Word of God. This is a prerequisite of becoming His bride. This is the process necessary in us becoming radiant, without stain, wrinkle or having any other blemishes. If we don't read, study and devote time to His Word, how can we be washed by it? Again, it is very clear that we are only holy because Christ gave Himself up for us, washed us with the Word and became our Savior.

*R*eady *A*nd *P*repared. Every Christian should be asking themselves each day how they can **be getting ready and prepared as the Bride of Christ.** Being ready plays a huge role in being prepared, but you can't be ready if you're not prepared. They are two very radically different things and we as a Church have gotten them all mixed up.

Getting ready so that we are prepared would be like knowing you have six months to get ready for the wedding, so you start making plans immediately. You work on the details daily seeing to it that you have all of the *i's* dotted and *t's* crossed. As that date gets closer you continue to get your house in order and you have plenty of time, no worries, no rush. You check your list again and find that you have completed that task and can move on to the next one. Before you know it, the day of the wedding is here. It flows as smooth and delicious as the chocolate fountain bubbling with yummy goodness in the celebration hall down the road just waiting for the guests to arrive and start dipping the strawberries.

Now swinging the pendulum to the other side of being prepared without being ready. This would be like, "What??? I know I am getting married, but it's not today, is it?? (Can you see the look of terror on my face?) I must have written the wrong day down in my calendar! Did you say the groom is in the church house and it's going down right now? I'm not ready! My hair's not done, my dress is not back from the alteration shop and the cake hasn't even been ordered!" Panic sets in as you take a step and your legs brush together and you can feel the fur. All of a sudden it dawns on you.... you know the worst part of all of this is that you haven't shaved your legs in over two months allowing your leg hairs to grow extra-long on purpose in the hopes of getting them waxed the day of the wedding for optimum smoothness for your new groom! You are now going to need a lawnmower. I think you get the horrifying picture! Please forgive my terrible sense of humor. My friends who know me well know how this side of me pops up often.

But seriously, after reading this book, I pray that your spirit has been awakened to the call to make yourself a *ready and prepared* Bride. I want you to be able to ask yourself and those God has placed in your care the hard questions that will naturally arise such as: "What must I do to get ready and be prepared? How can I help others to be ready and prepared?"

To answer this question, let's first take a look at one of the biggest areas that "making ourselves ready" is not. It's not doing greater works for the Lord than He has called you too. By greater works, I mean putting in longer hours teaching, preaching, counseling and serving in areas that God has not called you too. We have all walked down that road where we wear ourselves out in ministry as we take upon ourselves every need we see lacking in our churches thinking, "There's an empty spot, so I guess I'll fill it!" As a pastors' wife I can easily fall into this trap and often have. I also have seen many in my church try to fall into that trap on purpose because that's how they were taught, and they believe their works done through flesh will get them through those pearly gates.

I do appreciate these precious saints in our church knowing that most have a servant's heart like mine. I truly see them as a gift to the Body of Christ who just need to be taught that what really pleases God's heart is intimacy with Christ first, and only then can real ministry be birthed.

This is something my husband Greg and I pay close attention to, for it is usually five percent of the people who seem to do all the work. The enemy would love nothing more than to see God's people burned out with busyness. This is one of Satan's biggest strategic moves against Christians.

Many of us with Martha hearts have a hard time being intimate. We like to keep busy to avoid intimacy, but that leads to full-on wreckage. We are skilled at ministry yet know nothing about intimacy with God, so we do great for a while, and then our batteries run out. Because we don't get refreshed or renewed by the One who can truly renew us, all our good deeds are done in our own strength and we find ourselves tuckered out! Scripture clearly warns us that the enemy wants nothing more than to wear out the saints in the last days.

Another pitfall of the enemy is that a lot of Christians get into deliverance ministry without intimacy with Christ, and without learning to do warfare from the secret place, which is where the true power comes from. Matthew 7:22-23 is clear that some Christians will think that they are casting out demons in Jesus' name and in His power, but it's nothing more than their flesh, and they end up causing more damage to themselves and the Kingdom of God.

Dr. Michael K. Lake, addresses this issue in an online teaching he has done through Biblical Life College and Seminary entitled, *"The Enemy's Tactics For Wearing Out the Saints."* He states, "Most believers, if they are serious about spiritual warfare, tend to do so by the seat of their pants. For them, spiritual warfare is like occasionally confronting a bully on the playground in elementary school. They are aware of the event, but are never aware of the 'long game' of warfare." He goes on to say that, "Strategic warfare is a concept that is foreign to them. Unfortunately, the enemy is quite familiar with strategic warfare. In fact, it is the only game he plays. What is the end result of this? Most believers approach spiritual warfare like they are either playing checkers or, even worse dodge ball. Satan always plays chess! He strategically weaves things into the Church and society over decades and even generations. I believe this is one reason the 'Moral Majority' has become the 'Minority Without a Clue.'" [64]

We are all a vital part in keeping the church functioning smoothly, however, sometimes people work like this to show the Lord they love Him and hopefully to be rewarded by Him in heaven. But being made ready has nothing to do with this type of ministry in the church.

The parable of the talents in Matthew 25:21 gives us a wonderful example of being made ready. In this parable Jesus is teaching on what the end of times will look like. He tells the man, *"Well done good and faithful servant! You have been faithful*

---

[64] http://www.biblical-life.com/wearing_out_saints.html

with a few things." Do you notice that the Master says, "well done" and "few things," and not "much done" and "many things?" He was trusted with a few things and did them well.

This has been the hardest lesson for me to learn especially since I seem to have a Martha's heart. I have had to learn the hard way and I am thankful that our Father is patient. I do my best not to fill holes myself just because they are there. I would rather take six months to pray the right person into that position of ministry than have the wrong person fill it immediately and have them get burned out never to return to ministry again. I'd rather teach them about intimacy before all the other churchy stuff that just isn't important.

There Must Be Intimacy Before Ministry. Your "Ministry" may not be in a church. You might be a doctor or lawyer, musician or teacher, a soldier or a stay at home mom. No matter what God has called you to do, it must be birthed through intimacy with the Lord. You must pursue an intimate love relationship with Father God and Jesus His Son. It is only then that you will truly walk in your calling, anointing and gifting's. This is what will cause you to be able to bear good fruit, bringing others into the Kingdom of God.

Intimacy with God will cause you to be successful in all that you set your hands to do. If your ministry is being birthed through intimacy, your works will be granted to you as the "*righteous acts*" of a bride who has made herself ready (Revelation 19:8). They are described as, "*Fine linen, bright and clean,*" and they will be given to her and will last for an eternity.

The beautiful threads of intimacy and the importance of being a Bride who is ready for her King is weaved throughout several passages of the Old Testament, and its treasures and lessons are beyond compare.

Is your ministry being birthed through intimacy?

You Must Be Prepared Before You Are Presented.
One of my favorite Bible treasures is Queen Esther (Hadassah) in the Book of Esther. It's an amazing true story about a young girl who had to be adopted because her family had been killed,

and how God raised her up to be a queen. It's not a fairytale and we need to take a good look at the details.

Esther had to be prepared before she could be presented to the King. She went though 12 months of beauty treatments, and this even included what she ate. There was much training involved to be able to become the Queen of Persia, the largest nation in her time. But before she became queen, she only had one chance to catch his eye. One chance to impress him. One chance to win the heart of a mighty ruler.

Esther was only one of hundreds of virgins brought before this king. What did she do that one evening in the King's private chamber? What did she say to him? Did she make it all about Him or was it all about herself? She was selected to be the wife of the Persian King Ahasuerus (King Xerxes) because she pleased him in the secret place. In Esther 2:17-18 it says, *"Now the king was attracted to Esther more than to any of the other women, and she won his favor and approval more than any of the other virgins. So he set a royal crown on her head and made her queen instead of Vashti. And the king gave a great banquet, Esther's banquet, for all his nobles and officials. He proclaimed a holiday throughout the provinces and distributed gifts with royal liberality."*

Are you going to be able to win the heart of a King?

We also have the precious book, "The Song of Solomon" in our Bible. It comes alive as the one who waits eagerly for her beloved, and she can't eat or sleep until she finds him. She runs all throughout the city longing to find her love. This is a beautiful picture of one who is Beloved and focused on her Lover. The most awesome thing throughout the whole book is that she announces and decrees her love for her lover to everyone. All her friends know about her love for this King.

Do your friends know you are lovesick for your soon coming King?

Hosea 2:14-21 is a beautiful prophecy to Israel and a picture of God's heart for us. It shows how the Lord will allure us to the wilderness and "speak kindly" to us during intimate conversations even though we have been unfaithful. I can't read this passage without crying out, "Oh, be still my heart!" I feel like the Book of Hosea is so much a part of my life, and yet God loves me so very much.

Have you been allured to the desert?

As you have probably already noticed, Matthew 25:1-13 is a passage that is dear to my heart and it would take volumes to explain my reasoning for it being so cherished. But it clearly reveals the vital importance of intimacy between us and our soon coming King. We discussed this in a previous chapter, but I want to briefly remind you that all *ten virgins were* **ready** when they received a supply of oil to keep their lamps burning. However, it was only the *five wise virgins that had* **prepared** themselves with more oil while the Bridegroom was away preparing a place for them, who would be allowed to enter the wedding banquet with the King. That's fifty percent less than those who thought they were in!

Next time you are in church, imagine fifty percent of your church family not being able to come through that door. Picture them banging and begging to be let in. We are not only the virgins, but we are the lamps. The oil symbolizes the Holy Spirit, and we are either going to have enough or we are not. It is clearly our choice. The only way to light our lamp is to be covered in the precious oil and completely saturated with love for our groom. This is what ignites the fire within us.

Have you checked your supply of oil?

We know that the oil symbolizes the Holy Spirit because oil is frequently used as a symbol in Scripture. (See 1 John 2:20,27; Acts 10:38). Jesus plainly tells the foolish virgins who were *ready but not prepared* with enough oil, "*I do not* **know** *you*" (Matthew 25:12). Throughout Scripture, the word "know" which is "Ginosko" in Greek and "Yada" in Hebrew is a Jewish idiom for intercourse. Truly knowing someone is connected with intimacy. Jesus is clear in Matthew 25 that anyone who wants to enter the wedding feast and become His Bride must have that intimacy with Him while in this world. This is a vital and important part in being a *ready and prepared Bride.*

Are you having an intimate relationship with the King of Kings?

$\mathcal{T}$**he Bride and The End Time Battle.** Revelation 19:7 says that the Bride has made herself ready! What has she made herself ready for? Yes, she has made herself ready for the coming of her King and for eternity with Him. We need to be prepared to love our King more than the world and anything in it (1 John 2:15).

Are you prepared to not love the things of this world?

Are you prepared to die, or are you afraid of death? *"They triumphed over him (Satan) by the blood of the Lamb and by the word of their testimony; they did not love their lives so much as to shrink from death"* (Revelation 12:11).

But the story doesn't stop there! We must be prepared to go even a step further, to war.

All the prophets knew that there would be an end time battle that would have to be fought! All the saints throughout the centuries and followers of Jesus knew it! They were prepared for it. We have been made for a very specific time in history and should be prepared for it. It is time that we find our true position as the Bride of Christ. While we should be ready for the marriage supper of the Lamb, we have also been called to a last and final battle.

Revelation 19:11-16 reads: *"I saw heaven standing open and there before me was a white horse, whose rider is called Faithful and True. With justice he judges and wages war. His eyes are like blazing fire, and on his head are many crowns. He has a name written on him that no one knows but he himself. He is dressed in a robe dipped in blood, and his name is the Word of God. The armies of heaven were following him, riding on white horses and dressed in fine linen, white and clean. Coming out of his mouth is a sharp sword with which to strike down the nations. 'He will rule them with an iron scepter.' He treads the winepress of the fury of the wrath of God Almighty. On his robe and on his thigh he has this name written:* **King of Kings and Lord of Lords."**

Are you ready to go to war with your King?

*A*re *Y*ou *R*eady? Many who call themselves Christians are only thinking about getting ready for an eternity with Christ Jesus, our soon coming King. Our Father God is working on His Son's behalf to get the Church ready and prepared for the last and final battle that will bring death to all we know of this world. You and I need to choose whom we are going to stand with and serve in the last day. Make no mistake that you can be deceived, fooled and left banging on a closed door. The Bible warns us that just as the people of Noah's day were left screaming for Noah to open the door of the Ark, it will be no different for us. We must be prepared and ready.

You also need to know that before you go to the marriage supper of the Lamb, you will have to fight in the biggest battle that has ever been fought in the history of time. If we were to put every single battle that has ever been waged over thousands of years together it would be like child's play compared to this war that we will be fighting in. If you don't learn how to war in this world, how will you ever be able to war in the heavenly realms with Him?

In Revelation 19, the beautiful message of the marriage supper of the Lamb was brought to John through a powerful, yet humble angel who encouraged and assured John by saying, *"These are the true words of God!"* (Revelation 19:9). The angel relayed the coming judgment in which King Jesus would make war upon the nations with the saints or armies of heaven joining Him in battle. He had a message to deliver to us meaning that there is yet a prophecy to be fulfilled. In this continued vision John saw a white horse. Let me share with you about my King who is riding this white horse.

The Man on this white horse has risen from the dead and His Name is Faithful and True! He is my Warrior-Messiah-King. He will come to bring justice, to judge the earth and He will make war. His eyes are like blazing fire, and on his head are many crowns. He has a Name written on Him that no one knows but He himself. He is dressed in a robe that is dipped in blood and His Name is the Word of God. He will have the armies of heaven following Him and they will be riding on white horses and dressed in fine linen, white and clean. Out of his mouth comes a sharp sword with which to strike down the nations. He will rule with an iron scepter. He treads the winepress of the fury of the wrath of God Almighty. On His thigh he has a Name written:

KING OF KINGS AND LORD OF LORDS.

These two messages, of the marriage supper of the Lamb and the last battle are inseparable. I am encouraged because we have been given plenty of warning. If we are prepared, we have nothing to fear and everything to gain. There's so much more to being a Bride of Christ than just claiming to be His fiancé.

"Enter through the narrow gate.
For wide is the gate and broad is the road that leads to
destruction, and many enter through it. But small is the gate and
narrow the road that leads to life, and only a few find it."
Matthew 7:13-14

35
Morning Prayer

Just as we physically get dressed every morning, it is vitally important to get spiritually dressed every day. But because the concept of getting dressed in in our spiritual garments and armor can be uncomfortable until you become familiar with it, I would like to give you a shortened example of how I do this. This is how I pray.

Father, Your Word says, *"Blessed is he who watches and keeps his garments on"* (Revelation 16:15). Thank You for allowing Your Son, Jesus to sacrifice His life so that I can be cleansed in His blood and clothed in His garments. I am so grateful that because of Your Son, Jesus, I can draw near to You and come into Your presence at any time, anywhere, and that I am never turned away no matter the situation or circumstance, or even by the condition of my heart.

Thank You for creating my Tameion Chamber, my secret place of intimacy with You. As I have opened the doors of the deepest and most hidden places in my spirit to You, I will continue to invite You to enter. You are always welcome, and You have always been faithful to come. I want nothing more than to experience You and Your love in a very real way. My heart desires to learn from You and to be equipped and ready for the assignments You have prepared for me. May You never find the doors of my heart closed to You.

Each day, as I enter my chamber, I choose to connect with Your Holy Spirit who is my counselor and guide according to Your Word on which I stand. (John 14:16-18; John 16:7-13; Acts 2:33; Romans 8:16)

Cleansing. Father, I want to make sure that I leave nothing spiritually vulnerable because as an intercessor, a watchman and a warrior bride, I am on the enemy's most wanted list. You have taught me that he will always be looking for the smallest crack in my armor. I ask that Your Holy Spirit would daily illuminate and bring to my mind any sin, rebellion

213

or pride that I need to confess to You. I ask that You forgive me from all sin, my own, and any sin that has been brought against me according to 1 John 1:9.

Father, I am grateful that because of the price Your Son, Jesus was willing to pay, that I am being continually cleansed through the process of sanctification from sin by His precious and powerful blood. I am also grateful for the cleansing that comes as I bathe myself in Your Word as Ephesians 5:26 says... *"that He might sanctify and cleanse her with the washing of water by the word."*

Father, I sit down and I place my feet in the bowl of cleansing water that You have provided, and I ask that You would wash my feet just as Jesus did in Matthew 13 for His disciples. I ask that You would wash the dust and grime of the world off my feet. I know there are many places my feet have traveled and there are many things I might have picked up along the way, things that are not pleasing to You! I ask this of You as an act of the complete surrendering of my pride, which I put in the hands of Your Son Jesus, and under the purifying water of Your Holy Spirit so that my cleansing might be complete for this day. I also understand that in this place of humility, Jesus has become so much more than just my teacher, He is now my Lord. I ask that He be put in His proper place of authority in my life.

Getting Dressed. Father, I am overwhelmed with love for Jesus. My heart is in awe of His willingness and obedience to carry out Your plan of redemption for me that day on the cross. His selfless act of love has cancelled sin and death in my life so that I may live. I willingly choose to put on His **Garment of Salvation** and gladly step into Your plans and purposes for my life. I wrap myself in You and the life of Your Son. I commit myself to You today and I choose to be joined with You and Your Son, Jesus, to *cleave* to You both, forsaking all others. (Psalm 32:1; Isaiah 61:10, Matthew 19:5)

I eagerly put on the **Priestly Undergarments** that identify me as Yours. They set me apart as holy, consecrated, dedicated and worthy to minister to You and to be used for Your glory, a reflection of Your beauty. I recognize that these garments carry the anointing of *Sincerity of Heart* and the *Fear of* *the Lord.* They come with the authority and responsibility of representing You and Your Kingdom here on this earth. In humility I accept the specific purpose and calling You have on my life, and will keep myself pure, ready to be used by You. (Exodus 28; 1 Peter 2:9; Colossians 3:22)

Father, the name of Jesus is the name above every other name and is mine to claim each and every day. He is called by all of heaven, *"THE LORD OUR RIGHTEOUSNESS."* I gladly allow You to cover me with His **Robe of Righteousness**! His righteousness is what You see when You look at me! You no longer see my sin and shame and the imperfections of my flesh. You now see that I am Your child, qualified to be the Bride of Your Son. I am covered under His precious blood that is beautiful in Your sight.

Father, I accept this Robe of Righteousness with great joy as it qualifies me to be in the Your presence, and it protects me as I serve You. Father, I now secure my Robe of Righteousness with Your Son's **Belt of Righteousness**!

Father, You have taught me the importance of needing both the Robe of Righteousness and the Belt of Righteousness, because combined, they create Your precious gift of the **"Garment of Light!"** I understand that as I put these garments together, they are a reflection of You, their Designer. Thank You for the provision and protection of this heavenly garment.

I understand that I act on what I believe in my heart, and that my heart is what influences my thoughts and words. I desperately need the leading and guiding of Your Holy Spirit each and every day, not only to continue to cover me with Your Righteousness, but so that this righteousness will penetrate my heart and change it so that Your heart becomes mine, and I become more like my soon coming King, Jesus. (Jeremiah 23:6; Isaiah 61:10; Romans 13:11-12; Isaiah 11:5)

Father, I now accept Your Son's **Sash of Faithfulness**. I am so grateful that Jesus was faithful unto death that I might live for Him. And I pray that I may be found faithful to my last breath upon this earth. (Isaiah 25:1; Psalm 89:1-18)

I now put on my most beautiful **Garment of Praise,** for the Spirit of Heaviness tries to steal my joy and gladness. I will choose each day to praise You Father, no matter what the circumstances. In the darkest of nights, I will praise You in hopeful expectation of Your healing Light. In times of joy, I will praise You, keeping my eyes focused on Your great mercy. I choose to put on this Garment of Praise, which is also one of my most powerful weapons in defeating the enemy of my soul. I stand and trust in Your promises, that praise will cast off the spirit of heaviness each time it tries to enter the door of my heart. You are my light, my love, my shield, my hope and my very great reward. (Isaiah 61:3; Psalm 45:7-8; Psalm 150)

I now place upon my head my **Crown of Beauty**! Oh Father, this is my bridal veil and signifies that I belong to Your Son, Jesus and no one else! I am committed to Him, and will wait for Him in purity and faithfulness seeing with eyes through the veil of one who has been promised to a King. I will practice loving and serving You both, every day of my life.

Father, I am so grateful that You have chosen me to become the Bride of Your Son, Jesus. You searched me out and found me at the bottom of the sea of sin and shame. I will now humbly ask You for the help needed that I may see myself the way You see me, as a bride. I choose to cast off all the old filthy garments and the identities I used to wear. I remove and cast down all of the mindsets, habits and lies of the enemy that are attached to them. I choose to accept my new identity as the Bride of Christ. I choose to think and act as a bride preparing myself for my wedding day! Your Son is going to come and take me to Your home, and I will join in the Marriage Supper of the Lamb.

I choose to reject the guilt and shame of my past, and I wholly embrace the conviction of Your Holy Spirit that draws me close to Your heart. I choose this day and everyday from here on out, to allow You to use the ashes of my life to transform them into something useful and beautiful for Your Kingdom, Your honor and glory. (Ephesians 5:23; Revelations 19:7; Isaiah 61:3 NIV; Isaiah 62:3)

Thank You Father, for Your **Eye Salve.** Please anoint my eyes so I can see clearly through the obstacles that the enemy places before me. Please remove any and all unclean images, and bring healing to my eyes from any damage done by viewing ungodly sights. I obediently put Your **Spiritual Spectacles** over my eyes so that I can see through Your eyes with Your heavenly perspective. I need Your heart and discernment for navigating through the darkness of this world. I must be able to identify the deceiving look-a-likes from the Truth of Your Word with my spiritual sight. I need to see others through Your eyes of forgiveness, the way that You see them. I also understand that my responsibility is to protect my eyes from viewing evil and worthless things. (Colossians 3:12-14; Psalm 119:18; Ephesians 1:18; 1 Kings 3:9; Proverbs 15:21; Malachi 3:18; Psalm 101:3; Revelation 3:18)

I set a **Guard** over my mouth to remind myself not to gossip! I want no part in speaking deceptive, idle, hurtful, critical or judgmental words to others. Instead, I commit to speak the truth in love, to speak words of encouragement, and when directed, to speak words of correction. (Matthew 12:34; Luke 6:45; Psalm 141:2-4; Isaiah 49:18b; Psalm 32:9; Ephesians 4:29-32; Proverbs 6:19; Exodus 20:16)

Father, as You have clothed me in preparation for Your Son, I pick up my precious gift of the **Aroma of Christ**. There are no earthly words to describe its worth to me. I now anoint my body, my soul and spirit with the Aroma of Christ. I have read many times in Your Word of the price that You and He paid. I cannot even begin to comprehend what Your Father's heart must have felt that day as You caught and kept every drop of this costly perfume. In obedience to You, and because of Your love, compassion and Your plan for me, Jesus willingly chose to lay down His life on an old rugged cross.

Father, I always want to focus on the fact that this is all the work of Your Mighty Hand and Your Great love. It is hard for me to explain Your ways, but I do know that my heart is forever grateful that Your Son, Jesus was not swept away by the wrath of uncontrolled and angry men, but He was bruised and crushed by You, His Loving Father. I do believe that this was Your mysterious way at work resolving the tensions between a Holy God and a world full of sinful men and women separated from You, and that because You are a Holy God, the sin of man could not be ignored.

So I choose this day to lay my life down for You, and in that way, may I emulate You so that anyone or anything near me will be aware of Your presence. (Isaiah 53:10, 2 Corinthians 2:14-16; Psalm 45:7-8; Philippians 2:5-12)

I place the **Breastplate of Righteousness** upon myself. Thank You, Father, for guarding my heart as I choose to stand firm in my faith, steadfast and immoveable in my relationship with You. I understand that Your righteousness is my protection from all of the wickedness that comes against me, and that as Your righteousness covers my heart, I can love others the way that You love them. I ask You Father, to activate Your righteousness in me as I obey You, so that I can respond with the heart of Your Son Jesus, to the unrighteousness of the world. (Ephesians 6:14; Isaiah 59:17)

I tightly secure my **Belt of Truth** around my waist. Father, You are Truth, and I choose to study Your Word so that I will know the truth and will be able to identify the deception and lies of the enemy. I also want to be able to identify the false shepherds, prophets, teachers and the doctrine of demons; those who look like You, act like You, but don't have Your heart. I understand that this belt is the foundation that holds my Sword of the Spirit, Keys to the Kingdom, my spiritual gifts and spiritual fruit. My Belt of Truth also holds my garments firmly in place, enabling me to fight the good fight and to run with perseverance the race You have set before me. (Ephesians 6:14; Hebrews 12:1-2)

I put on my **Shoes of Peace**, choosing each day to walk in Your steps and in Your ways. I choose to bend my will to Yours, to submit to Your plans for my day. Please guide me in the way that You want me to go and lead me into divine appointments. I understand that in Your shoes, my step is firm, my heart is strong, and I am able to stand my ground. I am aware that while the spikes in the soles of my shoes hold me firmly in place, these spikes also fatally wound the enemy as I trample him with every step of obedience that I take. Father, I trust You for protection. (Ephesians 6:15; Psalm 17:5; 37:31, 39-40; Psalm 25:4; Proverb 4:11-12)

Father, thank You for giving me Your mind and the mind of Jesus Christ, Your Son. I place my **Helmet of Salvation** upon my head. Not only does it guard my mind, but it also assists me in thinking Your thoughts and discerning Your ways. I choose to study Your Word and to fill my mind with Your thoughts, which will be held in security under the protection of my Helmet of Salvation. I choose to take my thoughts captive each and every day, to reject, renounce and cast down vain imaginations and every high or proud thing that exalts itself above or against the knowledge of You and Your truth. I choose to be obedient and faithful to the commands that You speak into my mind. (Ephesians 6:17; Isaiah 59:17; 1 Peter 4:1; Ephesians 6:13)

I choose to faithfully put on the **Garments of Love and Humility** over all my other garments and armor each and every day. I know that without these, my other garments amount to nothing and will be rendered ineffective. I completely understand that everything I do and say must go through these garments of love and humility, for these are Your ways. (1 Corinthians 13:1-3; Colossians 3:12-14)

I thank You Father, for Your Precious Holy Spirit. He is the only **Anointing Oil** I seek. I ask that You will cover me completely, leaving no place untouched by this anointing. I ask that you anoint me with boldness to carry out all of the plans, mandates and visions that You have placed within my heart. I choose to obey You as I walk in this anointing, even when I feel weak, tired, inadequate or afraid. Through the anointing of Your Holy Spirit, You will give me the strength needed when I am weak and weary, and power that I need to step out in trust and obedience in spite of my feelings. May the Anointing Oil of Your Holy Spirit, cause my eyes to see, my ears to hear, my mind to discern, and my heart to love with the compassion of Christ. Increase my vision with Your anointing. Father, I can do nothing of lasting value without your Holy Spirits and His Oil of Anointing. (2 Corinthians 1:21-22; Isaiah 40:29-31; 2 Timothy 1:7; Acts 4:31)

Father, in everything, I choose to take up my precious and powerful **Shield of Faith**! I recognize my need for its protection, and I commit to holding it at all times as it quenches Satan's fiery darts and protects me from the evil one. I place each and every one I pray for behind its covering as I seek Your face and heart on their behalf. (Ephesians 6:16; Psalm 7:10-13; Zechariah 12:8; 1 Corinthians 16:13-14)

Father, my **Sword of the Spirit** is my greatest treasure and most precious inheritance here on this earth. It is Your covenant from the great courts of Heaven sent to earth, and I hold it in my hands today. I want to be faithful to You as I take my vows according to Your Word. This is also the ultimate weapon of warfare that You have strategically placed in my hands.

I thank You for Your patience as it has taken me many years to learn to use this weapon properly. I choose to study out its treasures and the wisdom of its ways. I want to understand its mysteries correctly, and I want it to be the guide of my life. I want to know, believe in and understand its truths. I want to declare it as the holy and uncompromised Word of the living God whom I love and serve. I understand that it is a weapon greater than all the others. With it I can defeat the enemy and destroy his strongholds! My Sword of the Spirit holds the keys to hope, healing, freedom and deliverance to anyone in bondage. How I thank You for this mighty weapon, for it is alive and active. Sharper than any double-edged sword, it penetrates even to dividing soul and spirit, joints and marrow; it judges the thoughts and attitudes of my heart. (Hebrews 4:12)

Father, I thank you for my many other powerful weapons. These are also of great importance, such as my **Spear** that is a restraining force against ungodliness and keeps the enemy from getting too close. (Ephesians 6:17; 2 Samuel 23:6-7; Habakkuk 3:11)

I also thank You for my **Rod of Authority**! It is a sign of Your authority that carries the anointing of the Holy Spirit for ruling territories as kings and priests to God and for supernatural miracles. It can be used for discipline or correction and for the rescue of God's people. Just as rods were used in making covenants, I choose to pass under the rod and to enter into covenant with You, my Father. I will stand firm in my faith. I will use the authority that Your Son Jesus has given me. I will accept Your discipline and correction and will use this rod as a tool and weapon as needed and as instructed by You. (Ezekiel 20:37, Matthew 10:1; 28:18-19; Luke 10:19; Exodus 4:17, 17:9; Psalm 23:4; Proverbs 13:24; Revelation 5:10)

Father, You are the true manna, the bread of eternal life. My **Hidden Manna** is a supernatural, spiritual resource. Your Son, Jesus said, *"I have food to eat of which you do not know...My food is to do the will of Him who sent Me, and to finish His work"* (John 4:32-34). I accept Jesus as the bread of my life, and choose to partake of and share in His life, so that in Him, I will have supernatural strength to accomplish Your will. (John 6:48-58; Revelation 2:17)

Father, in conclusion, thank You for Your great provisions and abundant love and care. Please be the center of my mind, will and heart today, and help me to please You in my attitudes, words and actions. *"Let the words of my mouth and the meditation of my heart Be acceptable in Your sight, O Lord, my strength and my Redeemer"* (Psalm 19:14).

Wardrobe Of The Warrior Bride

This list is only the beginning of the treasures that await those who open the door of their Tameion Chamber to Jesus the Son, the Father and the Holy Spirit. He will be faithful to provide and to reveal more of His Kingdom resources in His Word as we continue to seek Him.

Garment of Salvation

Priestly Undergarments

Robe of Righteousness

Belt of Righteousness

Sash of Faithfulness

Garment of Praise

Crown of Beauty

The Aroma of Christ

Belt of Truth

Breastplate of Righteousness

Shoes of Peace

Helmet of Salvation

Hidden Manna

Spear and Other Weapons

Outer Garments of Love and Humility

Oil of Anointing

Eye Salve and Spiritual Spectacles

Shield of Faith

Sword of the Spirit

Rod of Authority

Intercessor's Mantle

Names Of God

Yahweh	I AM (LORD: Father, Son, Holy Spirit)	Psalm 97:9
Adonai	My Lord	Genesis 15:2
Jehovah	Lord God, Self-existing One	Genesis 2:4
Jehovah-Roi	The God who sees	Genesis 16:13
Jehovah-Jireh	The Lord will provide	Genesis 22:13
Jehovah-Nissi	The Lord our banner	Exodus 17:15
Jehovah-Shalom	The Lord our peace	Judges 6:24
Jehovah-Sabaoth	The Lord of hosts, Lord of powers	Romans 9:29
Jehovah-M'Kaddesh	The Lord my sanctifier	Exodus 31:13
Jehovah-Rohi	The Lord my Shepherd	Psalm 23:1
Jehovah-Tsidkenu	The Lord my righteousness	Jeremiah 23:6
Jehovah-Shammah	The Lord who is present	Ezekiel 48:35
Jehovah-Rapha	The Lord our healer	Exodus 15:26
Jehovah- Nakah	The Lord who smites	Ezekiel 7:9
Jehovah-Gmolah	God of recompense	Jeremiah 51:6
Immanuel	God with us	Isaiah 7:14
El Elyon	Most High God	Genesis 14:18
El Shaddai	Lord God Almighty	Genesis 28:3
El Olam	The everlasting God	Isaiah 40:28-31
El Bethel	God is my sanctuary	Genesis 31:13
El Chai	God is my living truth	Joshua 3:10
El Elohim	God is the only true God	Daniel 11:36
El Gibor	God is my mighty helper	Isaiah 9:6
El Kanna	God is my righteous zeal	Deut. 4:24
Eli	God is my God	Psalm 22:1, 10
Elohey Tehillati	God of my praise	Psalm 109:1
Qanna'	Jealous God	Exodus 34:14
Baal-Perazim	The Lord of breaking through	2 Samuel 5:20

Adapted from: https://www.blueletterbible.org/study/misc/name_god.cfm
Unsure of the other resource....

JESUS, *"the name which is above every name*, *that at the name of Jesus every knee should bow, of those in heaven, and of those on earth, and of those under the earth, and that every tongue should confess that Jesus Christ is Lord, to the glory of God the Father"* (Philippians 2:9-11).

Yahweh, I AM	John 8:58	Yeshua, Jesus	Matthew 1:21
Jesus Christ, Messiah		Matthew 1:1	
Jesus of Nazareth	Acts 2:22	Alpha and Omega	Revelation 1:8
Anointed One	John 1:41	Beloved One	Matt. 12:18
Bread of Heaven	John 6:32	Bread of God	John 6:33
Bridegroom	John 3:29	Cornerstone	Mark 12:10
Deliverer	Romans 11:26	Door	John 10:9
Good Shepherd	John 10:11	Intercessor, Advocate	1John 2:1; Job33:2
Jesus, my Salvation	Isaiah 12:2	Lamb of God	John 1:29, 36
Light of the World	John 8:12	Lion of Judah	Revelation 5:5
Lord of Glory	1 Cor. 2:8	Master	Matthew 23:8
My Beloved Son	Matthew 3:17	Prince	Acts 5:31
Prophet	John 1:25	Redeemer	Isaiah 59:20
Righteous One	Acts 3:14	Son of God	Matthew 4:3
The Truth	John 14:6	The Way	John 14:6
The Life	John 14:6	The Word	John 1:1

Adapted from: http://www.hebrew4christians.com/Names_of_G-d/Yeshua/yeshua.html

Books by
Connie Stoffel and Nancy Bowser

 The Tameion Chamber By Connie Stoffel

 Watchman Warrior, Intercessory Prayer by Nancy Bowser

 The Soul Redeemer (Book One) by Nancy Bowser

 The Soul Redeemer, *From Victim to Victory* (Book Two) by Nancy Bowser

 The Soul Redeemer, *Kingdoms* (Book Three) by Nancy Bowser

Coming Soon: **The Power Of God Through The Blood Of the Cross,** *A Bible Study* by Connie Stoffel